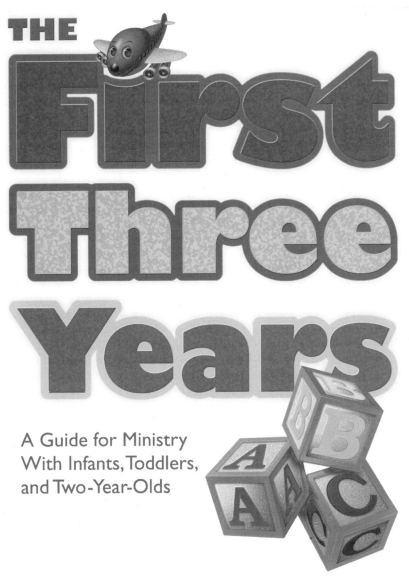

THE First Three Years

A Guide for Ministry
With Infants, Toddlers,
and Two-Year-Olds

Mary Alice Gran, Editor

DISCIPLESHIP RESOURCES

P.O. BOX 340003 • NASHVILLE, TN 37203-0003
www.discipleshipresources.org

A Child

I am a child—a miracle to see.
Look at me and get a glimpse of what the future will be!

I cry loudly, I bang furiously.
I giggle rapturously, I smile angelically.
I stare intently, I move quickly.

I look at you with trusting eyes.
You seem so big and very wise.

Please...
Hug me.
Hold me.
Talk to me.
Walk with me.
Feed me.
Play with me.
Sing to me.
Pray with me.

Teach me that the church can be
A loving, trusting place to be.

Through trust and love help me to see
That I am special and God loves me!

MaryJane Pierce Norton

Cover and book design by Joey McNair
Edited by Debra D. Smith, Heidi L. Hewitt, and Cindy S. Harris

ISBN 0-88177-324-7
Library of Congress Catalog Card No. 00-105382

DR324

Contents

Introduction

Mary Alice Gran
Nashville, Tennessee

Why Minister to Infants, Toddlers, and Twos?

Children are our special responsibility, entrusted to our care by God. Therefore, we want the church to be a place where they can grow in body, mind, and spirit; a place where they can meet Christ and be nurtured in a growing, life-giving faith. Just how do we do that? Frequently, as well intended as we are, we do not have a ministry for young children in our church. It isn't that we don't care. We do! We just don't know how.

We are concerned about the quality of care given to our children, and we are also worried about the talk of abuse and litigation. And we know that the facilities for young children are not what families might have at home, but children did use them in 1978. And we want children in worship, but they wiggle and make noise. And we love to see young families busy at the church, but they just do not think the same way we do. It is just easier to pretend everything is fine the way it is. We do not know what to do differently to make our church a better place for young children and their families.

The world is a different place now. If it seems that today's children and parents are different from their parents and grandparents, they are. Parenting styles are different. Parental expectations are different. Society is different. Parents' reactions to society are different. The choice of a quality nursery environment is important—so important that decisions about where to attend church will frequently hinge on how the nursery facilities look and how comfortable parents feel with the care their children receive there.

But expectations do not end with a clean and safe nursery. Parents and their young children need to be accepted for who they are, and they need to feel loved unconditionally. But is that any different from the expectations you and I have in our relationship with the church and the congregation? The prime question for the church seems to be not why but how.

This resource is prepared to help congregations have the tools needed to build a quality ministry with young children and their parents. Just as Jesus said,

"Let the little children come to me; do not stop them" (Mark 10:14), we should not only not stop them but should do all we can to encourage them to meet Jesus. And just as the African proverb says, "It takes a village to raise a child," we can adapt that wisdom to fit our situation: "It takes a whole congregation to raise a child." How true it is! From the first suggestion that a young family wants to raise their child within the faith community, the congregation begins to take seriously the pledge to be made at baptism: "With God's help we will proclaim the good news and live according to the example of Christ. We will surround *these persons* with a community of love and forgiveness, that *they* may grow in *their* trust of God, and be found faithful in *their* service to others. We will pray for *them*, that *they* may be true disciples who walk in the way that leads to life." (From Baptismal Covenant I, in *The United Methodist Hymnal*, page 35. © 1976, 1980, 1985, 1989 The United Methodist Publishing House. Used by permission.)

How to Use This Resource

The articles in this book focus on providing basic information on a wide variety of topics. Use what is helpful for you. Adapt the ideas and suggestions to fit your own situation. Take seriously the contents of the sections "The Child," "Legal and Financial Issues," and "Safety and Health." This book does not contain every answer to every question, but it will answer most of the questions you have. Some information is repeated in more than one article. That was a deliberate choice based on the importance of the information and on the expectation that most articles will be used as stand-alone pieces.

Become familiar with the table of contents (pages 3–5), and use it as a helpful guide as you work through this resource. Other leaders in your congregation who may also want to become familiar with the contents include the pastor, Christian educator, nursery coordinator, director of weekday programs, chairperson of the children's council. These people may wish to have access to this resource, or may need their own copy.

This book has the following features:

- Sixteen sections that define topics contained within the book.
- Each section divider lists the articles in that section.
- Each section divider also lists related articles, which are in other sections of the book.

Directions for Photocopying

The articles, forms, parent leaflets, and posters in this book may be photocopied and used within the purchasing congregation. When photocopying, be sure the copyright notice appears on each one. To make quality copies for your local congregation, place the outside edge of the paper against the copier guide and increase the page size from 106 percent to 110 percent to eliminate the spiral. To eliminate any shadows at the edges of pages, cover the book with a legal-size sheet of paper before closing the top of the copier.

May this book be a blessing to the young children and their families within your community.

Parent, Caregiver, and Congregation Expectations

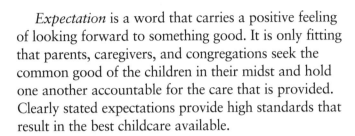

Donna Lee Strieb
San Antonio, Texas

Expectation is a word that carries a positive feeling of looking forward to something good. It is only fitting that parents, caregivers, and congregations seek the common good of the children in their midst and hold one another accountable for the care that is provided. Clearly stated expectations provide high standards that result in the best childcare available.

What Is Expected of the Caregiver

A caregiver is expected to

- demonstrate a sense of serenity, calm assurance, and love.
- exhibit maturity, confidence, gentleness, warmth.
- display a respectful manner.
- model appropriate behavior for the children.
- be attentive to the children's physical needs.
- understand children's developmental characteristics.
- know how to respond appropriately to the different personalities and temperaments of children.
- value each interaction involved in caring for children.
- seek to be involved with the children and not with the other caregivers.
- obtain pertinent information from the parents about the children's needs and habits.
- delight in playing with the children.
- be secure about personal childcare abilities.
- divert children's attention when they are unhappy or uncomfortable.
- provide an atmosphere of trust for both parents and children.
- respect parents' concerns, needs, and wishes.

What Is Expected of the Congregation

A congregation is expected to

- take seriously the congregational baptismal vows by providing a place where a young child's physical, social, emotional, and spiritual needs are met.
- hire the best staff possible or provide the best volunteers available.

- inform parents of all childcare procedures and expectations.
- provide a proper ratio of adults to children in the nursery.
- secure a nursery coordinator to oversee all aspects of the program.
- offer CPR and first-aid training for the caregivers.
- be aware of insurance, liability, safety, and security issues.
- provide airy, spacious rooms with appropriate furniture, decor, and toys.
- ensure a nursery area that meets the highest standards of cleanliness.
- take every precaution to ensure a safe, secure place for the children.
- provide a nursery home visitor (or equivalent) to keep in touch with parents about their children's needs and to be a contact person for the congregation.

What Is Expected of the Parents

Parents are expected to

- refrain from bringing a sick child to the nursery.
- provide all pertinent information to the caregiver (parents' location while the child is in the nursery, an emergency phone number, name of physician, feeding and nap schedule, any known allergies, and so forth).
- label with their child's name everything that is brought to the nursery.
- provide the caregiver with information about their child's needs and habits.
- bring appropriate and necessary items for their child, such as a change of clothing, bottle, diapers.
- promptly and personally pick up their child from the nursery.
- be informed about their child's experiences (both positive and negative) during the child's nursery stay.
- tell their child positive things about the nursery.

Using the Articles in This Section

The articles in this section provide basic information about children that is important for parents and caregivers to know. These articles could be used as part of a parenting class, in orientation packets for new nursery workers, or as part of ongoing training for caregivers.

Section One: The Child

Contents

Other Related Articles

Developmental Characteristics of Infants

Donna Lee Strieb
San Antonio, Texas

The Infant (Birth to One Year)

- is totally dependent on others for every need.
- relates to self.
- has no understanding of time and events.
- must have physical needs met.
- requires protection, love, care, and a safe environment.
- sees people as objects.
- likes to look at new and interesting things.
- is an active learner.
- needs to develop relationships with specific adults.
- begins to discover the results of cause and effect.
- develops language ability through crying, cooing, babbling.

The Growing Child

During the first few months of life, the healthy newborn can hear and respond to noises but lacks motor control and eye coordination. The child can feel comfortable or uncomfortable. The brain is actively developing during this time.

From four to six months of age, nerve and muscle coordination increase, allowing for smiling, turning and holding up the head, reaching out to grasp objects, and eating soft foods.

By six months, the young child is ready to try sitting alone, has doubled in weight, may cut the first tooth, and enjoys watching what is happening around him or her.

In early infancy most infants will accept unfamiliar people without distress. As children move into later infancy, they begin to show a strong preference for their primary caregivers, usually their parents. By eight or nine months of age, many infants exhibit stranger anxiety, becoming upset when they encounter unfamiliar people.

The next big growth indicator comes around ten months, when the child can stand and balance with help and takes more interest in self-feeding. By one year, the growing child usually begins taking the first steps.

Interacting With the Child

During these early months, it is important to interact with infants and to provide enriched environments in order to stimulate their brain growth. Talk to them. Sing to them. Mimic the sounds and facial expressions they make. Encourage them to move, listen, and interact with their surroundings.

Infants learn from two sources, the senses and the actions they perform on objects in their environment. In many ways, children learn more in the first six months than ever again, for it is during this critical time that they learn to deal with time, space, and energy. Experiences at this stage, whether positive or negative, can have lifelong effects on their psychological, social, and spiritual development.

As the infant matures during the first year of life, the primary developmental issue is trust versus mistrust, an issue that continues through the early formative years. It is essential for the child to develop a trusting relationship with adults who are involved in the child's life and to have opportunities to explore in a safe environment. It is important that the initial relationship between child and adult is secure and that the child's needs are met in a positive, nurturing way. Such a foundation allows new attachments to develop with other adults and children, and the child trusts more easily.

Developmental Characteristics of Toddlers

Donna Lee Strieb
San Antonio, Texas

The Toddler (Twelve to Twenty-Four Months)

- becomes an experimenter.
- distinguishes among self, objects, and others.
- has increased mobility and language and is in constant motion.
- develops a desire to please parents and other significant adults.
- exhibits growing curiosity and wonder.
- tests independence and explores cause and effect.
- desires routine and orderliness.
- has a short attention span.
- needs a secure, safe environment with set limits.
- engages in parallel play with little sharing.
- experiences the world as revolving around "me."
- enjoys repetition.
- imitates skills and develops pretending.
- needs much rest because the body is so active.

A Positive Self-Image

The child will continue to build on the strength of the trusting relationships that began to develop during the early months of infancy. In this period, the primary developmental issue focuses on developing a positive self-image versus a negative one of shame and doubt. (Guilt says, "I made a mistake." Shame says, "I am a mistake.") A positive self-image will help the child negotiate future life tasks in a healthy, fulfilling manner and will provide a foundation for the child to understand him or herself as a beloved child of God.

For the child, the world is experienced through the senses of touch, sight, sound, taste, and smell. A child will perceive a person's true feelings about him or her and will react to the insecurity or nervousness of another person. The tones and inflections of the voice convey more than words; therefore, what we are, what we think, what we do, and how we speak teaches the young child more than the content of what we say.

From the time a child takes that first step alone until about two and a half years of age, constant motion seems the norm. Exploring and testing one's freedom is an exciting adventure, which means that a toddler will take great risks and be unaware of the danger. And since the memory span is short, the child can quickly forget hurts or instructions given. Thus, a safe environment with close adult supervision is important for experimentation and development of large-motor skills.

Toddlers love pleasant sounds, such as recorded music, singing, lullabies, animal noises, and words. They like to touch and pat and tap, to be talked to, to be sung to, and to be laughed with. Language is developing, but the child has a limited vocabulary and has difficulty in understanding as well as in being understood. Stories, simple songs with motions, and fingerplays are not only enjoyable but also enhance language development. Toddlers also love direct eye contact with others. This conveys a sense of undivided attention and connectedness that is doubly important in this exploratory stage.

Children this age can become unhappy when their parent is out of sight. The child has learned to trust the parent, and when a stranger appears on the scene and Mother or Daddy leaves, the child must start all over again to build a relationship of trust. Although this is a demanding time for adults, the child is emerging from babyhood into an individual person with a unique personality. It is a time of great growth and excitement.

Developmental Characteristics of Two-Year-Olds

Donna Lee Strieb
San Antonio, Texas

The Two-Year-Old
- develops further motor and language skills.
- continues to develop body balance and coordination.
- views the world from an egocentric perspective, focusing on "me" and "mine."
- does not understand right and wrong.
- is curious and loves to explore.
- needs love, care, and acceptance.
- enjoys repetition.
- does not distinguish between fantasy and reality.
- learns primarily through the senses.
- begins to understand and use the word *no*.
- plays alongside others (parallel play) more than with others.
- is easily frustrated and may throw tantrums.
- enjoys simple stories, rhymes, and songs.
- has a short attention span.
- is affectionate and can also show feelings of jealousy.

An Exciting Age
The second year is an exciting time. Physical mastery makes life easier. The power to say no allows the child to be more assertive, more fully a person. Routine is important. Old familiar patterns, food, clothing, and toys are preferred over new ones. When things become unfamiliar, shyness and fear may cause the child to want the security of a parent. Knowing that Mom or Dad is near is important. The issues of developing trust and a positive self-image continue to play a crucial role in the child's development.

Talking With Two-Year-Olds
Increasing language skills enable the child to be understood more readily and to respond to what people say. The following are some suggestions for communicating with two-year-olds:
- Speak at eye level with the child. This may mean that you need to kneel down so the child can see you without looking up.
- Speak in a natural voice and avoid baby talk. Sometimes adults have a tendency to speak in a high voice and use exaggerated facial expressions. This should be avoided, since young children learn by imitating what they hear and see.
- Encourage children to name objects and noises. Add additional information to what the child is saying: "Yes, that is a puppy. The puppy is warm and furry."
- Listen patiently. Learning to speak is not an easy task. Give the children plenty of time to express themselves. Show by your words and actions that you are interested in what they are saying. Model courtesy, respect, and good listening skills.

Infants, Toddlers, and Twos— Watch Them Grow!

MaryJane Pierce Norton
Nashville, Tennessee

Age	Development	Things to Do
Sleepy-heads (birth to six weeks)	Children in the first six weeks may sleep as much as twenty hours a day. This does not usually take the form of long periods of sleep, however. It is more likely to include periods of restlessness, some moments of alertness, and periods of seeking sleep even while eating. Newborns show interest in human voices and quickly learn to follow their parents' voices. They can see, hear, feel, smell, and taste. They see best what is close to their faces and is either black and white or of a primary color.	• Hold newborns close. • Provide mobiles with bold colors. • Sing to infants or hum while holding them close. The vibrations of your body will soothe infants.
Charmers (six weeks to five months)	As babies begin smiling and then laughing willingly, they charm most adults and children around them. At this stage, infants begin to control their heads while lying on their backs. They learn to roll from back to stomach. They will begin experimenting with sounds. Hands become a fascinating discovery, and the infant will stare at the hand, move the hand, suck on the hand, wiggle the hand. In fact, this becomes the child's most fascinating toy.	• Smile back at the baby. • Provide unbreakable mirrors so babies can watch themselves. Also provide musical toys and brightly colored objects. • Move babies from one place to another frequently so they can see and watch a variety of objects and activities. • Talk and laugh with infants.
Sitters (five to eight months)	By six months, most babies have doubled their birth weight, gotten their first tooth, and begun to sit unaided. They will throw things, bang things, drop things, and enjoy these throwing, banging, dropping games with any willing adults. By eight months, babies often begin to exhibit stranger anxiety. Where before they were willing to laugh and go to just about anyone, now they are aware if an adult is unfamiliar and will cry and cling to those they do know.	• Play peekaboo. • Introduce toys with different shapes. • Link words to actions and objects. • Provide space and places for babies to move freely, kick their legs, roll over, rock on all fours, and scoot or crawl.
Movers (eight to fourteen months)	Children respond to their own names and imitate sounds. By age one, some children can say two or three words and understand many more. Most are scooting, then crawling, then walking and exploring every available space they can. They are no longer happy being confined and are intent on practicing their new movements. Children stare at people and objects as if they are studying every detail. Most are teething and experience some misery with this. They enjoy balls, stacking toys, shape toys, fill-and-dump toys.	• Provide safe places for babies to practice crawling and walking. • Read. Read. Read. Use board books or plastic books. Make up your own words and use lots of sounds as you read. • Talk. Talk. Talk. Help the child build vocabulary words to understand and to speak.

Age	Development	Things to Do
Motion Machines (fourteen to twenty-four months)	By twenty-four months, children walk well and have begun to run. They are in constant motion, exercising their legs and, in fact, their whole bodies every waking moment. They fight against confinement. Many parents tell scary stories of toddlers slipping from the confines of a car seat, highchair, or playpen. Any kind of no will cause a negative reaction from toddlers. They are concerned with their own needs and wants and are not concerned at all with others. They are learning independence and seeking independence in nearly everything they do. They are beginning to do some reasoning and problem solving. They enjoy talking and will go from single words to short sentences by the time they are two. They explore everything, usually with their mouth first.	• Talk to the children. Encourage them to talk, and listen intently to what they say. • Provide space for the children to walk, bend, climb, and crawl. Push-and-pull toys and riding toys are good for this age. • They can begin making pictures with paper and crayons. • Provide a routine toddlers can follow. They like predictability and distrust change. • Set limits in the classroom. Children this age regard other children as objects to be explored. You will need to protect the rights of each child with rules for treating others kindly.
Talkers (twenty-four to thirty-six months)	The most distinctive development of twos is their emerging language ability. Over a period of one year, children progress from knowing and using as many as two hundred words to knowing and using as many as one thousand. The more they master language, the less likely they are to resort to kicking, hitting, or biting to let their needs be known. Questions become an important part of adult-child conversations. Twos continue to be physically active, climbing, hopping, and running as they grow in coordination. Although twos still have a short attention span, they can engage in quiet activities. And activities with adults are especially appealing. Twos are growing in awareness of others as human beings like themselves, with thoughts, feelings, wants, and needs. Sympathetic action emerges, with one child comforting another. This is the year for toilet training. Although some children master this skill as toddlers, most do not until they approach age three. Having friends and being in a group become more important to twos. You will often see children imitating one another's movements and words.	• Continue talking to children. Name things you see and feelings when they occur. Encourage children to build sentences and to use words instead of actions to express themselves. • Be sure to provide adequate space for movement. As often as possible, pair words with actions to exercise the body while building vocabulary. Twos enjoy songs, stories, finger-plays, and poems using action. • Twos enjoy art and the sensory pleasure it brings. They are interested in colors and in creating colorful art. • Routine and limits continue to be important for twos. As they start developing a sense of time, they begin to expect and look forward to story time, music time, and snack time. • Continue to state rules so that twos will have a clear understanding of limits and expectations.

Faith Development of Young Children

Donna Lee Strieb

San Antonio, Texas

While being held in the arms of love, an infant begins to experience faith. The development of trust in infancy, along with love and acceptance, can become the cornerstone for the foundation of the child's faith. In this first stage of faith development, the child's understanding of God is a reflection of the care and nurturing he or she experiences from parents and caregivers. As children learn to trust the dependability of those who love and care for them, they learn to trust the dependability, love, and care of God.

As a child enters the toddler years, the groundwork for faith development is laid by developing a joyful attitude about learning and a positive self-regard, orientation toward others, and attitude toward life.

These attitudes must be reinforced by both parents and caregivers. Therefore, religious education for young children becomes attitude education based on faith, hope, and love. Concepts of God are accepted as single ideas, but are not formed into a cohesive whole. The toddler's self-worth and self-esteem need to be nurtured within the boundaries of the adult's love and care, which proclaim: "You are a child of God."

During the first three years, there are certain basic concepts the child understands about God, Jesus, the Bible, and the church. Children begin to learn that

- the Bible is an important book that is full of stories, especially about Jesus.
- Jesus loves God and people, taught about God, and was born as a baby with caring parents.
- God loves each person.
- they can express praise, wonder, joy, and thanksgiving.
- the church is a happy place where we hear stories of Jesus and offer prayers to God.

The Holy Spirit is a difficult concept for young children, which can be approached as feeling God's nearness.

Positive reinforcement of any action that encourages trust, dependability, love, and care should begin from the first moments of a child's life. Trust is the foundation of faith, for if a child learns to trust the parent, then the child will learn to trust God. In addition,

learning to have a genuine appreciation for nature opens up the ability to appreciate the Creator and to experience God's grace in all living things. Another attitude that nurtures faith is predictability in the orderliness of life, which allows for trust in the routine.

Parents need to teach their children positive self-regard and positive orientation toward others. The church can play an important role in assisting parents in the Christian nurture of their children. Talk to your young child about God's love just as you speak of your love for the child. Your actions will demonstrate your love and respect for each other as well as for your little one. You can express your own faith through prayer times with your child.

Caregivers help nurture faith when they radiate serenity and security; have nurturing attitudes; are patient but persistent when necessary; are comforting, flexible, and creative; and can respond to the different personalities and temperaments of children. Through the interaction of daily routines and appropriate play experience, caregivers can help children trust, love, and care.

Congregations can support parents by offering help and knowledge, providing the highest quality care possible with the best caregivers, accepting children in the worshiping community, and loving the children in their midst whenever the opportunity presents itself.

Parents, caregivers, and congregations have been given priceless treasures in the little children who enter their lives. Together, with God's help, we can all do our part to help our children know themselves to be children of God. Jesus said, "Let the little children come to me; do not stop them; for it is to such as these that the kingdom of God belongs" (Mark 10:14). When a child is baptized, the entire congregation, including the parents, promises to live according to the example of Christ, to nurture the child in Christian faith, and to pray for the child and for one another.

With Jesus' command ringing in our ears, and through the promise made each time a child is baptized, we are called to an important responsibility—the responsibility to the Christian nurture of children. May God grant us wisdom and understanding.

Nurturing the Young Child's Spiritual Nature

Judith Mayo
Livonia, Michigan

When a child is born, parents often purchase the latest books on infants and childcare. They learn the most modern thinking on immunizations, medications, diapering, feeding methods, and schedules. Most parents try hard to nurture their children so they will grow up to be strong and healthy. Parents often take classes on nurturing self-esteem in their children, listening skills, positive discipline, and teaching children responsible behavior. They purchase all the latest learning toys and study the newest learning theories. Many parents look for developmental nursery schools that will facilitate early learning. But how often do we, as parents, caregivers, and members of the congregation, give serious and intentional thought to another important part of our children's nature, their spirituality?

Children are born spiritual, coming into this world with a natural openness and sense of wonder. They begin their lives as intuitive beings. When they are nurtured and allowed to grow in healthy ways, they will have a persistent yearning for a deep and natural relationship with the Divine. Children respond to the miraculous and the wonderful. Their imaginations are capable of working with rich imagery and of incorporating it into their sense of reality. Young children are not yet able to think abstractly, nor are they prisoners of the rational. They know a truth that most of us forget: All truth is not understood in a totally rational way; some truth is intuitively perceived or left for a pleasurable experience of discovery.

Jesus said, "Truly I tell you, unless you change and become like children, you will never enter the kingdom of heaven" (Matthew 18:3). Jesus is not telling us to be childish, naive, and immature in order to enter the Kingdom. Rather, it is the openness of little children to be in personal relationship with Jesus Christ that we are to seek.

Nurturing Spirituality

While all children are born spiritual, the environment can do much to nurture their spirituality. Parents and caregivers must be deliberate about supplying the content for this spirituality. If you want your child to grow

spiritually as a Christian, you must make Christian content available to him or her. You must supply the Christian stories, images, and symbols from which your child can begin to fashion his or her own spirituality. Some developmental theorists tell us that there are specific tasks individuals must accomplish at every stage of development before moving on to the next stage. Only when each task is completed can the individual make a healthy transition to the next developmental stage. We can learn much from these theories to inform our understanding of the young child's spiritual development.

According to developmental theory, the first major crisis is birth—real, physical separation from the mother. It is through coping with this first stage of development that the infant begins to establish the trust or mistrust that will determine his or her expectations of all future relationships, including spiritual ones.

Parents and caregivers must respond consistently to the infant's cries, providing whatever the child needs in a calm and loving way. The establishment of routines of care and play, the extent and manner in which the child is held and spoken to, the amount of eye contact between the child and the caregiver—these are some of the absolutely essential elements in determining the foundation of trust or mistrust that the infant will bring to all future relationships. The establishment of trusting, caring, dependable relationships also determines whether the child will approach a relationship with Jesus Christ in a positive, trusting way, or whether it will be a relationship based on anxiety and mistrust.

With the emergence of language ability, young children develop the capacity for a rich imagination. They are able to construct vivid images that, in many cases, stay with them into adulthood. To nurture the young child's spiritual life, carefully select the sources that the child uses to construct these images. Telling appropriate Bible stories will supply the images that undergird the child's spirituality. By the same token, be aware of other images the child is absorbing from the media, other children, and the environment. Discuss what the child is experiencing. Help give language to and focus on positive Christian images.

Ways to Encourage Spiritual Growth

The work of children is play. Provide them with biblical images for assimilation and incorporation into play:

- Provide Bible storybooks.
- Visit your sanctuary.
  - Explore and become comfortable with the sanctuary.
  - Admire the banners, stained glass windows, and pictures.
  - Sing hymns.
  - Look at the baptismal font and feel the water.
- Tell the story of Jesus' baptism, and talk about the child's baptism.
- Provide an unbreakable nativity scene, and use these figures to tell the story of Jesus' birth.
  - Wonder together how the shepherds felt when they heard the angel choir.
  - Encourage the child to retell the story using the nativity figures.
- Provide other manipulatives that can be used to tell and roleplay Bible stories.
- Get a flannelboard with story figures for storytelling.
- Talk with God.
- Pray together.
- Admire God's creation.
- Wonder and think about God, Jesus, and people of faith.

Model your own spiritual nature for your child. Model how you pray, how you read the Bible, how you are a steward of all that is entrusted to you. Talk about your relationship with Jesus Christ. Let your faith show as a constant part of all that you do.

Most of all, surround your child with a loving, dependable environment that is filled with wholesome influences. Provide the contents for the child's spirituality through Bible stories and religious imagery. Respect the child's spiritual nature. Respect and encourage play that includes activities such as picnics with Jesus. Do not be anxious about an imaginary friend named Zacchaeus. Such play is an indication that the child has assimilated biblical images that will help the formation and reformation of maturing spirituality. Dorcas is a wonderful name for a doll. Encourage wonder and play to meet and develop the child's relationship with Jesus Christ in a way that is appropriate for maturity and individuality.

Brain Development of Young Children

Mary Alice Gran
Nashville, Tennessee

The first few years are a time of exceptional physical growth. Watch a baby quickly outgrow newborn clothes and move shortly into big-kids clothes. This is also a time of enormous mental growth.

With the advent of powerful technology, scientists are learning more about how the brain works. Every day new research uncovers added information that increases our understanding of the growth of the brain.

At the same time, there has been an increased interest in the learning and well-being of young children. Research has increased our understanding of what early childhood specialists have long suspected: The first three years are crucial for the emotional and intellectual growth of children.

At birth, the baby's brain contains about one hundred billion nerve cells (neurons), which have complex thinking capabilities. In order to function, these nerve cells must connect with one another. During a child's early years, brain connections are made that are used throughout a lifetime. These connections are made through experiences that shape the developing structures of the brain.

What can we do in the nursery environment to support the brain development of infants, toddlers, and two-year-olds? Here are some practical suggestions:

- **Be verbal**—Talk with each child. Listen to the child's speech, and mimic the sounds he or she makes. Watch the child's facial expressions, body language, and verbal cries for cues to what he or she is trying to say. Use language to express these cues. Also use language to express what you are doing and thinking. And read, read, read.
- **Move**—Encourage movement of large and small muscles. From hand grasps to leg movements, help children move. Play gentle games that get them moving.
- **Use music**—Sing to the child. Play games that use music, and repeat them over and over. Play music softly while the child is doing other activities.
- **Touch**—Encourage the child to reach, grasp, and touch. Use textures and shapes for play; stack and splash and squeeze. Caress the cheek. Pat the arm. Hold and rock and sway.
- **Experience the world**—Watch a streamer move in the breeze. Look at the baby in a mirror. Play in the box. Climb the step. Push the ball. Laugh and laugh and laugh.
- **Be responsive**—Observe the child and take cues from him or her to learn when it is time to repeat the activity, have a quiet time, or change to a different activity. Even infants communicate. Pay attention to what they are saying and you will learn from them.
- **Protect the brain**—Initiate habits of safety that protect babies' brains from injury. All babies fall as they learn to sit, crawl, walk, climb, and run. Continually strive for a safe environment where falls are minimized and learning is maximized.

As a caregiver, you have an important role to play in creating a positive environment in which to encourage the young child's brain to grow. Take your role seriously as you have fun caring for and loving infants, toddlers, and twos.

Additional Resources

Mapping the Mind, by Rita Carter (Los Angeles: University of California Press, 1999).

Rethinking the Brain: New Insights Into Early Development, from Families and Work Institute (212-465-2044, www.familiesandwork.org).

The First Years Last Forever video, from I Am Your Child (310-285-2385, www.iamyourchild.org).

Self-Esteem of Young Children

M. Kathryn Armistead
Nashville, Tennessee

Self-esteem means "how I value myself." Healthy self-esteem means that personal needs are fulfilled and given joyful, creative expression. Healthy self-esteem allows a person to behave unselfishly and to have a deepening capacity for joy, peace, patience, kindness, goodness, gentleness, and self-control. This is the direction in which we want our children to grow.

Here are ways that caregivers and parents can enhance infants' self-esteem:

The first step is to keep yourself healthy. A healthy caregiver or parent has a much better chance of having an easily soothed baby. By healthy, I mean more than physical health. I also mean emotional, relational, and spiritual health. Remember, a child's self-esteem will be, at least in part, a reflection of the parent's health.

The second step is for the family and caregivers to welcome the infant into a place that is safe, secure, and stable. After the birth, the parent brings home an infant, a real person with wishes, demands, delights, creative urges, and physical needs. A home should be a haven that provides predictable regularity and a place for play, a place where the child is touched, caressed, and cherished. The same is true for the church nursery.

The third step is to give empathy to and to take delight in the child. It is imperative that the infant experience empathy from the parent. This means responding to, confirming, approving of, and mirroring the infant. Every child needs to have a parent who feels and expresses delight in who the child is and what the child accomplishes. The child looks for the gleam in the parent's eye. The payoff in the child's later life will be appropriate ambitions.

The fourth step is a parent who lets the child idealize him or her. Idealization by a child may also enhance your self-esteem, but remember that idealization will not last much beyond the age of five; so be prepared to let it go. Through this process, the child experiences what it is like to be big and strong and to find comfort when it is needed. The payoff in the child's later life includes ideals, respect of principles, and the ability to sustain a sense of well-being and focus.

The fifth step is to let the child work and play beside the parent. In this the child is doing more than copying your behavior as a parent or caregiver. The child is exploring his or her talents and interests, as well as experiencing an essential alikeness that is reassuring. The child is experiencing what it is like to share oneself with another through participating together in an activity or task. The child is accepted during the primarily adult activity.

The sixth step is to put the no's of a toddler into perspective and to respect what the child is trying to accomplish. An infant may have a sense of self, but the parent and caregivers also project their own desires, feelings, and preconceptions onto the child. Between eighteen and twenty-four months, the child demonstrates the ability to organize experiences into categories. The toddler often introduces the categories by saying no. The child is not trying to make you angry or to get attention. The child is trying to assert who he or she is. Because the toddler is also beginning to reflect on his or her and your activities, you can also take this opportunity to express yourself in short, clear statements. Even if the child does not fully comprehend your reasoning, go ahead and briefly explain. This can help set a pattern for talking through differences. If you have to discipline a child, it is also important to express your reasoning coherently. Limiting the use of the word *no* increases its power and challenges you to find positive alternatives.

Healthy self-esteem enables a child to appropriately love self, others, and God with an ever-deepening capacity for the fruits of the Holy Spirit: joy, peace, patience, kindness, generosity, faithfulness, gentleness, and self-control.

Children's Play

Barb Nardi-Kurtz
San Antonio, Texas

Catalina is five months old. Today she is sitting in the swing in the doorway. Using her feet to push, she swings to and fro; and when she leans and pushes, she goes around or from side to side. Catalina crows with laughter, enjoying her play time in the swing.

Yesterday, when she was put in the swing for the first time, Catalina did not know what to do. Her mother pushed her once or twice, but Catalina was tired and became fussy and cried after a few moments.

Today, Catalina has learned to play in the swing, manipulating items in her environment and exercising her feet and legs, arms and hands, and back.

Children will learn an enormous amount in their first three years. Their sometimes seemingly aimless play has great purpose. The child is learning how to move, to communicate, to manipulate objects—how to do most everything! Language, movement, and discrimination are all part of the learning of the very young child. Play is the learning setting.

Josh was fifteen months old when he received a wonderful green wagon for Christmas. It has a gate on the side and a seat at either end. Josh had a good time tearing away the bag the wagon came in, but then he wandered off. All Christmas Day he kept coming back to investigate. By bedtime, he had learned to open the gate, climb in, and seat himself. He learned that he could hide by curling up in the well between the seats. In his off-and-on play with the wagon, Josh was manipulating the gate, exercising, climbing, reaching, using his imagination, and becoming more confident in his growing abilities.

How do we encourage this kind of play in young children? Three elements are especially important: (1) an environment that it is safe and convenient to explore; (2) toys that encourage experimentation and imagination; and (3) people who are willing to encourage seemingly aimless play while providing resources that will enable the child to grow.

Toys, Books, and Equipment

At twelve to eighteen months, children need lots of room to move and a few colorful, easy-to-manipulate, and easy-to-keep-clean toys.

Nesting boxes and stacking rings are great early toys, as are sets of measuring cups and spoons and nesting, unbreakable mixing bowls. Things to climb under and into encourage exploration. A small wagon, a soft sculpture, and a plastic age-appropriate jungle gym are good items for exploration.

As the child grows older, furnishings and equipment can grow in sophistication and size, but not necessarily in number. Too many objects can be confusing to young children. A few colorful, well-built toys and a few pieces of sturdy, basic furniture are always better than clutter. In a church nursery, several of one colorful, easy-to-manipulate toy is preferable to many different items.

As a child approaches age two, the addition of a table with attached benches provides encouragement to climb, to sit and work at simple puzzles or pegboards, or to build with large plastic building blocks. A little later, you might add washable markers and large newsprint for creating pictures.

A removable sandbox with built-up edges that you can set firmly on the table is a good addition for play. Fill it full of various sizes and shapes of beans and a few cups, spoons, and graduated strainers, and a child will stay busy for long stretches of time. Remember to never leave a child unsupervised.

Books are important from the very beginning of a child's life. They may go in the mouth endless times, but board, plastic, and cloth infant books are made to be chewed on. Picture books help the child differentiate objects. As they grow, children will begin telling stories with books, especially if someone reads to them.

Through play children reinforce their sense of identity, develop motor skills, learn to move about in their environment, and learn to trust themselves and others. Given the opportunity for play by loving caregivers in comfortable and safe surroundings, they will continue to grow as confident, healthy children.

Using the Articles in This Section

The articles in this section are directed toward the caregivers and teachers who will be with young children in the various ministries of the church. Use the articles in training sessions, in orientation manuals, or as part of one-on-one training.

Section Two:
The Caregiver/Teacher

Contents

Other Related Articles

Helping the Young Child Grow in Faith

MaryJane Pierce Norton
Nashville, Tennessee

Nurture Faith in Infants

Parents bring their children to church in order to help them grow in faith, and the foundation for their faith begins in infancy. All faith is based on trust; therefore, as children learn that adults can be trusted to satisfy their needs, this becomes the basis for trusting God.

As adults, we often separate the physical self from the spiritual self, forgetting that our whole being is intertwined. A young child does not make that sort of division of self. Fulfilling a physical need also nurtures the child's mental, psychological, and spiritual needs.

Respond to the Needs of Infants

The first step in faith growth for infants comes when adults pay attention to their needs. As a teacher, seek to respond in good time to each baby's needs to be changed, fed, talked to, played with, and rocked. This says to the child, "This person cares for me." It builds the foundation for the child to be able to say, "I know what it is like for God to care for me, because I have experienced care from adults." Trusting in God's love and care is the foundation of a child's faith. Through attitudes, feelings, and actions, we teach the infant about God's love and about our love for one another.

Talk About God

Long before they begin to talk, children can recognize words and know what they mean as adults use the same words over and over again. We help children grow in faith as we help them build the language of faith. Use CDs or cassette tapes with simple songs about God and Jesus. Say short prayers to God as you hold and talk with the baby.

Talk About the Children

Every child is a child of God. Beginning when the child is an infant, we say over and over again, "You are a child of God. God loves you. You are important." This helps the child begin to make the connection between God and him or herself. Having caring adults tell the child over and over, "You are a child of God" helps form the basis for healthy self-worth.

Play With the Children

It always makes me sad to walk into a room and observe adults talking and interacting with one another instead of with the children in their care. This says to the children: "You really do not matter much to me. I would rather talk over you than talk to you. Maybe when you're an adult you'll be important enough to get my attention."

As infants feel your arms around them, feel your body rocking theirs, see the pictures you point to, and play with you, they learn that they matter. They grow and learn. We build faith as we play with the babies in our care. We build faith because we are teaching this message: "You matter. You are important. I enjoy you. I like helping you learn. God loves you."

Practice Christian Values in the Classroom

We teach values in every word we say and every action we take. We teach forgiveness as we lovingly clean up a spill instead of demanding angrily, "Look at the mess you've made!" We teach hope as we say, "Just look at you turn over. My, how you're growing. Thank you, God, for growing children!" Ask yourself, *Do children in my class learn values that show love for God and love for neighbor?*

Nurture Faith in Toddlers and Twos

Most toddlers and twos have begun to communicate not just through their actions, cries, and laughter but also through words. Teaching the faith to toddlers is still much the same as for infants. Their religious concepts are related to concrete experiences; therefore, much of the way we teach is through the experiences we provide in the classroom.

Provide a Climate of Trust

For toddlers and twos, trust means having a dependable place with dependable faces. Toddlers and twos do not like change; they appreciate sameness: the same caregivers, the same classroom, the same schedule, and so forth. They like hearing the same stories, singing the same songs, enjoying the same activities over and over again. We might become bored, but for the toddler or two-year-old who is growing and changing so rapidly day by day, this dependability builds trust. It leads them to say, "I know the people I can count on. I know what's waiting for me." And since you, the teacher, are trustworthy and speak of God as trustworthy, the child says, "I can trust God because I trust my teacher, and my teacher tells me God loves me."

Model Caring

Toddlers and twos often have little regard for other children, except as objects to explore. But by age two, as they grow in their ability to play and interact, other children become more important as friends and play-mates. Children mimic adults. You, the caregiver, are modeling care and concern for others. Children will learn to show care and concern as they see you hug a child, take care of a scraped knee, and guard a child from being hurt by another.

Pray With the Children

Children learn their first prayers early. My son, Bradford, was saying two- and three-word prayers long before I expected it. Often, the only discernible word was *God*, but he had learned the attitude of prayer and the places of prayer even before he could really speak his prayers. He learned these prayers at church and at home. You, the caregiver, teach prayer as you pray. Pray often with the children, praying short prayers of thanks for what you do and see, for food, for hurts, and for each child.

Sing With the Children

Songs help us express our faith in God. Pair words with actions so that toddlers and twos can learn the songs more quickly. Sing songs about Jesus, God, church, and children.

Tell and Read Stories

Books that talk about God, Jesus, and the church help toddlers and twos grow in knowledge and in faith. They enjoy hearing stories and having books read to them. Twos also enjoy using flannelboards and putting up pieces of the story as you tell it. Short Bible stories about God's love and care are good choices. Keep a Bible in the room, and refer to it as the book adults read to help them know more about God.

Play With the Children

We cannot separate religious growth from total growth. As the whole child is nurtured, spiritual growth is nurtured. Play is the work of the child. Through play children learn and grow, exercise their minds and bodies, explore the world and their place in the world, learn about God's creation and their place in creation. Through play they learn that they can create. As you, the caregiver, play with the children, you teach faith.

Help! I'm Not a Nurse!

MaryJane Pierce Norton
Nashville, Tennessee

Although it was not really a laughing matter, we used to laugh about "Tuesday morning sniffles." Parents pointed out to me that their babies often had sniffles on Tuesday morning after they had been in the church nursery on Sunday. As much as we worked to provide a safe, healthy environment for children in our church, illnesses were still passed from child to child.

As the teacher or caregiver, you can take steps to ensure a healthy classroom.
1. Use the highest standards of cleanliness for everything in infant/toddler rooms.
2. Familiarize yourself with children's illnesses.
3. Enforce an illness policy approved by your congregation.

Developing Guidelines

Parents should not bring children who are ill to the nursery, but occasionally it will happen. What do you do? How do you know when to ask the parent to take the child home? And when do you know that, although the child may be uncomfortable, there is no risk to the other children in your care?

First of all, ask the education committee or children's council of your congregation to adopt a written illness policy. Distribute it to parents and post it near the door of the nursery. Clearly indicate which illnesses are easily spread from child to child. Become familiar with signs of illnesses common to infants and toddlers. In fact, working with many children as you do, you may be better able to spot illnesses before parents (especially first-time parents) are aware of them.

Illness

Exclude children from the nursery for the following illnesses and/or symptoms:
1. Diarrhea (more than three times in the last twenty-four hours).
2. Vomiting (two or more episodes in the previous twenty-four hours).
3. Temperature above 101 degrees.
4. Skin infections or infestations (impetigo, head lice, ringworm, or shingles) until at least twenty-four hours after treatment begins.
5. Pink or red eye with eye discharge.
6. Nasal discharge that is greenish in color.

Rashes

Occasionally, a child will arrive in the nursery with spots. This could indicate a skin irritation, heat rash, or allergic reaction. But sometimes it is chickenpox or another illness that can pass quickly from child to child. Here is a list of six common rashes and their symptoms:
1. **Chickenpox**—Symptoms include a small, red pimple-like rash that develops into blisters. These will crust and then heal. Children who have been exposed to chickenpox develop the rash twelve to twenty-one days after exposure. They are contagious one to two days before the rash appears and until all the blisters have formed scabs.
2. **Measles**—Symptoms include a red rash, high fever, red eyes, and cough. While most children are immunized for measles, some are not. After exposure, children may develop the disease in ten to twelve days.
3. **Roseola**—Symptoms include a high fever that goes away and is followed by a red rash that lasts twenty-four to forty-eight hours. After exposure, children may develop the disease within seven to fourteen days. This disease commonly affects children between the ages of six months and two years.
4. **Impetigo**—Symptoms include a skin infection that starts as a single round bump surrounded by a red area that turns into a crusty lesion. The contagious period usually ends within twenty-four hours of starting treatment with antibiotics. The incubation period is usually one to three days after exposure, during which the disease can spread easily to other children.

5. **Fifth Disease**—Symptoms include a "slapped-cheek" rash on the face, a low-grade fever, and a lacy rash that moves from the upper to the lower body. Although it is not as well known as some of the other rashes, it is important to be aware of it, as it can be harmful to unborn children. The incubation period is four to fourteen days.

6. **Herpes Simplex Virus I**—Symptoms include mouth sores, swollen glands, fever, and a red, weepy rash. This disease can be transmitted by adults who have cold sores. The incubation period is two to twelve days.

Communicating With Parents

When a child who was present in the nursery is found to have a contagious illness, check to see which other children were exposed. Parents will greatly appreciate being told of potential exposure. They may want to contact their physician for advice.

While it may be difficult for you to confront a parent with an ill child, remember that you are the caregiver for many children. Your role is to provide a safe, healthy environment for the children present. And remember, an ill child needs one-on-one care and does not need to be with other children and caregivers.

Will You Please Sign In?

MaryJane Pierce Norton
Nashville, Tennessee

I am part of a small church where there are often fewer than fifty in Sunday school on Sunday morning. Recently, something happened that helped us remember the importance of forms. As one of the toddlers was walking across the floor, she tripped and fell. Nothing was on the floor that made her trip; it just happened, as it often does with toddlers. Her shoes just got in the way, causing her to fall with such force that she split her lip. Blood and tears began to pour. One of the caregivers picked her up and started searching for her parents, but neither parent was in the place where he or she could normally be found on Sunday morning. They were found quickly enough, but not without some anxious movement through the halls and in and out of classrooms. If we had been using a sign-in sheet, they could have been found more quickly, and Allison could have been comforted by her parents in a more timely manner.

As a teacher, you have an extra bit of security when using a sign-in sheet. You can tell at a glance where parents will be if they are needed. You have ready information about medications, feedings, and naps to help you know how best to minister to the child.

Do not hesitate to gently remind parents of the importance of completely filling out the sign-in sheet each time they come to the nursery.

(Note: A full-page sign-in sheet is on page 174.)

Sample Sign-In Sheet

Today's Date _____

Child's Name	Parent's Name	Parent's Location	Comments	Arrival Time	Pickup Time	Signature of Parent Picking up Child

Saying Goodbye With a Smile

MaryJane Pierce Norton
Nashville, Tennessee

It's Sunday morning, and a parent and child are approaching the church nursery. With each step, the parent's steps drag. With a burst of energy and an "I'm not going to let this get the best of me" smile, the parent enters the nursery.

"Here we are!" the parent announces cheerfully as she hands her eight-month-old to the waiting teacher. Quickly she turns to beat a fast retreat. The baby's face immediately crumples, and the crying begins.

Now a new dilemma begins for the parent. Does she walk out while her baby is crying? Does she turn to comfort her child, knowing that she may end up spending the entire time in the nursery? The mother thinks to herself, *Why now? We've been coming to the church nursery for weeks. Why do I now have a crying child?*

This scene is not unusual. Over and over again on Sunday morning and through the week, children seem to go almost overnight from being quite happy being left with a teacher to crying brokenheartedly. What has happened to those happy babies? What can you, the caregiver, do to reassure parents as they leave their children in your care?

Separation Anxiety

Most young infants make a smooth transition into the nursery, smiling happily at parents as they leave and at caregivers who take them. But around six to eight months, most babies experience separation anxiety. This is actually a healthy sign, as infants are beginning to realize that they are separate from their parents and that their parents are actually leaving and are not simply where they cannot see them. This is a natural part of growth, so it should be applauded. The baby is growing as he or she should be.

However, separation anxiety can be hard for parents. As the teacher, you know that the infant will most likely stop crying soon after being left. But when a parent leaves a crying child, you can bet he or she will be thinking, *Maybe I shouldn't have left him this time. I wonder if he's still crying. Am I a bad parent to have walked out with my child wanting me?*

For some children, separation anxiety does not completely end until age three.

What to Do

First, it is important for parents, especially first-time parents, to realize that separation anxiety is normal and healthy. Explain that this is normal and that it is simply a sign that their child loves them and wants to be with them.

Encourage parents to arrive early enough to allow time for a routine: signing in, placing the child's belongings in a cubicle, hugging, and waving goodbye.

Greet all parents and babies warmly and cheerfully, refraining from negative comments.

Encourage parents to observe the group but not to get down to play with their child, as this raises the child's expectations that parents are going to stay.

Talk with parents, explaining that prolonging the goodbye time can sometimes make it more difficult. With each successive hug, kiss, pat on the back, and goodbye, children build up hope that the parent will stay. Thus, when the parent leaves, the protest becomes even more vocal. Each child and parent is unique, so if the child or parent seems to be experiencing particularly intense separation anxiety, encourage the parent to stay.

Help the parent and child with their goodbyes. As a parent, I have often been frustrated when teachers did not notice my dilemma and help me involve my child in an activity or offer to hold my child to help the transition. Remember favorite toys and activities, and be ready with these for children who have difficulty separating from parents. One of my son's teachers always greeted him with, "Bradford, I've been waiting for you! Let's go get your favorite book." He had something to look forward to, I felt relieved, and we both began the day happier.

Help parent and child by reinforcing when the parent will be returning (for example, "Daddy will be coming back for you at the end of Sunday school"). If you can, peg the routine of the parent to an activity the child will recognize, such as "right after snack time" or "after nap time."

Create a partnership with parents. Be honest about how the child handled the goodbye time. It helps the parent with the next separation if you say, "Jason cried for five minutes after you left, but he was fine and cheerful after that." It is also helpful to say, "Melissa cried most of the hour after you left." Then you can suggest ways to ease the transition the next time.

A familiar routine for leaving the classroom is as important as a familiar routine for entering it. Children handle the return of parents in many different ways. Some rush to their parents with open arms. Some ignore their parents or refuse to leave and cling to their teacher. Suggest that parents follow a familiar pickup routine: signing out, checking the child's cubicle for belongings, and saying goodbye to friends, favorite toys, and caregivers. Try to include an easy goodbye song.

What Does Not Help

Sporadic attendance makes it difficult for children to adjust. Encourage parents to attend regularly, if possible. This helps children recognize you as their teacher, friend, and trusted adult.

Slipping out unnoticed, without saying goodbye, tears down the feeling of trust. The child will miss the parent and then usually cry when he or she realizes the parent has left. Trust is the basis for faith at this age, so it is hard to build this foundation for faith when trust is shaken.

What Makes It Harder

Some circumstances make separation anxiety even more difficult. As a teacher, you should be prepared to help even more in these situations:

- When English is a second language for a child, separation anxiety may be more severe. You can help by learning a few words of comfort in the language of the child's family.
- When a child has little experience being with other children and in group-care situations, separation anxiety can be especially hard. Encourage the parent to visit with the child at least once before leaving the child, and more often if necessary.
- When the child has had a bad experience in group care, separating from parents can be more difficult. Ask parents about experiences in nursery or childcare. Talk through what you, as teacher, will do to help both parent and child separate.

With infants and toddlers, we are building the foundation upon which they will form their first impressions of church. Helping children feel cared for and loved by their church includes helping them move from parent to classroom with as little upset as possible.

Discipline With Infants, Toddlers, and Twos

MaryJane Pierce Norton
Nashville, Tennessee

You have four children in your care: a three-month-old infant, a ten-month-old crawler, a twelve-month-old, and a fifteen-month-old. Imagine the following situations:

The three-month-old is crying. It seems as if every time you put him down, he begins crying. What do you do?

The ten-month-old is clinging to her mom, refusing to enter into any activity. What do you do?

The twelve-month-old and fifteen-month-old have handfuls of each other's hair. What do you do?

In each of these situations, your approach to discipline, to guiding a child's behavior, will influence your actions. Think for a minute about the word *discipline*. Did you know that *discipline* and *disciple* come from the same root word? In both cases, something is taught and something is learned. As disciples of Jesus, we live by his example and follow his teachings. In the classroom, the children we teach live by our example and follow our teachings. They are learning a way of living through our example.

One of the goals of discipline is to establish controls for children to help them grow in a healthy, safe manner. Through discipline they learn adult controls until they can move to self-control, self-discipline. Infants and toddlers benefit from caregivers who guide their behavior in appropriate ways. The next question is, What is appropriate discipline for infants and toddlers?

Young Infants

Our primary concern as caregivers is to create a trusting, caring environment for infants. When they cry, do we care for their need? Babies who are attended to quickly in the early months cry less as they grow because they learn that the world around them is a good and trustworthy place. Are we gentle and soothing as we change diapers, give bottles, rock, and play with infants? An infant may be attended to quickly, but the manner and kind of attention may not build trust. Being gentle and speaking in soothing tones teaches that this is a safe place. This is discipline for the young infant that establishes a climate of love and trust.

Older Infants

As infants become more interested in the world around them, they need interesting experiences to help them grow. They need to see action, play with toys, interact with adults. As infants grow and increase their mobility, they may become bored and cry more often. As a caregiver, your role with older infants includes providing a stimulating atmosphere for them.

Move older infants from infant seats, to playpens, to the floor, providing them with appropriate toys to explore. Hold them, carry them, rock them to reassure them of your presence. Provide a variety of stimuli. As their attention is captured, there is less crying. With less crying, you are less likely to worry about spoiling the child by holding or carrying him or her. One reason babies cry is that they want to be carried, to receive constant stimulation, to see more things, to move around, to be close to others. Try to anticipate this need by moving the baby from place to place, providing different toys to stimulate the child.

Another concern with the older infant is stranger anxiety. You are often a stranger to the infant, and the child lets everyone know by crying, clinging, or screaming. Actually, this is a healthy sign that indicates love for the adults who are primary caregivers. It also shows that the child is now able to distinguish between those who are close and those who are not. As a caregiver, how you handle this in caring, loving ways is part of discipline with the infant.

Toddlers and Twos

Toddlers and twos are off to discover the world. They know no limits and have no understanding of danger. They know only that they want to go, go, go. They declare their independence with their frequent no's and their ability to get into something each and every minute of the day.

Toddlers and twos need a safe environment in which to explore the world. They need limits since they have none themselves. They need a safe place to touch and learn, as they are curious and inquisitive. The world is opening up to them, and this early curiosity helps them as they learn to care for themselves and others and develop imagination, language, and motor skills.

This great curiosity leads to situations that can be unsafe to themselves and to others. Remember the two children pulling each other's hair? Most likely they are not pulling hair to hurt each other; they are pulling hair to explore each other. Unfortunately, they are also hurting each other as a side effect, and they need limits and rules to guard against harm.

The no's of toddlers and twos emerge as they begin developing autonomy and self-control. Seemingly overnight, compliant children become stubborn and determined to have their own way. And they say no even when they want to say yes or actually mean yes.

As a caregiver, you can help your toddlers develop self-control when you do the following:

- Provide a safe environment, a room with safety features, such as receptacle covers on electrical outlets and toys without sharp corners. Always have at least two adults present.
- Reassure children, continually letting them know you are there to love and care for them. Hugging, rocking, holding children when they are out of control are important ways in which we let children know that we are still there caring for them.
- Have faith in children. As the children you teach move from the total dependency of the young infant to the growing independence of the toddler, build their confidence and move them closer to self-discipline by pointing out what they can do: "Look how you can jump!" "You put all the puzzle pieces into the puzzle. Good for you!" "I'll help and together we can pick up these toys. You're a big helper placing these toys back on the shelf."

- Offer limited choices: "You may play with the ball or with the pillow. Which do you choose?" Learning to choose is an important step in self-control. Limiting choices helps build early success for the child.
- Set two or three rules for your class, and be consistent: (1) Use gentle touches. (2) Take care of toys by picking them up. Toddlers benefit from hearing these rules. Talk about being gentle with one another and taking care of the things in the classroom.
- Act the way you want the children to act. Remember, you are teaching by example. Remove children from situations when they are hurting others. Often, a toddler or two-year-old will lose control and begin kicking, screaming, and crying. Holding children so that they cannot kick and thrash about can help them calm down and regain control.

Some Final Thoughts

Express pride in the way infants and toddlers in your care are growing. Show interest in what they are learning. Enjoy their development. Respect their feelings. Remember, they grow and learn from the example you set of care, assurance, and positive expectations.

Any kind of negative physical reactions to a young child's behavior (hitting, spanking, slapping) is never appropriate. Always act as though the parent were by your side.

Children With Special Needs

Marti Biegler
Burnsville, Minnesota

The key to working with children with developmental, behavioral, or emotional limitations is to communicate with the family. You will have to deal with two different situations: (1) the first-time or visiting child and (2) the child who will be in your nursery on a regular basis.

If the child is a visitor, remember that parents of a child with special needs generally spend a lot of time with their child and are usually quite willing to discuss information that will help you care for him or her. You may want to ask, "Do you have any special instructions that will help me care for your child?" Actually, this is a good idea for any visiting child. In addition, ask the parents of a visiting child if the child knows any children in the nursery. Again, this is a good practice for any visitor, as it demonstrates your desire to make the child feel comfortable.

As with any child, if you serve a snack, be sure to ask the parent if the child may partake. If at any time the child is having a difficult time, you may either try to have one person care for the child or place him or her in a group with fewer children per caregiver.

When the child is picked up, be sure to take time to discuss with the parents how things went. What did their child enjoy? Did their child need to be comforted? How? Did their child connect with another child or caregiver? Any visitor needs to know that his or her child's needs are going to be acknowledged. And the parents of the child with particular needs will certainly appreciate that their child has been included in the ministry of the church.

A Home Visit

If the visiting child is now in your nursery weekly, the nursery coordinator should phone the parents not only to welcome the child and the family to the congregation but also to set up a time for the coordinator to visit the family. The purpose of the visit is to get to know them better and to ask and answer questions about their expectations of the church and of the nursery care. Relax, take notes, establish a comfortable rapport with the parents so that they will feel comfortable discussing their child and his or her special needs.

During the visit with the family, ask specific questions regarding their child's care. Most are standard questions caregivers ask regarding any new child, so no one should feel uncomfortable about this discussion. Document this information for the benefit of nursery workers so that they will also be able to meet the needs of the child. Suggested questions include the following:

- Is there any information the caregivers need to know about your child's likes and dislikes?
- Does your child prefer to be in a large group or to receive individual attention?
- Are there any physical concerns the caregivers need to know about?
- Are there any dietary concerns?
- What is the best way to comfort your child?
- If your child requires special equipment, could you demonstrate how it is operated?
- Is there anything else that the church can do for you? (Listen carefully, and be ready to ask if you may tell other leaders this information.)
- Would you be interested in volunteering in our nursery? (This is important, as it gives them a way to connect with other parents in the church.)
- In which room would you prefer your child to be placed?

Parents of a child with mental disabilities may prefer to have him or her in a classroom with children of the same chronological age. Or they may prefer to have their child in a classroom with children who are developmentally at the same stage as him or her. If your church has more than one nursery, divided by age or developmental level, explain how each room focuses on specific needs. Include information about the ratio of child per caregiver. Whatever the parents decide, be sure to honor their request.

You need to become aware of the child's personality and usual behavior, as with any child at the nursery level, so you can detect if there is a problem with the child while in your care. While visiting in the home, spend time playing with and getting to know the child. This will help the child recognize yours as a familiar face and feel more comfortable in the nursery.

Beyond the Nursery

Outside the Sunday morning nursery, the parents of a child with disabilities or special needs may feel isolated and exhausted. If they are new to the area, they may not have a support system that would allow them a respite from caring for their child. The child may have a severe disability requiring special training for a caregiver. The parents may need support from other parents of children with similar needs. Here are some potential ways for the church to support these families:

• Know your community resources so you can direct the family to the appropriate support. The chaplain's office at the local hospital can give suggestions. Newspapers often list information about community support groups.

• Sponsor a support group for parents of children with special needs. A parent of a child with special needs in your church may be willing to be in charge of contacting others in your congregation who may wish to participate. If appropriate and consistent with the parents' wishes, publicize this group in your church paper, from the pulpit, and in the community. Invite families with children who have learning disabilities or emotional problems, as well as families with children who have physical or mental disabilities.

• Consider putting a person or family who has experience with individuals with special needs in contact with the child's family to provide a needed respite. Provide names of responsible teens in your congregation who provide childcare. In some cases, the family can train a volunteer to perform any procedures necessary for competent care of the child.

Caring for the child with special challenges can be a rewarding experience. Communication, compassion, and sensitivity will make it a positive experience for all involved.

Language Development of the Growing Child

MaryJane Pierce Norton
Nashville, Tennessee

In the first years of life, much of the learning time for babies and toddlers is spent on the development of movement and language. As a teacher of infants and toddlers, you have an important role to play in helping the child in both areas of development. Children learn to walk and talk on their own, but they benefit from interaction with adults helping to promote their development. What should you expect? See the list below for age-level characteristics and suggestions for ways you can help children with language development.

Birth to One Month
Their crying seems unconnected to specific meanings.

One to Three Months
They have different cries to indicate hunger, fear, pain, fatigue. They begin cooing.

Three to Six Months
They babble, coo, and laugh.

Six to Nine Months
They mimic sounds with changing pitch and inflection.

Nine to Twelve Months
They may speak their first words.

Twelve to Eighteen Months
They may speak up to twenty words.

Eighteen to Twenty-Four Months
They build a vocabulary of up to three hundred or four hundred words. They speak in phrases.

Ways You Can Help
- Imitate the sounds the baby makes. "Ah-boo, coo-coo, brrr" are more than phrases; they are talking with the infant. When you say them back, you encourage the infant in this talking and encourage practice in these sounds.
- Play games (peekaboo, pat-a-cake, and so forth) to encourage listening/response.
- Sing songs with motions and words to reinforce listening and imitation.
- Read books, beginning as young as six months, using one-picture board books or plastic books. Point to the picture and say the word clearly to help babies link the object with the word. Select books that say "God loves you," "Jesus loves you," and "I love you."
- Repeat words and phrases over and over to help children learn and remember the names of things they do and see.
- Use religious words with children: *God, Jesus, church, Bible.* Hearing these words again and again from an early age will help them develop a religious vocabulary.
- As children grow, increase the complexity of your conversation with them. Remember, children can understand many more words than they can say. Language development is both speaking and listening. As you carry on conversations with children, they learn to listen for longer periods and begin to know more and more words.
- Use consistent terms. Settle on one name for yourself and say it over and over. This also applies to religious words. Do not confuse children with too many names for one concept. For example, use the names God and Jesus. It is too early for Lord, Savior, and other similar names.

Remember
Most children learn to speak quite well without any formal instruction, but we have the opportunity to help them in their development. And we can introduce children to words of faith that will be important for them to know as they continue to grow.

For the First-Time Nursery Worker

Marti Biegler
Burnsville, Minnesota

Getting Ready

The following hints will help you prepare for the children.

1. Survey the room. Take a look around, locating important areas: changing table, diaper bag storage, food/snack areas, toy storage, and so forth. Read all posted policies and procedures. Survey the room for potential dangers (open outlets, broken or unsafe toys, and so forth), and report them to the nursery coordinator immediately. If cabinets are locked, locate the keys. Put your coat, purse, and other personal items away from the children's reach.

2. Prepare for check-in. A sign-in sheet or card should be completed for each child. If you cannot locate one, have a paper and pen ready to note each child's name, age, parents' names, name of person picking up the child, and any specific instructions. Use masking tape or nametag stickers to label diaper bags and make nametags for each child's back. Also label toys, blankets, pacifiers, and any other items that children bring with them. Store all diaper bags out of reach of the children.

3. Read and review diaper-changing procedures. These should be posted above the changing table. Wipe down the changing table, sink, and counters with disinfectant. Make sure gloves, disinfectant, and paper towels are available, as well as an emergency supply of diapers and wipes for children who arrive without them.

4. If you will be caring for children needing bottles, determine how bottles will be warmed. Check with parents regarding the temperature preferred by their child. Run warm water over a bottle to take off the chill. Do not use a microwave oven, as it can deteriorate the nutrients in milk and possibly scald the baby's mouth. If you are providing a snack for older infants and toddlers, prepare it just before the children arrive.

5. Prepare for emergencies. The nursery should have a first-aid kit and manual readily available. You will probably find this either in a high cupboard or shelf or in a secured lower cupboard. Take the time to scan the exits in case of an emergency. Look near the door for exit procedures. Check communication procedures: If help is needed, who should you call? Where is a phone/intercom?

6. Place a few inviting toys on the floor or table for older infants and toddlers. The children will be more apt to enter cheerfully if they see something appealing that is ready for them.

As the Children Arrive

When a child arrives, talk to the parent about the child's needs, likes, and dislikes. What comforts the child if he or she becomes upset? Is the child used to taking a nap? Will the child need to be fed?

Interact with the children as they are ready for you. Sit on the floor. Talk about what they are doing. Sing. Pray. Play. Enjoy your time with the children. Always treat the children as though a parent were watching.

Swings and music boxes are favorites with small infants (sleepers or creepers). Young toddlers (walkers and talkers) enjoy push toys, interactive toys (jack-in-the-box), and books. Older toddlers (players and prayers) enjoy Bible stories, blocks, ride-on toys, coloring, bubbles, and large-muscle equipment. Children this age will do a lot of interacting. If a child is truly inconsolable, you may want to seek out a regular caregiver or the child's parents. An unfamiliar caregiver may be more than the child can handle on that particular day. Do not take rejection personally.

As the Children Leave

During checkout time, refer to registration cards/sign-in list. Ask people picking up children to state their names and the names of the children (unless you know the child and parent personally). Parents will never complain about your being too careful.

Straighten and clean the nursery for the next visitors. Wipe down the changing table with disinfectant and tie up the trash. Many nurseries double as daycares during the week or are used by other ministries. Leave the room as you found it.

Using the Articles in This Section

The articles in this section will help a congregation consider how young children and their families are incorporated into the total life and ministry of the congregation. These articles will be helpful for church councils and other groups within the church that are seeking to create a welcoming and nurturing environment.

Section Three: The Congregation and the Young Child

Contents

Other Related Articles

The Congregation, the Young Child, and Baptism

Ron Anderson
Indianapolis, Indiana

What is it that we do when, as a congregation, we baptize young children? Perhaps at its simplest, we extend an offer of God's grace previously extended to us, recognizing that God acts in grace before we know of or can request God's help. As a community formed by that grace, we stand as a sign of God's readiness to receive every person, regardless of age or ability.

The baptism of children is a powerful reminder of God's grace and readiness to be in relationship to us. It is also an act of faith on our part as we respond with children and their parents to that grace. Baptism is the way we, as the church, incorporate people into God's mighty acts of salvation and initiate them into Christ's holy church, into membership in the community of faith, witness, and nurture founded in Jesus Christ.

In the baptismal service (*The United Methodist Hymnal*, pages 33–39), the congregation engages in four distinct actions: (1) We confess our faith in Jesus Christ. (2) We renew our commitment to faithful participation in the life of the church. (3) We commit ourselves to the Christian nurture of one another and to those presented for baptism. (4) We welcome the newly baptized into the family of Christ and promise to surround them with a community of love and forgiveness.

The Baptismal Covenant presumes a community of faith that is ready and able to receive the newly baptized into its shared life. Through this life of love and support, Word and sacrament, the congregation offers the family a model of Christian life in the world. Through individuals in the congregation—teachers, caregivers, pastors, and others—as well as through its life together, the congregation enacts the gracious invitation of Christ to be in living relationship with God.

These are all things we do as a congregation when we baptize a child. But these acts of commitment, renewal, and invitation all point toward our ongoing responsibilities for the child and the child's family. We have a lifelong commitment to the parents and children with whom we celebrate baptism.

One way to describe this commitment is to think of the congregation's life together as encompassing the tasks of believing, welcoming, and holding.

As a believing community, the congregation identifies who and whose it is. The church is a people of God, called together in the name of Jesus Christ by the power of the Holy Spirit. This is the faith we confess together in creed and song, Scripture and prayer, preaching and sacrament as we gather to worship and praise God. As a people of God, we have both a history that reaches beyond our immediate community and a history in a particular place and time. We offer the gift of this story and identity to parents and children when they begin the process leading toward baptism, as well as in the days and years that follow. As a believing community, the congregation both proclaims and enacts the good news of Jesus Christ in word and deed. In the baptism of a child or adult, we remind ourselves of this good news and of our commitment to life together in prayer, presence, gifts, and service.

As a welcoming community, the congregation is called upon to enact ministries of invitation and hospitality. A welcoming community asks: "How do we reach out to and receive families into our faith community? What place do we give children in worship and in other parts of our life together? What do we do to ensure the quality and safety of our nurseries and classrooms? What training do we give to those who will care for and teach these new members of our Christian family?" The child becomes a full member of the body of Christ through baptism. Our invitation and welcome must be full and honest, not waiting for that day when the child can participate as an adult.

As a holding community, we explore the ways our Christian life requires nurture, care, and support throughout the life span. We focus particularly on the character of our Christian education and worship life. We must offer resources and systems that will nurture children and their parents so that all may accept God's grace for themselves, profess their faith openly, and learn to lead a Christian life.

In the baptism of a young child, the church names itself as God's creation in Jesus Christ. As a believing, welcoming, holding community, we stand ready to receive each child as God in Christ receives us.

Caring for Young Children and Their Families

Susan A. Patterson-Sumwalt

Denver, Colorado

Mary and Joe Smith have not participated in a church family. Their first child has arrived, and their relatives and friends are asking when Nicholas is going to be baptized. Mary and Joe decide to call the church where they were married to inquire about baptism, and a date is set. What next?

Too often nothing happens except the baptism itself. The church community fails to take advantage of this opportunity to bring a new life and family into its midst.

We know that transition times in people's lives provide open doors. The birth of a child is one of those times. Parents feel receptive to the church that is concerned about their baby. This opportunity may not surface again until the child is ready for schooling in the religious faith. Most new parents are eager and excited about the birth of a child and want to be the best parents possible. If they think the church can help them in this, they will respond.

We, as the church community, participate in each child's baptism. We, like the parents, take important vows. We commit to caring for the newly baptized child and family. We say that we will nurture, love, teach, and pray with and for them as they grow in their relationship to God and as Christ's disciples in the world. How can we live out the promises we make? How can the church fulfill these promises and care for young children and their families? The following is a variety of suggestions to help make the church a caring place.

Provide a Nursery Home Visitor

A nursery home visitor is a caring, knowledgeable adult who visits parents upon the birth of a child to extend hospitality on behalf of the congregation. He or she can take a gift, information about baptism, a nursery handbook, a statement about the church's philosophy on caring for the young child, a message from the pastor, a book on parenting, and so forth. The nursery home visitor embodies the message that the church cares about parents and their children.

Acknowledge Births

A rose on the communion table, an announcement in the bulletin and church newsletter, or a banner with the child's name on it are all ways to acknowledge births.

Hold Classes on Baptism

These classes for parents, grandparents, and sponsors provide training in understanding the sacrament and an opportunity to network with others in the same stage of life.

Provide Quality Nursery Care

Knowing that their children are being loved, hearing Bible stories, enjoying Christian music, and being cared for in a safe environment is important to parents. Nursery workers and caregivers should be trained to be good listeners and to be supportive of parents' concerns.

Welcome Children in Worship

Parents should have the option of choosing provided nursery care or taking their child to worship with them. They should feel congregational support for either of these choices.

Provide Supportive Ministries

Consider parent support groups, Sunday school classes for parents of young children, parenting classes and seminars, reading lists of parenting books, and marriage enrichment weekends. Provide support for single parents, blended families, grandparents serving as parents, and stepparents. Link parents to mentors.

Other ministries are daycare, parents' day out, music classes, activity classes, picnics, field trips, and play groups. It is crucial to have a comprehensive ministry that includes opportunities for parent and child involvement, as well as parents-only programs.

Celebrating Births, Adoptions, and Baptisms

Phyllis Tyler, Lloyd Brockmeyer, Jerry Owyang

Alhambra, California; Cedar Rapids, Iowa; Orange, California

A child is important, whether his or her parents are married to each other, are not married to each other, are divorced from each other, are adoptive parents, or are foster parents with primary care of the child. The birth of a child is a blessed event, regardless of the circumstances of birth. It is appropriate to celebrate the birth or adoption of each child, no matter what the family circumstances.

Welcoming a newly baptized child into the Christian family is important for the entire congregation. At every baptism we are called to remember our own baptism. As children grow, seeing and participating in the baptisms of others creates opportunities for hearing stories of their own baptisms.

Be creative as you plan ways to celebrate births, adoptions, and baptisms. Consider the following ideas:

- Create a committee on births, adoptions, and baptisms to plan celebrations. In addition to births and adoptions by church members, this group can invite new parents in the church neighborhood to celebrate the births and adoptions of their children.
- Plant a tree, make a toy for the nursery, or refurbish a specific place in the church in honor of a child. Give the parents a certificate that says something such as "In honor of the (adoption, birth) of (name of child), a (tree, rocker) was (given, planted, created)." Avoid permanently placed plaques. Instead, consider a permanent record book that can be displayed in the church.
- Create a college scholarship fund. Encourage people to contribute to the fund in honor of births, baptisms, or adoptions. In this way, the congregation declares its belief in the future of the children.
- Place a single rose on the altar in honor of a birth or adoption. Deliver the rose and any congregational announcements to the family.
- Invite members of the congregation to write a letter of welcome to the child. Children can draw pictures to welcome the new child into the church family.
- Make a sign for the family to put on their lawn to announce the new child as a child of God and a part of your church.
- Display a photo of the child on a bulletin board. Invite people to write messages of blessings to post around the photo.
- Dedicate a musical presentation during worship in honor of the child. Greet the child using the liturgy from *The United Methodist Book of Worship* (pages 585–87) or from *The United Methodist Hymnal* (page 146).
- Announce births on the church sign.
- Provide meals for the family, as appropriate.
- Have a Love Feast (*The United Methodist Book of Worship*, pages 581–84) at a time convenient for the family. Invite the congregation to bring to the child gifts of poems, stories, blessings, or needed items.
- Design and create a baptismal banner to place in the sanctuary on baptismal Sundays. Suggested headings include "You Are a Unique Miracle of God" or "You Are Family." Place names of children baptized and the date of their baptism on the banner.
- Make a banner based on Isaiah 43:1: "I have called you by name, (child's name); you are mine." Display the banner at the baptismal service and then give the banner to the parents.
- Sing "Child of Blessing, Child of Promise" (*The United Methodist Hymnal*, 611). Use it regularly so that it becomes a familiar ritual for the congregation.
- Light a baptismal candle at baptisms, and give the candle to the parents to light on each anniversary of the child's baptism.
- Take a formal photograph of the baby with the pastor by the baptismal font, with the family gathered around. Give a framed enlargement of the photo to the family along with the baptismal certificate.
- Videotape the baptism and give the parents the tape.
- Send cards to children on the anniversary of their baptism.

Whatever you do as a congregation, do it consistently for each new child. A new child, a new promise, is a blessing for us all. The whole congregation needs to have opportunities to celebrate this occasion as the family of God.

Using the Articles in This Section

The articles in this section focus particularly on the administrative aspects of the nursery ministry. Nursery coordinators or others with administrative responsibilities for the nursery ministry will find these articles helpful as they work with paid or volunteer staff to create a high-quality ministry for younger children. While some specific articles have been listed under "Other Related Articles," nearly every article in this book could have been listed.

Section Four: The Nursery Coordinator/ Administrator

Contents

Other Related Articles

The Role of the Nursery Coordinator

Betty Orum
Indio, California

The role of the nursery coordinator or nursery administrator requires wearing many hats, whether the person is a Sunday morning volunteer or a full-time, paid professional. You will need to consider (1) a system for keeping important information about each child, (2) safety and security expectations, (3) health standards, (4) programs to educate and nurture the caregivers, and (5) programs to educate and nurture parents.

Getting Started

Visit all programs for young children within your church, as well as church programs in other congregations in your area. Do not exclude those you may have heard are not quality programs, for you will learn from these what you do not want to do. During the visits, try to take as many notes as possible and interview both caregivers and administrators.

In addition, visit local community colleges or universities that offer an early childhood program. This is an important connection that will help you set up your program and make it ongoing. Later, this connection can also help in staff training and parent education.

Establishing Good Communication

Positive communication with the church family is essential. Prepare reports on a regular basis so that all interested people/groups are informed of the nursery status. Do as much as possible to be an advocate for the nursery within the church community. Make training and education available to all volunteers. Stay in contact with church staff and members.

Is your facility going to be used by several groups during the week and on Sunday morning? Clear guidelines on the use of the facility will help avoid confusion and inappropriate use of space and materials. Make sure you understand the needs of others using the same area, and help them understand your needs as well. Meet often with the pastor or whoever needs to be aware of concerns as they arise. Prepare a checklist of tasks to help each group leave the area ready for the next group. When concerns arise, discuss them honestly and quickly before they become problems. Open and frequent communication is a top priority for all who share space.

Safety and Security

Arranging security procedures for the children and staff of the nursery is an important responsibility. What are the assurances that the appropriate people will pick up the children? What are the assurances that strangers will not wander into the nursery facility? Look at the layout of the facility and think about security issues. Gather a group of creative people to think about how your church can plan a checkout system for the children and parents. Put your plans in writing and inform the congregation and the parents.

As parents arrive with their children, either for a short period of time or for several hours, have a sign-in process (notebook or clipboard) for registering each child. Include space on the form for the date, name of child and parents, location of parents while the child is in the nursery, signing in, and signing out. Make sure there is a space for information about the child's likes and dislikes or particular needs and specific helps (feeding/napping information). Clearly indicate safety procedures to ensure that the appropriate person picks up the child when it is time to leave.

To set policies and implement procedures to help keep children safe while at church (and to help protect caregivers from false allegations of abuse), use as a guide *Safe Sanctuaries: Reducing the Risk of Child Abuse in the Church,* by Joy Thornburg Melton. (This book can be ordered from Discipleship Resources, 800-685-4370 or www.discipleshipresources.org.) It will help you as you work with other church leaders in children's ministries to develop a churchwide plan for keeping safe the children and the youth and adults who work with them.

Once established, closely follow the policies and procedures set in place by your church to assure the safety of children and of caregivers. They are designed to protect children and to reduce the risk of tragic incidents.

Physical safety is of primary importance. Make a written safety checklist to distribute to all caregivers. The person performing the safety check should date, time, and sign it. Personalize your own safety checklist, but the following tasks are recommended as basic: rug vacuumed, floors clean, bathroom clean and sanitized, toys clean, electric plugs covered, half-doors in place, cupboards closed and childproofed.

Of equal importance is the cleanliness of the area. Since toddlers are often on the floor, the area must be kept as clean as possible, with all small objects removed. In many toddler centers, caregivers wear inside shoes or slippers to ensure cleanliness and safety. If food is prepared for the children, all sanitary precautions should be followed. All items belonging to a particular child should be clearly labeled to prevent use by other children.

Never use microwaves for heating milk, as they can deteriorate the nutrients in milk and possibly scald the baby's mouth.

Proper diaper-changing procedures are important for health and safety. Post diaper-changing policies in a visible place in the diapering area.

Training and Recruiting Staff

Use the available expertise of people within the community to enhance your program. Fire department personnel can help you with safety concerns. Hospital nutritionists can help you choose healthy, safe foods for young children. The Red Cross can train youth as assistant caregivers and assist in infant/toddler CPR classes for caregivers, parents, and ushers. Other early childhood directors/administrators can help you find where to purchase supplies, toys, equipment, and so forth. Physical therapists can help train caregivers on how to pick up children, how to rise from the floor, and so forth.

As a nursery administrator, you will want to search for caregivers who genuinely love children, have enormous amounts of patience and energy, and work well with other adults. The caregivers themselves, paid or volunteer, are key to having a successful, caring program for young children. Selection and nurture of caregivers is your most important responsibility.

Record Keeping

Record each step you take in setting up and continuing to improve your nursery. This record will be a valuable training tool for others, provide help in selecting training needs, support insurance needs, and help you realize how far you journey in your task. You are a most important link in assuring that God's children receive the care they need in a safe, loving environment.

Managing the Nursery

Sarah Heckert
Brentwood, Tennessee

The necessary components to managing a nursery are the physical and financial needs of maintaining the nursery, providing for the needs of the children and their families, nurturing relationships with and between the caregivers, and developing a vision for ministry within the congregation. Each component requires a variety of skills and knowledge.

Maintaining the Nursery

In order to manage the physical aspects of your nursery, you must have a general understanding of what infants, toddlers, and older children require to be safe, healthy, and happy. In order to have a successful nursery that will meet your congregation's needs, you must also know what will make the parents happy. To establish and manage the facility, you will need to work closely with the church staff to ascertain when childcare will be needed, how long it will be needed, the approximate number and ages of the children to be served, and the number of caregivers necessary. This will help you know how many rooms, how many staff in each room, how much space, and what supplies you will need. You will also need established budget information and a criteria for hiring childcare workers, both paid and volunteer.

A nursery does not have to be elaborate to be efficient. Work with trustees to ensure proper facilities. Rooms should be well lit, freshly painted in a light color, and sparkling clean. Bright pictures and colorful posters on the wall will set the tone for a cheerful room. Toys should be in good condition, age-appropriate, and clean. Stuffed animals and dolls should be washable. Clean cribs with fresh sheets are a must, along with a highchair or two. A sink in each childcare room allows for hand washing after diaper changes and before snack time. A shelf, series of hooks, or cabinet is needed to keep diaper bags off the floor and away from curious hands. Provide an emergency phone to call the church office or the 911 service.

Providing for Children and Their Families

What can we, as managers, do to help our families feel comfortable with leaving their children in our care? Develop ongoing relationships with the parents to achieve mutual trust, have open avenues for communication, and provide support for you and for them. Know the children and their parents. The attitude of the nursery manager is critical in providing a vital ministry to the families in the church. Realize that parents will not be able to participate fully in worship or Sunday school if they are concerned about the well-being of their children in the nursery. Do everything possible to reassure parents. Check each childcare room to make sure it is clean and safe. Rooms should be inviting for parents and children, but secure from others. Make sure the rooms are open and the staff ready for work when the families start arriving. Greet children by name and welcome visitors. Remind parents to register their children. Label the diaper bags.

If at all possible, separate babies and crawlers from walkers and toddlers. Walkers and toddlers fare beautifully in a large open room with climbing toys, riding toys, big building blocks, and a small table and chairs for snacks and coloring. These are the types of things crawlers can get into trouble with: choking on crayons, climbing up and then falling down the slide, getting run over by an overzealous two-year-old on a scooter. Older children are also great at flinging toys across the room. So, for the peace of mind of both parents and caregivers, keep babies and crawlers in separate rooms, if at all possible. If that is not possible, set up a protected area for them.

Although it is your task to make sure children are safe and well cared for, you are not alone. Work closely with pastors and staff regarding these nursery needs and opportunities for care. Draw on God and supportive people for the strength and help you need to guarantee that the children in your care have what is needed.

Stay current with child development research and literature, as well as safety issues. Professional groups provide resource support for childcare programs housed in churches (Ecumenical Child Care Network, www.eccn.org) and for weekday programs (National Association for the Education of Young Children, www.naeyc.org). Local childcare networks are also available to provide support for people involved in managing early childcare programs. Colleges in your community are also good sources of current information and resource people.

Nurturing Relationships With the Caregivers

Recruiting the best caregivers possible for long-term work not only reassures parents and provides children with familiar faces, but it also provides a caring network among the caregivers. With your encouragement, support, and training, caregivers will have the joy of caring for young children and the satisfaction of providing a valuable service for their congregation. Greet caregivers each time they arrive, and provide them with current information. At transition times, thank staff members (whether volunteer or paid) for their time, and ask for a brief evaluation of their experience. Remind them of any upcoming childcare needs. Do little thoughtful things (writing notes, giving small gifts) to regularly thank caregivers for their time and care. As frequently as possible, provide public recognition for their work. Provide training, social time, an understanding ear, and support. By showing that you respect and value the caregivers, you will set the tone for the congregation. Through your attitude, public recognition, and professional training and support, they will be respected and valued by the families who use the nursery, by the church staff, and by the congregation. In turn, the caregivers will value one another and the children.

Developing a Vision for Ministry in the Nursery

You are in a position to help the congregation see the nursery as a place for ministry. Become an advocate. Write articles for the church newsletter, or ask a parent to write. Give public recognition to the caregivers. Provide programs on ministry in the church nursery, complete with video or slides for adult classes, women's groups, men's groups, youth groups, and committee meetings. At every opportunity educate people about the quality of care, policies, child-friendliness, and other features of the nursery facilities. As a way to recruit other advocates, recruit people to participate in the care. Help the congregation see the nursery as their ministry with young children and their families.

Helps and Hints for the Nursery Administrator

Sarah Heckert
Brentwood, Tennessee

Questions for Parents of Infants

- Does the baby prefer sleeping on the side or back? Does the baby like to be rocked to sleep, or put down in a crib and allowed to fall asleep on his or her own? Does the baby usually take a nap during this time?
- Is the baby due for a bottle soon? Does he or she like a bottle at room temperature? warm? cold? If the baby is nursed, when was the last time he or she ate? Will the nursing mother check back between Sunday school and church?
- Does the baby prefer infant seats that bounce or baby swings?
- Is the baby attached to any special blanket or toy?
- When was the baby's diaper last changed?
- Is the baby allergic to anything?
- Is there any reason the baby should not go outside?
- Does the baby have a pacifier? Does he or she use it all the time, or only when sleepy?

Caring for Infants

- Infants' diapers need to be checked every thirty minutes, as they have frequent bowel movements.
- Be sure stuffed animals and dolls in the nursery are machine washable.
- Remind parents that baby gates are up to keep the walkers and crawlers in the nursery, not to keep the parents out. Parents are welcome any time.
- Always change sheets on a crib between babies, and let the parents know about this policy.
- After each childcare session, wipe the cribs down with a solution of one-fourth cup bleach to one gallon of water to disinfect them.
- Have cloth diapers or cotton receiving blankets to use for burp clothes.
- Wash teething toys after each use in the bleach-water solution mentioned above. A dishpan or sink can be kept filled with bleach-water solution, so that toys can be tossed in as necessary. Remember to keep the bleach solution out of the reach of children.
- Do not allow babies to use teething toys other babies have used, unless the toys have been washed again.

- Wash your hands after each diaper change or nose wipe.
- Label diaper bags as children arrive. Provide labels for bottles, blankets, and other items that may be removed from the bags.
- A ratio of five or six babies to two caregivers is recommended. Remember, the higher your ratio of caregivers to children, the better parents will feel about entrusting their child to your care.
- Keep on hand extra diapers and emergency changes of clothes in a few different sizes.

Working With Walkers and Toddlers

- Encourage loving but timely goodbyes between toddlers and parents. If a parent wants to check on a child later, ask the parent to request a report from the nursery supervisor or other adult. It is difficult for a toddler to separate twice.
- Toddler rooms need to have small tables and chairs, climbing structures, and some riding toys. This is a an active, exploring age.
- Have a supply of graham crackers or animal crackers, since children this age love to snack. Make sure parents know if snacks will be served.
- Provide a separate area with a child-size toilet and sink. If this is not possible, at least set up a private corner with a potty chair.
- Encourage all parents to leave the nursery area as soon as they have dropped off their children. Any adult standing nearby indicates to toddlers that their parents are on the way. This interferes with the caregivers starting activities and play time.
- Keep a clean supply of washcloths (one per child) for wiping faces and hands.
- Toddlers love structured activities, such as taking walks to look for rocks and flowers and playing hokey-pokey.
- Ask parents if their child is potty-trained and when the child last went to the bathroom. Ask what words the child uses to indicate he or she needs to go to the bathroom.

To Support Staff

- Attend meetings for church staff and planning, in order to make visible the importance of childcare to the entire congregation.
- When Sunday school caregivers are recognized, remember the nursery staff. They have been the children's first caregivers. Work with the Sunday school superintendent, Christian educator, or education committee chairperson to coordinate efforts.
- Keep the nursery rooms well supplied with whatever the caregivers have requested, making it easier for them to do their jobs.
- Inform the staff as early as possible of any expected change in schedule, and ask the same from them.
- For paid workers, establish a minimum guaranteed sum that caregivers can expect for their time. If a committee or group has requested childcare and no children show up, pay the caregiver for a minimum of two hours. This indicates to the caregiver that his or her work and effort are of value.
- Occasionally bring in cookies or other treats, hand out chocolate kisses, distribute thank-you notes made by older children or by parents, and so forth. (Caregivers should not eat while the children are present, unless they eat a snack with the children.)
- Realize that caregivers are working on Christmas Eve, Easter morning, and weekends. Show them special appreciation for their willingness to work when everyone else is celebrating.
- Keep supplies of hand cream and mild soap on hand, because frequent washings dry hands.
- Tell the staff about any positive comments or notes. The nursery coordinator frequently hears nice remarks about the quality of care offered, but the staff members rarely do.
- Pray for your staff regularly.
- Occasionally have lunches delivered to the church to eat after the children have gone, or go out together as a group. Special social time helps the staff appreciate one another and work as a team. However, do not expect paid staff to want to stay extra time on weekends.

- Arrange for the pastor and other staff to stop by to offer a word of thanks.
- Ask any senior staff member whose program was particularly enhanced by childcare to tell the caregivers about it.

Necessary Features of Childcare Areas

- Adequate light and attractive, bright wall decorations. Babies notice the contrast between light and dark.
- Plenty of age-appropriate toys, games, books, and puzzles; art supplies for older children.
- Toys in good repair with all their pieces. Broken toys (equipment and furnishings, too) should be discarded because they can be dangerous and are not fun to play with. Provide containers for toys with several pieces, in order to keep all the pieces together and to make pickup easier. Small toys should be discarded if they are small enough to fit into a choke tube (or a cardboard toilet paper tube).
- An adequate supply of cleaning supplies: disinfectant spray, paper towels, hand-washing soap, disposable gloves, broom, and dust pan. Keep them in a locked cupboard, safely out of reach of the children.
- An extra supply of diapers, wipes, and various sizes of clothing in case parents forget.
- Sign-in sheets in a prominent place, with space for each child's name, parents' names, location of parents while the child is in the nursery, name of person who will pick up the child, signing in, and signing out. Be sure that parents understand that their child will not be released to anyone other than the parents unless arrangements have been made with the nursery supervisor. This understanding will avoid hurt feelings from grandparents, favorite babysitters, and big brothers and sisters.
- A sink in each room to allow for frequent hand washing.
- An appropriate place for diaper changing.
- Nametags for the children's backs. Caregivers need to use the child's name frequently, with loving tones.

Planning for Memories

Lloyd Brockmeyer, Jerry Owyang, and Mary Alice Gran

Cedar Rapids, Iowa; Orange, California; Nashville, Tennessee

Memories are important. Even if children do not remember specific details, they will remember that their church was a place where they felt loved and cared for. Develop a calendar and plan specific ways for creating memorable occasions. Be alert for spontaneous opportunities.

- Create a special card to go to the child shortly after birth to welcome him or her to the congregational family. You could use a design created by an older child. Include a photo of the nursery staff and information about nursery services, including a phone number parents may call if they have questions.

- Take a photo of the baby's first Sunday in the nursery. Post the photo, with the baby's name and date of the first visit, on a bulletin board entitled "Our Special Friends" or "God Bless Our Children." Send the photo to the parents on their child's first birthday.

- Record nursery participants by taking photos regularly and making a scrapbook that is well labeled with names and dates. Each year, let the scrapbook travel with the children through the Sunday school classes. This will be a great reminder of how they have grown up in the church.

- For special occasions, help the child create something to give to his or her family that can become a keepsake: handprint in plaster of Paris, footprint painted on a small banner, drawing framed with construction paper, and so forth. Mark each gift with the child's name, date, and name of the church.

- Take a class picture at least once a year to give to parents and the church historian. Label each picture with children's names, ages, date the picture was taken, and name of the church. Include childcare providers/teachers in the picture as well.

- As a gift to the child, take a photo of the child with the caregivers and mount it with the words "God loves you, and so do we!" Be sure to include names of caregivers, name of the church, and the date the photo was taken.

- Prepare a children's pictorial directory. Take a photo of each child, label it with the child's first name, and post the group of photos in a location in the church where adults will see it. Encourage adults to greet the children and call them by name.

Hiring and Recruiting Nursery Personnel

Sarah Heckert

Brentwood, Tennessee

When staffing your nursery, it is important to remember why families need childcare. Parents entrust their children to church caregivers in order to attend Sunday school, worship, and midweek activities. As childcare providers, we can facilitate their worship experience by creating a loving, nurturing atmosphere. Whether paid or volunteer, the caregivers in your nursery are the heart of your facility. A caregiver's attitude and demeanor can either inspire trust and confidence or doubts and reservations from the parents we are serving.

A church makes a strong statement of commitment to its families by choosing to employ nursery personnel. This tells families that we understand how important childcare is to the congregation and that we value the presence of that family enough to ensure consistent, loving care. Churches willing to make this statement are on the right road to attracting and keeping new families.

Recruiting a Coordinator

Whether the congregation is large or small, and regardless of whether the nursery staff is paid or volunteer, the nursery coordinator will set the tone for the quality of care provided. This person should enjoy caring for young children, understand developmental needs, be articulate with adults, and be empathic with parents.

The church staff and supporting committees (children's council, nursery committee, administrative council, education/nurture committee, staff-parish relations committee, and so forth) can assist in the effort to identify a nursery supervisor. These committees will need to work together to develop a job description.

The supervisor or coordinator of the nursery must be nurturing, loving, efficient, energetic, and organized. He or she is often the first person the parents of young children meet when visiting the nursery. The impression this family has will play a critical part in their worship experience within the church. Educating both the congregation and the church staff about the importance of the nursery coordinator position will help elevate it from the job of babysitter to a ministry

as a church ambassador. Once the consciousness of the church has been raised, and caregiving is understood as a ministry, people from within the congregation may be more inclined to become nursery workers.

Whether hiring a coordinator or recruiting a volunteer, it is essential to check references to ensure safety. You should also have a clear line of accountability.

Once a nursery supervisor is in place, he or she will need to evaluate each event for which childcare will be offered to determine when and how many caregivers will be required. The coordinator may also decide if the childcare needs will be best met by paid staff, volunteer staff, or a combination of both.

Staffing With Volunteers

A church nursery staffed by volunteers has many benefits. If members of the congregation care enough to sacrifice their personal time in worship and/or Sunday school, they usually provide wonderful care. Loving children and understanding the importance of childcare are the primary qualifications. The volunteers do, however, need training in safety and health procedures. A second benefit to an all-volunteer nursery staff is a financial one. The funds saved on staff salaries are a big bonus for any church budget. A third benefit is that the volunteers feel connected to the church and think they are contributing to the overall well-being of church-related families. The nursery is an excellent place to provide an opportunity for the gift of service to one's own congregation. A fourth benefit is that volunteers meet new people within the church family.

Talk with the pastor and many church members to discover people who would be good nursery volunteers. Make a personal visit to recruit these people. Screen volunteer nursery workers with the same care and standards you would use to screen paid workers.

Consider contacting the parents of your nursery-age children. Most parents who regularly use the services of the nursery are more than happy to take their turn at providing care. Parents of teenagers sometimes enjoy time with young children, as do grandparents whose families live far away.

Volunteers can be an effective means of staffing. When working with a volunteer system, be sure to maintain a list of people who are willing to serve as substitutes and last-minute fill-ins as needed.

Volunteer staffing has some disadvantages. Scheduling volunteers on a rotating basis can be a time-consuming chore for the supervisor. In addition, when the commitment is not taken seriously, volunteers may not show up on their appointed Sunday. When parents rotate a few times a year, there is little opportunity to learn procedures for both safety and fun; and there is not enough time for the parents to establish a relationship with the children. Furthermore, since the children do not know the adults who are caring for them, separation from their parents is much more difficult.

Sometimes, volunteers do not want to follow the usual pattern of care already established in the nursery. Regular routines, methods of separating from parents, play time, snack time, cleanup, and so forth give toddlers and other children a feeling of security and belonging. Having different staff each week makes routines difficult to follow.

Most importantly, this type of rotating system lacks the consistency and training that is preferred in a quality nursery. Lack of consistency will lead to parents not trusting the safety of the nursery system and will increase the likelihood that children will be upset when left in the nursery.

Using Youth as Caregivers

The youth of the church are often a rich resource of childcare staff, both paid and volunteer. Many teenagers who are active in the church enjoy baby-sitting and may already be experienced childcare providers. They usually appreciate meeting and working with the families of young children in the congregation, as this often leads to more childcare opportunities. Parents of young children are always happy to add trusted, familiar names to their list of sitters. So, employing trained church youth in the nursery is a mutually satisfying technique for staffing, but it is not without pitfalls.

Volunteering occasionally in the nursery is fine, but the nursery supervisor must assure that the teenager is not frequently missing the opportunity to participate in worship and in programming for youth. The nursery coordinator needs to avoid being in the middle of a conflict between youth and parents over Sunday school and worship attendance.

Communicate with the parents. A phone call or note goes a long way in avoiding misunderstandings.

Let the parents know how frequently the youth may be asked to work in the nursery and how many hours he or she will spend during each visit. This will avoid the possibility of a teenager providing care when his or her parents assume that their teen is attending worship, Sunday school, and so forth. In addition to communicating with the parents, the nursery supervisor needs to clarify expectations with the youth.

Working in the nursery is not an opportunity to socialize with other youth. Their primary responsibility is caring for and interacting with the children. The teenagers must be given instructions for age-appropriate games, puzzles, and toys, in addition to clear guidelines for changing diapers, washing hands, distributing snacks, and so forth.

At least one adult should always be in a supervisory role in each room. This is important because of liability issues if a mishap occurs. Bottom line, the nursery supervisor needs to protect teenagers from assuming too much responsibility. The way to do this is to train teens adequately and to have them work in rooms with older caregivers.

Consider providing a certified baby-sitting (childcare) course in return for a specified number of hours of childcare in the church nursery. The extension office of a state university will have childcare training support, as will a local civic youth group, hospital, school, or the Red Cross.

Staffing With Paid Caregivers

The need to create an effective, reliable team of caregivers is the strongest argument for budgeting for paid staff. The nursery supervisor can train and direct staff to meet the ever-changing needs of the congregation. Familiar faces will be in the nursery each time the children arrive, whether on Sunday or on weekdays. Such continuity is invaluable when caring for children. The nursery supervisor can establish specific and high expectations for child caregivers and train the staff to provide that quality of care.

To attract paid nursery staff, the nursery coordinator should first search the congregation. Consider parents of older children or teenagers. Parents of young children may wish to work a few hours a week, especially if they can bring their children along. Consider contacting local high schools and colleges (particularly child development classes). Frequently, they will have a student center or other area where part-time employment opportunities are posted. Better yet, ask a professor or child development coordinator to recommend a student. Consider contacting local daycare centers.

Advertising in local newspapers and posting on local bulletin boards should be used only as a last resort. Applicants from these avenues may lead to hours of interviewing people and checking references of those who may have few or none of the characteristics required to provide quality care. Another option would be to call other places of worship within your community that have worship at hours other than your own. They may have members who are likely candidates.

When hiring caregivers, the nursery supervisor must be aware of several responsibilities. Work with the staff-parish relations committee, the church's business administrator, or other church officials with knowledge in this area to establish criteria for hiring. They will have access to federal and state laws regarding child labor, techniques for screening out people convicted of a felony or child abuse, and guidelines for interviewing candidates and checking their records. The business administrator or trustees should have knowledge of any restrictions in the church's insurance policy regarding age of employees. Develop an application for both volunteer and paid positions that is in keeping with your church policies. In congregations with no administrator, contact a church member with hiring experience for advice.

When initiating formal application processes, gain support from pastor, staff, and all interested committees, boards, and councils. Discuss what the process is, and why. Report information in the church newsletter. If someone refuses to participate in the process, remember that your first priority is the safety of the children and the integrity of the church. Other caregivers can be found.

As with volunteer staff, there are advantages and disadvantages when most or all of the nursery staff are hired. The most obvious is the payroll involved. A church that is able to pay more than minimum wage will attract and probably keep a higher caliber of staff. Employees who earn more than minimum wage are more inclined to stay on the job and work harder. With less turnover, children and parents have an opportunity to become familiar and comfortable with the caregivers.

Staffing With Paid and Volunteer Caregivers

Many churches choose a combination of both paid and volunteer staff for their nursery. Having one or two paid caregivers in each room will provide a familiar face and the foundation of consistent care. They will know the routine established for the children. Because of their ongoing relationship with the children, their presence will make it easier for the volunteers to care for the children. This will provide a safety net for the volunteers, who are in a new situation and may initially feel unsure about their work.

This system usually makes recruiting volunteers an easier task. When the nursery supervisor can request congregational support on the basis of increasing the ratio of childcare workers for the babies and toddlers and, at the same time, offer an experienced, knowledgeable coworker, more volunteers may step forward. The task is not overwhelming.

Consider using an application for all people who work in the nursery. With liability issues as they are today, this is not an area to be taken for granted. Investigate each person thoroughly before making a job offer or using him or her as a volunteer. Include documentation of the investigation in the personnel file. Include a check with the police department or other agency for reports of abuse. These procedures will assure the safety and integrity of church-sponsored childcare and will provide safeguards for the employees.

Both paid and volunteer caregivers need clear job descriptions. The staff-parish relations committee can provide leadership in writing job descriptions. Once job descriptions are written, provide copies to church leaders, parents, and caregivers. Reevaluate the job descriptions frequently, and make sure all caregivers understand church policies and procedures related to childcare.

Once the recruiting and hiring is completed, the training accomplished, and the nursery care both dependable and of high quality, the nursery coordinator and other staff members must remember to show appreciation to the nursery staff. Every program in the church benefits from a strong nursery because a well-run church nursery will attract new members and sustain families with young children. Caregivers need to feel that their work is valued and makes a difference to church members and to other staff. Although nursery caregivers have a low-profile job, regularly expressing appreciation for doing it well will help keep morale high. An occasional public acknowledgment, a plate of cookies, or a warm thank you can help affirm this dedicated team.

Developing Policies

Kim Giana
Jacksonville, Florida

Why Does Our Church Need to Have Policies?

The nursery area of your church is probably used several times during the week. The caregivers and volunteers may rotate on a regular basis. Without established policies and procedures, confusion and chaos will result. This leads to unhappy parents and caregivers, and to the children not having a positive church experience. Children feel more secure when the adults around them are knowledgeable and comfortable with policies and procedures in the nursery area.

How Do We Develop Policies?

If your church does not have a committee already assigned the responsibility, a good starting place is to form a task force to assess your church's individual needs. Be sure to include people who have knowledge and experience in the nursery area.

Look at nursery policies in use in similar settings at other local congregations. The Ecumenical Child Care Network (www.eccn.org) and the National Association for the Education of Young Children (www.naeyc.org) publish resources that provide helpful information. (For addresses, see "Resources for Nursery Coordinators," page 66.)

The actual process of writing the policies will evolve during a series of meetings. Distribute draft copies to parents, staff, and other appropriate people for input. Rewriting may occur several times before the task force is satisfied with the finished product. The process can be long and frustrating, but do not despair. Think ahead to the end result: happy, secure children and happy, secure adults each time the nursery area is in use.

Should We Revise Our Current Policies?

Determine if the current policies are still effective. Has it been several years since they were written? Have insurance or state requirements changed? Has the nursery area changed? Has the number of children requiring care increased or decreased? Have the caregivers changed? All are reasons for revising.

Are certain policies or guidelines not working smoothly? If so, those parts may need to be revised. Check on the proper procedures within your church for amending or revising policies, and be sure to follow them. Frequently, policies become obsolete and are increasingly ignored as years pass. Establish a regular schedule for reviewing and updating policies. Look at the current policies, and date any revisions made.

What Should We Include in Our Policies?

Consider developing three categories of policies: general policies for nursery use, guidelines for parents, and guidelines for nursery workers.

Provide a complete set of policies for all workers, parents, and appropriate committee personnel. Keep one copy in the church office for general use. Post one copy outside the nursery area and one in the nursery for easy access by caregivers.

Consider policy statements addressing health, security, facility/equipment usage by outside groups, and gifts to the nursery. Include guidelines for emergency procedures, illness, infectious disease, hand washing, caregiver application process, laundry, diaper-changing procedures, room cleaning, record keeping, CPR training, administering medication, taking children out of the building, and appropriate ages of children to use the nursery facilities. The resource *Model Child Care Health Policies,* which is available through the National Association for the Education of Young Children, provides model heath policies that can be adapted to meet the needs of your church. (For the address, see "Sample Illness Policy and Procedures," page 61.)

We Have Policies. Now What?

Communicate the policies to the congregation, parents, and caregivers. Train all childcare providers in the policies, and emphasize the importance of following them. Having policies that are not followed can become a liability issue in case of an incident. Post appropriate procedures within the nursery. For example, post the diaper-changing procedure in a visible location at the diaper-changing area.

Nursery Procedures for Caregivers

Sarah Heckert
Brentwood, Tennessee

1. Greet parents and children at the door with a smile. Help with any separation problems. Ask parents appropriate questions about the child's care (name, feeding and bathroom procedures, and so forth).

2. Remind all parents to sign in their children.

3. Write each child's name on masking tape and attach it to his or her back as soon as the child enters the nursery.

4. Label all diaper bags, bottles, pacifiers, and all items you take out of the diaper bags.

5. Play on the floor with the children. Be at eye level with them, and do not sit in a chair watching them play.

6. Diapers need to be checked at least every hour and before feedings. Any child in your care more than an hour should be changed. Soiled diapers should be changed immediately.

7. Wash your hands after each diaper change and nose wipe.

8. Pick up toys after they are played with. Leave the room as clean as possible.

9. Take notes about each child's time with you, and tell the parents about it.

10. Follow checkout procedures. Make sure children are picked up by the appropriate people.

Sample Illness Policy and Procedures

MaryJane Pierce Norton
Nashville, Tennessee

All children are important, for they are God's gift to us, given for our care and love. We strive to provide a healthy, safe, clean, loving place in which children can thrive. We depend on you, the parent, to help us. Please do not bring a sick child to the nursery.

If your child exhibits any of the following symptoms, please keep him or her at home:
- Diarrhea (more than three times in the last twenty-four hours).
- Vomiting (two or more episodes in the previous twenty-four hours).
- Temperature above 101 degrees.
- Skin infections or infestations (impetigo, head lice, ringworm, or shingles) until at least twenty-four hours after treatment begins.
- Pink or red eye with eye discharge.
- Nasal discharge that is greenish in color.

The following are some of the diseases common to infants and toddlers, and the contagious times for each. Please keep your child at home during these times.

Chickenpox

This is highly contagious as long as the pox are open and weeping. When the pox are scabbed and dry, the child can return to the classroom.

Ear Infections

While ear infections are not contagious, the upper respiratory infections that cause the ear infections are. In addition, at the early stage of an ear infection, children are often uncomfortable and cannot be cared for adequately with other children around.

Impetigo

Children need to be on antibiotics for twenty-four hours before returning to the classroom.

Pinkeye

This is another highly contagious disease. Most children need twenty-four hours after treatment has been initiated before returning to the classroom.

Strep Throat

Once a child has had twenty-four hours of antibiotics, he or she is not contagious and may be brought to the class if he or she is feeling better.

Infectious Diseases

Staff should follow universal precautions recommended by the Centers for Disease Control and Prevention in handling blood or body fluids:
1. Wear gloves unless the fluid can be easily contained by the cloth being used to clean it up.
2. Be careful not to get any of the fluid in your eyes, nose, mouth, or open sores.
3. Clean and disinfect any surfaces on which the body fluid has been spilled.
4. Discard the contaminated material in a plastic bag and securely seal it.
5. Mops used to clean up body fluids should be cleaned, rinsed with a disinfecting solution, wrung as dry as possible, and hung to dry completely.
6. Wash your hands thoroughly after cleaning up spills.

Consider this as a guide. You may wish to address additional concerns in your illness policy. The important thing is to have it in writing and distributed to all parents and caregivers, so that everyone knows what is expected.

Additional Resources

Model Child Care Health Policies. This book was prepared by the Pennsylvania Chapter of the American Academy of Pediatrics and is available from the National Association for the Education of Young Children (NAEYC). It is an excellent resource to use when developing health-related policies. The NAEYC address is 1509 16th Street, N.W., Washington, DC 20036-1426. The website for NAEYC is www.naeyc.org.

The ABC's of Safe and Healthy Child Care. This booklet was prepared by the Department of Health and Human Services, the U.S. Public Health Service, and the Centers for Disease Control and Prevention in 1996. It is on the Internet in PDF format (www.cdc.gov/ncidod/hip/abc/abc1.pdf).

Ministry With Other Church Workers

Mary Alice Gran
Nashville, Tennessee

Nurturing Positive Relationships
- Keep lines of communication clear and open.
- Listen.
- Exchange information.
- Tell stories about what the children are experiencing.
- Discuss the importance of staff support for the nursery ministry.
- Ask how the nursery ministry can support the efforts of other congregational ministries.
- Pray for the other ministries.
- Ask for prayers for the nursery ministry.

Working in a church facility is all about relationships: relationships with children, relationships with parents, relationships with the childcare staff, relationships with church staff, relationships with members of the congregation, relationships with your governing board, and, most importantly, your relationship with God.

You share in ministry with many individuals and groups: Christian educators, church office staff, custodians, choir directors, youth ministers, weekday ministries staff, church treasurer or other financial officers, pastors, the staff-parish relations committee, and the trustees.

Christian Educators
Some churches have a minister or director of Christian education or a program director who coordinates the educational ministries of the congregation. In other congregations, the chairperson of the education/nurture committee may fill this role.

This person is a key member of the nursery ministry team. He or she may be the designated supervisor for the nursery coordinator or childcare director. Work closely with this person in planning, developing policies, visioning for the future of the nursery, hiring staff, and setting policies. Educators are usually interested in the nursery ministry and can be strong advocates for quality childcare ministries.

Church Office Staff
Often, the church office staff are your key contact for communication with the church. Cultivate a positive relationship by providing copy for bulletins, newsletters, and the calendar in a timely manner. Provide the office staff with up-to-date information regarding nursery policies, hours, and other pertinent information.

Custodians
Custodians are important people in the life of the nursery because it is essential to keep the nursery facilities clean. Be appreciative of their efforts, and ask what you and other members of the nursery staff can do to help them do their job better. Meet regularly to talk about the children and the importance of a clean environment. Praise their efforts at staff meetings or other appropriate places. Encourage nursery personnel to leave the rooms ready for cleaning.

Choir Directors
The church choir directors or other staff involved in music ministry can be helpful resource people when selecting music to use with young children.

In many churches, the most common use of the nursery outside of Sunday mornings is during choir practice. It is important to maintain good communication with the music ministry staff members to ensure that the childcare needs of choir members are met and that the nursery standards are maintained.

Youth Ministers
A director of youth ministry or a youth coordinator deals with many of the same types of safety issues as the nursery director. Work together to set policies and support one another in carrying out strategies.

Additionally, the adults who work with youth may have children who need nursery care during youth activities. Work closely with them to provide needed care for their young children in a safe and loving environment.

Weekday Ministries Staff

If you share nursery space with other programs, such as a daycare program or parents' day out program, make every effort to work closely with them. Discuss the following with leaders in the other programs: What supplies and equipment will be shared? How can the storage be best used by all? What are your common visions and goals? What curriculum issues do you hold in common? Where are the pinch points that can erode a relationship if allowed to irritate.

Church Treasurer or Other Financial Officers

Work closely with the church treasurer, financial secretary, or chairperson of the finance committee as you develop the budget, check-writing processes, and other financial matters. Provide the appropriate people with complete and timely information, and consult with them when considering a change in budget, salaries, or number of staff.

Pastors

The pastors will need to have frequent and clear information about the nursery ministry, in order to support the nursery when making visits to families, attending meetings, and planning for the future. You will need to initiate regular meetings or at least develop a communication link. Remember that many people also want time with the pastor, so be prepared and ready to listen as well as tell information. Always keep the pastors in the communication loop before making major decisions.

Staff-Parish Relations Committee

Someone from the committee on staff-parish relations may be your supervisor or designated to relate to the nursery ministry staff. This committee can be helpful in writing nursery staff job descriptions. Depending on your church's policies, they may be involved in any nursery hiring or firing decisions.

Trustees

The church trustees carry a heavy responsibility for all congregational property, including the nursery. You can assist the trustees in learning about safety issues, appropriate facilities, and other property issues related to the nursery. Invite the trustees to meet in the nursery facilities for one of their meetings. Give them a personally guided tour, telling stories of the ministry that occurs there. Talk about the needs of children, parents, and staff who use the facilities. Provide them with resources and copies of appropriate articles from this book that deal with safety, liability, facility, and financial issues.

Working Together

Periodically meet with other appropriate staff to talk about nursery processes: What is working well but needs some enhancing? What is not working and needs resuscitation? What needs to die and have an appropriate burial? Select one issue or process and ask these questions: What is the issue? What is the goal? What additional information do we need? What are some solutions/possibilities in reaching that goal? What are the steps needed to reach that goal? What procedures will we implement?

One such issue might be: Older children are playing in the nursery when it is not being attended. Goal: To assure the safety of each child and the cleanliness of the nursery for very young children. Needed information: When are older children present? What draws them to the nursery? Who else is in the building at the same time? What needs to be happening for these children that is age appropriate for them? A little detective work and gathering of answers will then help the group plan for the needs of the older children as well as assure the safety of the nursery for younger children.

When working together as a team, solutions happen. In order to grow and maintain a healthy, productive team, it is important to honor one another's work as a ministry. Using good communication skills is essential. Working and playing together helps the good times be delightful and the hard times easier.

As with all relationships, the journey together is not always easy, but it is always worth the effort. God is with all of you, and together you make the nursery a safe place for children to experience God's love and care.

Helping Others When a Young Child Dies

Charlotte T. Brent
Welsh, Louisiana

You answer your phone on Monday morning and can hardly believe your ears when you hear your pastor say, "I have some sad news to tell you. The Giles baby has died. We don't have much information right now. I'll be going to their home in a few minutes, but I wanted you to know so that you could notify the nursery workers. I'll call back when I know the time and place of the funeral. In the meantime, I'm counting on you to get our care plan going. Thanks a lot." As you hang up, you recall that the baby was just in your nursery the day before. He seemed fine and was as lively and active as the other babies. What went wrong?

As you gather your thoughts, you remember the carefully designed care plan that the pastor and nursery staff have worked out. You breathe a sigh of relief that at least you have someplace to start in making a response to this grieving family.

Where to Begin

Your presence is the most meaningful gift you can offer in the first shocking days of loss. Make contact with the grieving family as soon as possible. Check with the pastor about making your first visit. Notify other nursery workers so that they can be prepared as well. When other parents hear of the death, they will be concerned and anxious about their own children. They will need to be reassured about the possibility of any communicable disease that might have been involved. Because you have already begun to have a close relationship with this child and his or her family, you and the other nursery workers will experience grief over this loss as well.

Design a Care Plan

A care plan in the event of serious illness or death of a child can be an invaluable resource for you and the nursery workers. If you do not already have such a plan, meet with your pastor and take with you a copy of this article. Perhaps you will want to set a planning session with your Christian educator, pastor, and other congregational care leaders for help in designing a plan. The plan should answer the following questions: How will we get information about a death? Who will make the initial and follow-up calls? What will we do about the child's personal belongings? Who will provide childcare for siblings? Who will schedule a memorial time sometime during the year? How will we keep in contact with the family throughout the year (birthday of the child, church holidays, and so forth)? You may think of additional questions requiring specific planning. Keep a copy of the plan where many have access to it. Review the plan yearly.

It is also helpful if you and the staff can participate in workshops or seminars on the grief process, especially in relation to the death of a child. Parents facing the loss of a child are in a unique situation that forces them to deal with an experience that is out of the natural order. The expectation of parents is that they will die before their children. This reversal of order adds to their burden of grief. While grief is a personal experience, having basic information about bereavement and mourning will help equip you to minister to parents, siblings, and others who will feel the loss of this child.

Set a time annually or semiannually to meet with church and nursery staff to talk about special circumstances related to the death of a young child. This session should be co-led by the pastor and by you. Use this article as a guide for the content of the session. It is better to be prepared and never need to use the knowledge than to never have met.

What Should I Say?

The grieving are in shock immediately after a death. The early days of grief are not a time to try to offer explanations for the death. Your presence and reassurance of God's love are the most appropriate response to the question of why. Avoid such clichés as "It was God's will" or "God just needed another flower for heaven's garden." They are not helpful and can be painful.

When speaking to children about the death, remember that young children are very literal. Children between two and three years of age will ask about a child who is absent from the nursery. You need to respond simply, directly, and truthfully, using a calm, kind voice. Avoid saying that the child has "gone to sleep" or "gone to be with Jesus." These statements can be frightening to children and can raise doubts and concerns about what will happen to them. Respond to the questions asked and say, "(Name) has died." You do not have to elaborate. Respond to their questions as they naturally arise. This can be a time to help children begin to see that death is a part of the cycle of life. Many good books and stories are available that can assist you in helping children deal with the mystery of death. (At the bottom of this page is the name and address of a catalog that lists many resources designed to help in responding to children and their parents during times of loss.) Contact your local hospice for other resources.

Some Ways to Continue Care

You will want to plan ongoing care for the parents after the funeral and flurry of concern are over. Many parents appreciate the remembrance of their child's birthday with a card or a call expressing your thoughts and prayers for them. These gestures show that their child has not been forgotten by the church. Your church may want to provide an opportunity to remember loved ones who have died during the year. Parents who have lost children should be included in this memorial. The use of candles, balloons, or other symbols can be meaningful ways to commemorate the life of the child who has died.

Consider grieving stages of caregivers who may have spent many hours caring for the child. Remember to minister to their needs as appropriate.

You are part of a ministry team that can share the love and care of Christ as you respond to the needs of a grieving family. Your presence and continued care will enable these families to walk through their grief experience knowing that they are not alone.

Additional Resource

For more information about grief, see the resource catalog from the Centering Corporation (402-553-1200, www.centering.org).

Resources for Nursery Coordinators

The First Three Years: A Guide for Ministry With Infants, Toddlers, And Two-Year-Olds, edited by Mary Alice Gran (Discipleship Resources, 2001). This comprehensive resource is a must for every ministry to young children. This guide offers practical advice on issues critical to creating, managing, and sustaining a ministry with very young children and their families. This book tackles issues such as safety/health, parenting, finances, and liability. Permission is granted to the purchaser to make photocopies of the articles for use in the local church. (Order by calling 800-685-4370 or online at www.discipleshipresources.org.)

Safe Sanctuaries: Reducing the Risk of Child Abuse in the Church, by Joy Thornburg Melton (Discipleship Resources, 1998). This book outlines why and how congregations must reduce the risk of child abuse in the church. Unique features include a plan for developing policies and procedures to prevent child abuse, suggested training models, forms, and sample worship services. Clearly written and easy to use, this book is a must for every congregation's nursery ministry. (Order by calling 800-685-4370 or online at www.discipleshipresources.org.)

Hand in Hand: Growing Spiritually With Our Children, by Sue Downing (Discipleship Resources, 1998). This book contains ideas, suggestions, and hands-on activities to help children make prayer and the Bible a vital part of daily life, live out the Word by example, and develop faith traditions. This is a good book for you, for caregivers, and for parents. (Order by calling 800-685-4370 or online at www.discipleshipresources.org.)

Teaching Young Children: A Guide for Teachers and Leaders, by MaryJane Pierce Norton (Discipleship Resources, revised 1997). In addressing the needs of infants and young children, Norton provides many practical teaching tips and describes the basic materials and equipment required for the classroom. (Order by calling 800-685-4370 or online at www.discipleshipresources.org.)

Toddlers and Twos curriculum resources (Cokesbury). This curriculum gives support for teaching toddlers and twos about God's love. Basic resources include a leader's guide with a CD, activity pak (games, storytelling figures, classroom activities, posters), and Bible story cards. (Order by calling 800-672-1789.)

The First Years Last Forever is a video from the I Am Your Child organization that is made available by the Rob Reiner Foundation and funded by Johnson & Johnson. This video, which is based on current brain research, helps new parents (and caregivers) understand the importance of the first three years of life in the healthy development of their children. It is available in English or Spanish for five dollars. (Order by calling 310-285-2385 or online at www.iamyourchild.org.)

Young Children journal. This resource is published by the National Association for the Education of Young Children (NAEYC), along with other resources related to the education of young children. For more information, contact the National Association for the Education of Young Children, 1509 16th Street, N.W., Washington, DC 20036-1426. The website for NAEYC is www.naeyc.org.

The Ecumenical Child Care Network (ECCN) is an organization that advocates quality childcare in faith-based settings. ECCN publishes a variety of booklets on childcare-related issues. For more information, contact Ecumenical Child Care Network, 8765 West Higgins Road, Suite 405, Chicago, IL. 60631. The website for ECCN is www.eccn.org.

The General Board of Discipleship website (www.gbod.org/children) includes articles, links, and other resources related to children's ministry.

Using the Articles in This Section

Many curriculum resources are available to support your ministries with younger children. The articles in this section will help nursery coordinators, caregivers, and teachers think about a variety of issues that relate to curriculum for young children.

Section Five: The Curriculum

Contents

Other Related Articles

What Is Curriculum?

Mary Jane Van Hook
Bloomington, Indiana

So, it is your job to plan curriculum for the infants and toddlers in your church. "Easy," you say. "They don't really need any curriculum. We'll find someone to take care of them for an hour, and we'll ask for some donations of discarded toys. Then we'll be all set." Right? Wrong! Yours is one of the most important jobs in your church. The first three years are extremely important in the physical and mental development of children. Current research demonstrates how crucial the first years are in the development of the brain. This is just as true of faith development as it is of any other area of development. Now, let's think about your job.

A good definition of curriculum for young children is what happens during the time they are in their church school room or nursery. Everything the child experiences from the time the child enters the room until the parents return for the child contributes to the curriculum. Several elements shape a child's perception of what happens: environment, the caregivers, interaction with the caregivers, and play. These are the things that facilitate the curriculum, or what happens.

The basic curriculum requirement for infants and toddlers is that their experiences be both faith forming in nature and appropriate to their stage of development. The curriculum itself is made up of four concepts: trust, mutual respect, play, and natural curiosity.

Trust

The first of these concepts is trust. If, in the first three years, a child learns that church is a trustworthy place, a strong foundation for faith development will be laid. How can you be assured of a trustworthy environment? Safety and physical security are essential. Be sure the space is clean and free from hazards, such as unprotected outlets, splinters, toys that are broken or small enough to be swallowed, and so forth. Make sure outside doors are secure and procedures are in place to keep strangers out of the nursery area. Make every effort to schedule consistent caregivers, so children can expect to be greeted by a familiar face each time they enter the nursery. Children handle separation from

parents much better when they know there will be no surprises in the nursery. Therefore, it is important to pay attention to how we achieve successful separation. Be sure to let parents know that they may stay with a distressed child until separation happens calmly.

Mutual Respect

Mutual respect, the second concept in our basic curriculum, results when a child is accepted as is and begins to know that at church he or she can make a mistake and still be loved. Curriculum is at its best when adults accept individual differences and styles of learning and show interest in whatever the child likes at that moment. Caregivers need to learn how to guide children's behavior in positive ways. It is actually possible to avoid saying no to a toddler, although the toddler will probably still say it to you. It is the toddler's most powerful word. A teacher who models careful listening—to cries, to words, and to behavior—is making a good start toward communicating mutual respect and trust. A teacher who also talks about his or her own feelings, makes polite requests, and helps children see the consequences of their behavior is teaching peacemaking in a very real way.

Play

Play, the third concept in our basic curriculum, is the child's way of participating in the world. Therefore, the child's need to play must be respected. How can you best facilitate children's play? And what makes play in the church setting different from play anywhere else? Begin by carefully choosing the equipment, toys, and other materials available for children to use. Tables, chairs, shelves, and other equipment for toddlers should be appropriately sized. Place wall decorations at the child's eye level. Choose sturdy equipment that will withstand use by many children over a period of years. Young children gain the most when they have enough space to freely explore and choose the toys or activities that interest them. This means that the space is not cluttered with materials that are inappropriate for the age level. Children who are two years olds need different toys than those who are seven months old. If it is necessary for both ages to share the same space, a low shelf can be used as a divider.

You may certainly accept donations of toys, but do not hesitate to screen them carefully. The church nursery is not the place for television-based toys, play weapons, coloring books, or passive toys that do all the actions themselves. Instead, choose open-ended toys, such as blocks, baby dolls, vehicles of all sorts, sturdy puzzles, manipulative toys, rhythm instruments, and so forth. These toys will allow children to use their imaginations and to play in a constructive way. Children do not tire of these toys quickly, because they use them differently at each stage of development. Rotate the toys in the room frequently.

Creative art experiences are important for toddlers. Try painting with water on a chalkboard or on dark construction paper, fingerpainting with shaving cream, making a paper collage on the sticky side of contact paper, drawing pictures with jumbo crayons on large sheets of newsprint. Remember, it is the process of creating that is important for the young child, not the product. It is better not to show a child a model you have created to use as a guide. The child's creation cannot possibly look like yours, and self-esteem and creativity may suffer. A printed curriculum such as *Toddlers and Twos* from Cokesbury (800-672-1789) provides many ideas for play experiences.

Natural Curiosity

Natural curiosity is our last concept in basic curriculum. As children play, their curiosity is continually aroused. In the church nursery we can use this curiosity to develop a sense of wonder about God's world. For our youngest children, it is the beginning of worship. Make sure to include pictures and real items from nature every week. As a child touches a starfish, smells a flower, or watches a goldfish, offer a simple prayer: "Let's say thank you to God for planning for fish. Thank you, God, for fish. Amen." An open Bible that adults read frequently and biblical pictures on the wall are good conversation starters.

Curriculum is what happens. When children experience trust, mutual respect, creative play, and wonder in an age-appropriate setting with caring and trustworthy adults, their faith journey has begun with a strong foundation.

Space That Teaches

MaryJane Pierce Norton
Nashville, Tennessee

Picture This

On Sunday morning, eager parents enter the room with their infants and toddlers. They stop briefly at the door to complete the sign-in sheet and then store their children's items on the hooks or in the cubicles provided. Parents and caregivers help children choose a place to go, move to an area, and begin work. Caregivers reach out and hold infants or toddlers who are having difficulty moving into the room. Parents or caregivers place infants in beds, playpens, infant chairs, or swings. They make sure all have toys to occupy busy hands. Soon the room is full of happy, active children playing in the various areas of the room. If asked about their room, caregivers say, "We have few problems. The children are happy and involved as soon as they come in. We think they are learning on their own and helping one another learn."

What has happened? The caregivers have turned their room into a room that teaches. The room is clean, neat, bright, and uncluttered. It has well-placed pictures and objects that reinforce the study unit, a predictable schedule, and learning centers. Let's look at each of these to see how it contributes to creating a great learning environment.

Clean, Neat, Bright Rooms

Rooms that are clean and neat command respect from the users. Children learn early to help with cleanup when there is an orderly plan for storing materials and the room is neat and clean when they enter. This literally gives them a mental picture of what to work toward at cleanup time. Disorderly rooms give a mental picture of clutter and disorder, so that's what we usually get when we ask for cleanup.

Parents are more apt to help clean up and put away items if they entered a neat, clean room at the beginning of the morning. With a messy room, adults as well as children are likely to think, *So what if the puzzle pieces aren't put back into the puzzles? It was a mess when I came in, so it's no different as I leave.* In addition, a neat room helps parents locate personal items that might otherwise be left behind week after week.

Bright lighting also contributes to making an area inviting. Combine natural and artificial lighting to provide a well-lit room with no dark corners. This makes a room look cleaner, encourages people to keep the room clean, and helps cleaning staff identify areas that need cleaning. Most important, good lighting creates a cheerful atmosphere.

Uncluttered Space

Sunday school rooms are great magnets. Anything that enters the room seems to stick there. By summertime, various corners of the room may be hiding Thanksgiving pictures, an Advent wreath, Christmas bells, and Easter lilies made from handprints. Sometimes it is hard to find anything current. And in infant and toddler rooms, we add to the clutter with diaper bags, special blankets, bottles, and sipper cups that have been left week after week. Rooms where more than one group meets may have an even more difficult time with clutter.

All of us, when we enter a room, quickly take in all the stimulation offered in that room. While we are in the room, our eyes return to these stimuli again and again. If a room is overly full, children have a difficult time concentrating. Along with pictures, banners, or objects, children need clear space, imagination space, space where they can visualize the Bible story as you tell it or picture things from their own lives.

Well-Placed Pictures

Look at the work areas in your room. If you have a block area, where can you put a poster or picture to help the children focus on what you are studying? If you have a book and puzzle area, how can you display these in a way that invites children to sit down and read or work a puzzle? What about the home living area in your room? Can you place pictures showing care of children close to where dolls are kept? Think about other objects you can use in your room in addition to pictures. What about a Bible? What about a worship area where objects appropriate to the children's age are displayed to remind them to say thanks to God? These objects focus their attention and enhance the teaching atmosphere of the room. Remember, pictures should be placed at children's eye level, not yours.

Predictable Schedule

Most infants in your care will be on their own eating and sleeping schedule. For toddlers, however, you will need a schedule as a guide. Divide time loosely into categories of play, group time (but do not be concerned if they do not all come together in the group), snack, play, and cleanup. Toddlers like predictability, so they enjoy knowing that after the story comes the snack. This helps them feel more in control. If they can anticipate what comes next, they will move better from one activity to another. Create a pictorial schedule on colored paper, using symbols to indicate activities or photos of the children doing the activity. Place it in a transparent folder and post it as a reminder for you and for parents. Also, as the children mature, they will begin to know what the pictures mean, and this will serve as an early stimulus for language development.

Learning Centers

I have taught Sunday school since I was seventeen. I have taught classes of one age, from infants through high school; and I have taught classes where children two to six years old were together. I have taught in large, well-furnished rooms, as well as in what was more like a closet than a room. I have taught both with and without learning centers. Learning centers remain my number-one choice. With learning centers, children can

- exercise choice, picking activities suited to their abilities and mood.
- work alone or with others.
- become self-directed learners, selecting materials and choosing their own way to proceed with the activity at the center.

With learning centers, behavior problems decrease. When children have choices, when they are free to work at their own pace, they are less likely to act out.

Learning centers for toddlers can include an activity table for art or other small-group activities; home living area with kitchen items, dress-up clothes, table and chairs, dolls and doll beds; block area with fabric blocks or hollow cardboard blocks for building; manipulative table for puzzles, stacking and nesting toys, and sorting boxes; movement area with large-muscle toys, such as rocking boats and indoor slides.

What about planning with learning centers? Setting up centers at the beginning of a unit takes time for looking ahead and planning what will go into each area. Once the centers are set up, less time will be involved. Your sessions will begin to fall into a pattern, and all you will need to do is change the supplies week by week. Use as a guide *Toddlers and Twos* curriculum from Cokesbury (800-672-1789). It is designed to use in learning centers.

Can learning centers work even if you do not have a teacher for each center? Certainly. Here are some guidelines:

- Set up only two or three centers at a time.
- Include only one really messy or involved activity each week, so that you can supervise that activity while the children work independently in the other areas.
- Remove items you do not intend to use. If you do not need blocks this week, cover them with a sheet or put them out of the way.
- Guide the children by talking even when you are at another center. As you help make a handprint banner, you can say, "Mike, the book you're reading is one of my favorites. I'm glad you're enjoying it." Or, "Hayley, turn your puzzle piece around. It will fit that way."

For safety it is important to have more than one adult in a classroom. If you are the primary teacher, recruit parents and others to help out. Provide on-the-job training for future teachers.

How do children learn? They learn first from caregivers. You are more important than any planned activity or craft. They learn, too, from the rooms. Well-kept rooms with appropriate activities contribute to children's learning. Your room becomes an active part of your teaching plan.

All God's Children— Valuing Diversity

Mary Pat Martin

Chicago, Illinois

As Christians, we are called to tear down barriers of hostility and division (Ephesians 2:19-22). We are called to love one another and to be the family of God.

Scripture tells us to

- value the worth of all children, helping them develop healthy self-esteem and identity (Genesis 1:27; Matthew 19:14).
- value the diversity that God has created (Genesis 1:31; Galatians 3:28).
- stand against injustice and oppression (Micah 6:8).

Divisions and hostilities among people due to race, culture and ethnicity, lifestyle, gender, religion, age, and disabilities have been around from the beginning of our history. Clearly, as Christians, we are called to be a force for reconciliation in the United States and in the world.

Our responsibility as caregivers includes:

- Caring for children in a way that is as similar as possible to their own family and cultural setting.
- Helping children value diversity.
- Exposing children to experiences that counteract biases and stereotypes.

Our Role

We need to be aware of our own biases and prejudices. We all have them, so it is critical that we spend time looking at the biases in our own lives. Examine the messages you received growing up about people who were different from yourself. How did these messages influence your ideas and beliefs about a person's inferiority or superiority?

We can begin to try to understand the "isms" in this country (racism, classism, sexism, and so forth), their beginnings, history, and current impact on all of us. We live in a race-based society, so it is critical that we understand as much as possible about how that came about and has been perpetuated and continues both individually and institutionally.

A Child's Experience

At a very young age children become aware of differences among the people around them. By age two, children recognize physical differences. They stare, point, touch, and begin to ask questions. At this age, children are not aware of which attributes are permanent, such as skin color, and which are not, such as body size. They absorb attitudes from those who care for them.

By the time children are nine years old, they will have formed most of their attitudes about race. We can assist young children as they develop attitudes, ideas, and values that will help them grow into healthy individuals who feel positive about their own ethnic and cultural identity and also value the diversity that God has created.

Young children try to make sense of something different based on their own experiences. They are able to classify based on color and size. Children watch to see how adults react to differences. Are they comfortable or uncomfortable with these differences? Is it acceptable to notice differences?

Children observe and pick up both spoken and unspoken messages about reactions to differences. When my two-year-old godson saw a man in a wheelchair, he stopped, stared, thought, and exclaimed, "Big stroller!" My African-American friend baby-sat a European-American toddler who said, "Dirt," when she touched Jackie's skin. We know children who think girls cannot be truck drivers or boys cannot be nurses, simply because they have never seen a female truck driver or a male nurse. As caregivers, we correct misinformation, we expose children to diversity, and we ask questions to help them understand.

Culturally Relevant Childcare

For infants and children to feel safe, secure, and cared for, they need to be treated in a way that is as consistent as possible with the care they receive at home. Our cultural background affects our childcare practices. Toilet training, feeding, acceptable ways of showing affection, setting limits, sleeping arrangements, and types of play are all influenced by cultural standards and expectations. Caretakers need to be sensitive to the cultural values of the children.

An Environment That Values Diversity

Begin by looking at the pictures and posters on the walls. What groups are represented? Is there diversity of race, age, class, ability, and family structure? Are men and women portrayed in a variety of roles, both inside and outside the home? Is Jesus portrayed as races other than just European? Do pictures avoid reinforcing stereotypes of cultural or ethnic groups?

Examine the books in your rooms. Are children of different ethnic groups portrayed in a positive manner? Is there diversity in the men's and women's roles? Are different family configurations portrayed? Do Bible stories depict characters who do not look European? Are there books, pictures, and stories that include children with disabilities?

Look at dolls, puzzles, dramatic play figures, dramatic play equipment, art supplies, and musical instruments. Do you have dolls of various races? Do you have both girl and boy dolls? Does the play equipment encourage play in a variety of roles, and do caretakers avoid guiding children toward certain activities based on gender? For example, are boys encouraged to play in the housekeeping center and girls in the block center? When doing art projects, do you have a wide enough variety of colors in paper, crayons, and paints to allow for the depiction of different skin tones? Do you sing songs and have musical instruments from different cultures?

After checking the environment and materials, review and make recommendations of materials to eliminate and to add.

Modeling Loving Attitudes

Our behavior and attitudes set an example for our children. We show that we value diversity in the way we respect each child and each family. We show it in the way we talk about differences: "This baby doll has beautiful brown skin." We show it in the way we correct misinformation and handle reactions to differences. (Some children around two years of age show fear about differences, especially physical disabilities.) We watch ourselves and work with others we trust to get and give feedback on any biases we might have (for example, praising boys for doing well and girls for looking nice). And we trust God in our own process of looking at our prejudices as we learn to celebrate diversity and stand up against injustice in our society.

Activities for Infants, Toddlers, and Twos

Sandra McGee
Cedar Rapids, Iowa

Activities for infants, toddlers, and twos differ greatly, as each age has different abilities. However, each age group shares the need to explore and to learn. Activities should provide a variety of experiences to help children learn about themselves, their surroundings, and their world. Activities should use the child's need to explore using the senses (for example, giving an infant a bright rattle that can be looked at, touched, tasted, and heard). Developmentally appropriate activities help children build self-confidence in their achievements and successes.

An activity coupled with loving praise, encouragement, and positive responses will encourage a child to continue to explore and to learn. Never force a child to participate in an activity.

Your attitude and interest in the child are more important than the activity itself. Be flexible. Every child is different, and every group of children is different. Change the activity to fit the child, not the child to fit the activity. Each activity can be added to or scaled down, lengthened or shortened to fit the child's needs, attention span, and mood. Remember, it is your attitude, interest, flexibility, and presentation that will determine the outcome of any activity.

The following are a few activity suggestions. The possibilities are endless and are limited only by your imagination.

Infants
So Big
With the child on your lap, ask, "How big is (child's name)?" As you raise the child's arms over his or her head, say, "Soooooo big."

Pat-a-Cake
Sit the child on your lap and hold his or her hands in yours as you say, "Pat-a-cake, pat-a-cake, baker's man. Bake me a cake as fast as you can. Roll it, pat it, mark it with a B. And put it in the oven for baby and me." (*Clap baby's hands together for pat-a-cake, and do rolling, patting, marking, and putting actions for the rest.*)

This Is the Way
Act out motions as you say or sing:
"This is the way the baby does, clap…clap…clap."
"This is the way the baby does, peekaboo, I see you."
"This is the way the baby does, creep…creep…creep."
"This is the way the baby does, sleep…sleep…sleep."

Wiggle
Wiggle the child's fingers, toes, and so forth as you say, "I wiggle my fingers; I wiggle my toes; I wiggle my shoulders; I wiggle my nose. Now no more wiggles are left in me, so I will be still, as still as I can be."

Peekaboo
This can be done with more than one infant at a time. It teaches and reinforces that when someone leaves, the person comes back. It can be as simple as putting your hands in front of your face, moving them away, and saying, "Peekaboo." This can be repeated over and over again. Or hold the child's hands in front of his or her face, remove the hands, and say, "Peekaboo!" Or say, "Where's (child's name)?" Then remove his or her hands and say, "There's (child's name)!"

Where's Your Nose?
This can be done with more than one child at a time. Say, "Where's (child's name)'s nose? Where's your nose? There it is! There's (child's name)'s nose!" Ask each child in turn. Ask about chin, ears, eyes, fingers, toes. This is a wonderful way for children to learn more about themselves and to feel good about themselves.

Baby
Say. "B-A-Bay, B-E-Bee, B-I-Bye, B-O-Boh, B-U-Boo, Bay-bee-bye-boh-boo!" (*When you say "boo," gently put your forehead on the child's.*)

Books
Select books that are cloth, soft, or stiff board, since infants will want to put them in their mouth. Hold the infant on your lap and let him or her look at the pictures, pointing to objects on the page and naming them. The child, depending on his or her age, can point to the pictures and begin to say the words.

See the Baby

Use an unbreakable mirror to let an infant look at him or herself. Point to the child in the mirror and talk about him or her. Say, "Who's that? Is that (child's name)?" In the mirror point out the child's nose, eyes, smile. Use the mirror to play peekaboo.

Motor Skills

Encourage the children to crawl by crawling along with them. Place an object just out of reach and say, "Let's get the (name of toy)." Help the child get the toy. Do not tease or frustrate the child. Give praise when the child gets the object. As children are beginning to walk, use lots of praise, smiles, and encouragement to get them to come to you. Do not be so far away that the child becomes frustrated.

Put It Here

Put a toy or block in a pile of toys or blocks. Encourage the child to pick one up and put it in the pile.

Drop It

Stand up and drop a toy into a pail. The infant can stand or be held to drop a toy into the pail. Take turns and give lots of praise.

Sound Games

Ring a bell or shake a rattle next to the infant. Wait for him or her to look. Smile and say, "What is that? It's a (bell, rattle)." Repeat a few times with a variety of sounds.

Music

Sing to the infant. The song can be one you know or can be made up as you go along. Dance with the child in your arms. Infants love music and rhythm. Help them clap to the music. Sing along with CDs, cassette tapes, or a music box.

Fingers and Toes

Children love activities involving their hands and feet. Play This Little Piggy with their toes. Or count their fingers by singing, "One little, two little, three little fingers; four little…" through "ten little fingers of (child's name)."

Toys

Provide the child with a variety of toys that stimulate the senses of taste, touch, hearing, sight, and smell. Interact with the child, giving smiles and praise, touching, cuddling, and talking. Personal interaction is by far the best activity you can provide for an infant.

Toddlers and Twos

Toddlers and twos are becoming more sure of themselves and their abilities. They like to stay active: running, climbing, grabbing, pushing, and pulling. They have a short attention span, so creative activities need to be brief and varied.

Children this age play alongside one another fairly well in small groups. This is an ideal age to teach simple fingerplays that use large muscles, or the children can imitate you and others in the group. Many wonderful action plays are available that teach children about their bodies. The following are simple fingerplays:

Head and Shoulders (traditional)

Head and shoulders, knees and toes, knees and toes,
Head and shoulders, knees and toes, knees and toes,
Eyes and ears and mouth and nose,
Head and shoulders, knees and toes, knees and toes.
(*Point to body parts while singing.*)

If You're Happy (traditional)

If you're happy and you know it,
clap your hands. (*clap clap*)
If you're happy and you know it,
clap your hands. (*clap clap*)
If you're happy and you know it,
then your face will surely show it. (*point to smile*)
If you're happy and you know it,
clap your hands. (*clap clap*)

Jack in the Box

Jack in the box, sitting so still,
won't you come out? Yes, I will!
(*Crouch down on the floor. On the last line, jump up with both hands reaching for the sky.*)

I Stretch My Fingers

I stretch my fingers way up high,
until they almost reach the sky.
I lay them in my lap, you see,
where they're as quiet as can be.

Stand Up Tall

Stand up tall, bend down low.
Jump up and down and touch your toes.
Stretch up high and wave goodbye.

Teddy Bear

Teddy Bear, Teddy Bear, turn around.
Teddy Bear, Teddy Bear, touch the ground.
Teddy Bear, Teddy Bear, show your shoe.
Teddy Bear, Teddy Bear, that will do.

Teddy Bear, Teddy Bear, go upstairs.
Teddy Bear, Teddy Bear, say your prayers.
Teddy Bear, Teddy Bear, turn off the light.
Teddy Bear, Teddy Bear, say good night.

Two Little Feet

Two little feet go tap, tap, tap.
Two little hands go clap, clap, clap.
A quick jump from the chair.
Two little hands fly up in the air.
Two little fists go bump, bump, bump.
Two little feet go jump, jump, jump.
One little body turns 'round, 'round, 'round.
And one little child sits quietly down.

Creative Materials

Fingerpainting

A wonderful fingerpaint for young children is non-menthol shaving cream. Paint on freezer wrap paper or on the tabletop itself. Give each child a small scoop of shaving cream with a little food coloring added to give it color. (Some coloring may stain some tabletops, so be sure to test a small area first.)

Playing Dough

Children this age love different textures and experimenting with them. The following is a wonderful playing dough recipe that lasts well:

3 cups flour
1 1/2 cups salt
3 tablespoons alum
Boil together:
3 cups water
3 tablespoons oil
a few drops of food coloring

Pour the boiling mixture over the flour mixture. Mix with a spoon, and then knead when cool enough to touch. Knead in two tablespoons hand lotion. Store in a covered container. It does not need to be refrigerated. Give the children rolling pins and cookie cutters to use on the playing dough.

Water Paint

If you can go outside, give the children paintbrushes and water to paint on a sidewalk, fence, or wall of a building. If you are inside, have them paint a blackboard or black paper with water.

Hands and Feet

Children are proud of themselves and their body parts. Trace around each child's foot, and let the child color it or draw a face on it to make a puppet. Trace each child's hand, and let the child color it for pretend gloves or mittens.

Scribbling

Providing scrap paper and pencils for a child encourages creativity. Use colored or textured paper for variety. Write on each creation the child's name, the date, and any comments the child wants noted.

Puzzles

Many simple puzzles are available for this age group that help build coordination and, with success and praise, their self-esteem.

Music

Many wonderful children's CDs and cassette tapes featuring sing-along songs are available. Choose some with music and dance (children love to dance), or make up your own songs. Have the children fall down when the music stops, then get back up and dance when it starts again. This gives them time for rest and helps the motor skills, and it is fun. Have a parade by marching around the room to music and clapping hands or stomping feet. Songs for transition help toddlers and twos move on to another activity. Sing to the tune of "London Bridge": "Now it's time to pick up our toys, pick up our toys, pick up our toys. Now it's time to pick up our toys. Won't you come and join me?" (You may also use the words "eat our snack," "read our books," "sit on the floor," and so forth.) If you start the activity yourself, singing about it and making it look enjoyable, the children will want to join in the fun.

Follow the Leader

Sing: "I can pat my tummy, my tummy, my tummy. You can do it too!" (You may also use the words "wiggle my finger," "blink my eyes," and so forth. Let the children suggest things to do.)

Grocery Store

Children love imitating activities in the adult world. Save boxes from cereal, gelatin, macaroni and cheese, and so forth. Add paper sacks, children's shopping carts, some larger boxes for pushing and carrying, and you have the makings of a grocery store.

Go on an Adventure

Take the children for a walk down the hall, to the next room, or just out the door and back in again. Have a destination in mind, such as another room to see a decoration, eat a snack, or get a new toy. Make it exciting by talking about going on an adventure to see or discover something new.

Go to Worship

Travel to the chapel or sanctuary. While there, sing a song, say a prayer, and collect a pretend offering. Let one of the children be the preacher giving a sermon and then greeting the other children at the door as they leave.

Nature Walk

Go outside for a walk. Talk about all the things God made: trees, grass, flowers, birds, and so forth. Take along a sack for the treasures the children may find along the way. When you get back to your room, you can talk about them and thank God for each item.

Be an Animal

While looking at a book about animals, imitate the way they move and the sounds they make. Waddle and quack like a duck. Or be an elephant, dog, cat, rooster, and so forth. Sing to the tune of "Mulberry Bush": "This is the way a bunny hops, a bunny hops, a bunny hops. This is the way a bunny hops so early in the morning." Imitating an animal is great for transitions: "Hop like a bunny to the table," "Fly like a bird to the door," and "Quiet as a mouse to the books." Then ask what the animal says. Children this age love to imitate animal noises and movements. Animal hand puppets or stuffed toy animals can be lots of fun for this activity.

This Is the Way

To the tune of "Mulberry Bush" ("This is the way we wash our clothes"), you can sing "wash our hands," "eat our snack," "sit at the table," "fold our hands," "pick up our toys," "quietly sit," and so forth as you do the activity. This is a great way to get children to join in.

Pretend

You can do so many wonderful pretend things. Line up chairs to make seats on a bus. The children can get on, pay a fare, sit down to ride, and sing "The Wheels on the Bus."

Or the chairs can be a movie theater. Sit down with your pretend popcorn and talk about the pretend movie you are watching. Ask the children for ideas about the movie.

Use the chairs as seats on a boat (or sit on the floor) and sing, "Row, row, row your boat..." Row your boat with your pretend oars. Ask the children if they see the fish in the water under the boat, and pretend you got splashed with water.

Pretend you are popcorn kernels in a pot. As the pot gets hot, you pop. Pretend to have a tea or an indoor picnic. This can coordinate with the snack or lunch. Spread a blanket on the floor and have the children sit on it. You can eat your snack, lunch, or pretend lunch on the blanket. Talk about picnics: "Do you see ants? bugs? Should we give a scrap of food to the pretend bird that is hopping by?"

Mirror

Provide an unbreakable mirror. Encourage the children to make a face (happy, sad, funny, scary, surprised) in the mirror.

Group Activity

Encourage the children to build a tower with blocks, with each child contributing to the construction. Talk about how it is growing with everyone's help. Sing to the tune of "Mulberry Bush": "This is the way we build a tower, build a tower, build a tower. This is the way we build a tower, when we work together!" Then, of course, you can enjoy knocking it down and spreading out the blocks. You could even sing: "This is the way we knock it down...." Be prepared to sing this portion at any time, as toddlers can suddenly decide they have had enough and knock it down before you or others are ready. The song may help others join in who may have been upset about the tower going down. Likewise, build a worship area. When they are done playing, sing: "This is the way we go to worship, go to worship, go to worship" and "This is the way we finish worship." Use familiar worship activities: pray, collect the offering (blocks in a bucket), sing "Jesus Loves Me," and so forth. Help worship be fun.

Remember, the activity is not as important as the child! Every child needs to be treated as a special individual. Sometimes the best activities will be initiated by the children themselves. Circulate among them, see what they are doing, and join them. Describe what you see them doing. Add an idea to the activity: "I see you're building. That really is getting tall! Shall we start another one beside it?" Or: "It looks like you're making breakfast. May I have a glass of orange juice?" After a while, move to join another child or group of children. Every child needs to feel special, to feel that you have sought him or her out. In an ideal setting, one person would rotate among the children while another is doing organized activities that are scheduled. Just be sure the activity is what is scheduled, not the child.

Using the Articles in This Section

The articles in this section will help nursery coordinators and administrators create safe, effective facilities for young children. Use these articles as you work with trustees, custodians, and others who have responsibility for the church facilities.

Section Six: The Facilities

Contents

Other Related Articles

Room Size and Location

Mary Alice Gran

Nashville, Tennessee

You are indeed fortunate if you are planning a new building with unlimited finances and an already successful children's ministry ready to move into it. However, most of us must work with what we have, making changes with limited resources, making the best decisions possible, trying to be creative with the resources at hand. The following guidelines will help you assess room space, location within the church complex, and number of children for which your facility is suited.

Plan for a minimum of thirty-five square feet of playroom floor space per child. This does not include bathrooms, closet space, or hallways. This may seem like a lot of space, but do not compromise this guideline. Children need space to explore, to rest, and to be.

For security reasons, locate the nursery facility in a central area within the church. Although it may be tempting to place it near the sanctuary entrance for the convenience of parents on Sunday morning, consider that area in relationship to the rest of the church building and access during the week. Certainly, the nursery should be clearly accessible to parents, with signs posted at each church entrance indicating the location of the nursery. A primary hallway with visual access into the nursery provides an excellent feeling of security for the caregivers, children, and parents. However, the arrangement should not distract children from their activities.

Bathroom facilities should be a part of the nursery with, ideally, a sink low enough for toddlers and twos to wash their own hands. Place a potty-chair within the facility. Include a diaper-changing area within the main nursery facilities or, if located in the restroom, make it visible from the main room as a protection for workers and for children. For additional information on setting up a diaper-changing area, see the article "Supplies and Procedures for Changing Diapers," on page 82.

Include storage space for caregiver supplies (crib sheets; washcloths; cleaning supplies; caregiver smocks, coats, and personal items; laundry; bulletin board supplies; and so forth). If the storage space is in low cupboards, add plastic door guards to prevent children from opening doors and then shutting them on their fingers. If the storage space is a closet, remove any lock that might allow children to become locked in the closet. Mount a small key-locked storage cupboard for cleaning products in a location that is inaccessible to children.

The main nursery area should be open, bright, clean, and home-like. If there are lots of young children in your congregation, it is better to have multiple medium-size rooms than one huge room. In planning an area, allow space for parents to gather as children are signed in and picked up, either inside the nursery or in the hallway. This is an excellent location for a bulletin board featuring information for parents. Near the entrance or in each room, hang pegs for diaper bags and children's coats. Allow a space for security procedures (pickup of children by parents).

Consider how the nursery facilities are prepared for emergencies. Include the following:

- Phone or buzzer alarm for emergencies;
- Emergency numbers posted by the phone (abuse hot line, church office, fire department, hospital, police, poison control, and so forth);
- Evacuation plan, including multiple exit strategies, posted near the door;
- First-aid kit and current first-aid manual;
- Poster of step-by-step instructions for choking and breathing emergencies.

The facilities set the tone for what happens within the nursery. Provide an area that encourages children to explore, to discover, to choose, to relate to caring adults, and to be all that God created them to be.

Supplies and Procedures for Changing Diapers

Stephen D. Krau
Nashville, Tennessee

Diaper changing is a critical health routine for infants. Not only will the child be uncomfortable if not changed, but it could lead to severe diaper rash and various other problems. Although this is often thought of as a distasteful part of caring for children, it does provide a time for caregivers to interact with the child on a one-on-one basis.

The first part of any childcare routine is to prepare the area before bringing the child to change. A specific area of your nursery/classroom should be set aside just for diapering. Set up the area in a way that is convenient for changing diapers, yet is safe for the child, with none of the supplies within the child's reach. The diaper-changing area should be in an open area near running water.

As there should be at least two adults in the area, it is desirable to have one adult do the diapering and a different adult handle bottles and feedings. Naturally, these tasks can be rotated from time to time, but, if possible, the person changing the diapers should not be the person handling food.

Diapering Supplies
- Diapering board/table (or nonporous, noncloth surface that can be wiped down)
- Garbage pail with secure lid
- Plastic bags
- Washcloths
- Paper towels
- Disposable diapers
- Baby wipes
- Extra diaper pins
- Disinfectant in spray bottle (one-fourth cup of bleach to one gallon of water)
- Paper/chart for the parent report
- Pencil
- Disposable gloves
- Facial tissues
- Liquid soap
- Nonporous hard toys (to keep child occupied while in the area)
- Cleaning supplies

Parents' Instructions
As the children arrive, have parents write down diaper-changing instructions. A small slip of paper, an index card, or a form designed for each child works well. Provide space for the child's name and for notes on lotions or powders to use when the child is wet, has a bowel movement, or has a rash. Include space for indicating allergies. Although it may not pertain directly to diaper changing, it may prove useful later and will be easy to access. Asking the parents these questions helps you not only provide the child with optimal care, but it also lets the parents know that you care about their child. This can be a great source of comfort to any parent, especially to those who are not accustomed to leaving their child.

Preparations
Obviously, diapers should be changed whenever a child has a bowel movement or is wet, but sometimes the child does not let you know when this has occurred. Check each child's diaper before he or she is fed and within the half hour before the parents are to arrive. When it is time for a change, have everything ready before you bring the child to the area. This assures that you will not have to leave the child alone. Check the parents' instructions, and get what you need from the bag the parents brought. Be sure to have a wet washcloth or commercial wipes within reach. Get the diaper ready. If the child is in a cloth diaper, the parents may have brought more. If not, you may need to use a disposable diaper provided by the church.

Diapering Instructions
Remove the soiled or wet diaper with gloved hands. Move it out of your way and out of the child's reach. Clean the child. Apply ointments/powders only as suggested by the parents. Be sure to put powder in your hand and apply rather than shaking the powder on the child and clouding the air. If the child has a rash, apply ointments as suggested by the parent. If the parent did not mention a rash and you notice one, be sure to mention it to the parent.

Put on the clean diaper by slipping it under the child and bringing it up between the child's legs. If the diaper is cloth, always hold your fingers between the child and the pin, so that the child is not pricked. If the diaper is disposable, use the adhesive pull tabs to connect the back of the diaper to the front.

This is a great time to interact with the child beyond the actual diapering task. Be sure to protect the child at all times, keeping pins and the dirty diaper out of reach, and keeping at least one hand on the child at all times. It is amazing how quickly a child can squirm from a diaper table to the floor!

If clothes are wet, you should also change them. While doing this, check the child's face, wiping his or her nose with a tissue and washing the face with a clean cloth as needed. Then take the child out of the diaper-changing area.

Area Cleanup

Cleanup should begin only after the child is out of the diaper-changing area and both of your hands are free. First take care of the soiled diaper. Soiled cloth diapers may need to be taken to the toilet to be rinsed out. Be sure to keep on the disposable gloves. Once a diaper is rinsed, place it in a plastic bag, seal it, and put it in the child's diaper bag. Disposable diapers can be placed in the garbage pail, with pull-tabs firmly in place. Disposable diapers cannot be flushed!

Clean up other supplies you used, including putting lids back on ointments. Throw away any paper towels you used. Rinse out the washcloth you used and place it in a plastic bag to be washed later. If you used any toys while diapering, wash them in a bleach solution, and let them air dry before another child uses them.

Clean the diaper-changing table or area after each use with a solution of one-fourth cup bleach to one gallon of water. Wipe the area down and dry with paper towels. Keeping the diaper-changing table clean for each child is essential in reducing the spread of contagious diarrhea and other infections.

Hand Washing

When the diaper-changing area is clean, wash your hands with soap and warm water, rubbing your hands briskly together. Be sure to do this after changing each diaper. This protects you and the children from catching diarrhea and reduces the spread of colds and other infections.

Parent Note

When finished, make a notation on the form you had the parents complete when the child arrived. Note when the diaper was changed and if the child was just wet or was soiled. When several parents show up at once to get their children, there may not be time to communicate this information verbally.

Furnishing the Nursery

Janellen Evans
Livonia, Michigan

The facility for caring for infants, toddlers, and two-year-olds needs to be a healthy, safe place for young children. It should allow the children to experience love and care and to develop self-esteem. The room may be the first setting where children experience the church family; therefore, it should be pleasant and comfortable and radiate God's love. It needs to convey to both the parents and the children the feeling that they are loved and that God loves them. In addition, the room should provide an atmosphere of warmth and friendliness to encourage parents and caretakers to communicate with one another.

Space

The furnishings should suit the children's physical, emotional, spiritual, and social developmental needs. Depending on the number of children in this age category and their attendance, the church needs to be flexible in deciding how many rooms are needed and the appropriate furnishings. Individual rooms for infants, for toddlers, and for twos would be ideal, but for most churches this is unrealistic because of lack of space and room availability. The required floor space per child varies, depending on state childcare licensing departments. Generally, you should plan on thirty-five square feet per child. An open space is needed for crawlers and toddlers to move freely without feeling confined or restricted while they play. Play is important because it provides a way for the children to work out their feelings, develop large- and small-motor skills, stimulate their creativity and imagination, and learn to be a part of God's world. The design of your room and placement of the furniture will determine the usefulness of the space.

Entrance

A half-wall separating the entrance to the nursery from the play area allows for ease in dropping off and picking up the children. It also creates less disturbance if one child leaves before the others. Install a counter on top of this wall to provide space for signing in children upon arrival, filling out registration forms, and distributing notes. To interest the children as they arrive, securely mount bookshelves or cubicles along this wall to house dolls, blocks, balls, books, soft toys, and other small toys. Position additional low open shelves in the play area to organize available toys. Watch for sharp corners on shelves, tables, and so forth.

Floors

Many types of materials are available for flooring. Vinyl and wood floors are easy to clean and sanitize; however, carpeting is a good choice to provide comfort for the crawling infant and protection for the child who is taking lots of tumbles during the first months of walking. The carpet must be durable, colorfast, gentle to the child's skin, made of hypo-allergenic materials, easy to clean, and meet fire codes. A short nap and dense weave are best for easy movement of push-and-pull toys and for preventing small items from becoming lost in the carpet pile. The carpet selection for children who are frequently on the floor should balance the least amount of chemical additives (soil repellents, mothproofing, and waterproofing) needed with cleanliness and sanitation needs. Wait several days after the carpet is laid before using it with children, in order to allow strong fumes from the carpet, padding, and glue to ventilate.

Equipment/Furnishings

Basic equipment for the room includes cribs, rocking chairs, and a diaper-changing area. Depending on availability of funds, equipment may be purchased new, or donations may be requested. Remember to accept only donations that meet predetermined safety guidelines and special needs. Sometimes a gracious "no, thank you" is necessary if a donation is not something suitable for your room or for the age of the children. (See the article "Policy for Donations and Gifts to the Nursery," on page 146.)

Cribs should have safety features, including slats spaced less than two and three-eighths inches apart; dropped railing latches that are inoperable by infants inside or toddlers outside; snug-fitting, extra-firm, easy-to-clean mattresses; and teething rails that are flexible and will not crack or splinter. The corners should be smooth and free from protrusions. The end panels should be solid, with no cutouts where a child might catch his or her head or hands. Cribs should be placed in a quiet section of the room away from the windows, toy shelves, and large-muscle activity equipment. Cribs need to be placed two feet apart or have a sneeze barrier placed between them. If the crib can fit through the door and has sturdy casters, it can be used to transport several children in case of a fire.

Rocking chairs should be sturdy, comfortable, and stable. They should have a high back with large arms to provide comfort for the caregiver and to allow for babies to be cradled securely. Loose seat cushions are not recommended, as a toddler's legs may get entangled while attempting to climb into the chair.

The diaper-changing area can be a built-in counter or a sturdy, moveable changing table. It must have a washable surface that can be disinfected easily. Cupboards equipped with safety latches should be available above or below for storage of tissues, diapers, wipes, disposable gloves, spray disinfectant, paper towels, and bags for disposing of diapers. Water should be available for cleaning the children and also for the caregivers to wash their hands. Toilet facilities should be easily accessible for children who are in the process of toilet training.

Other items to furnish your room might include any or all of following, depending on space and need: a playpen constructed of tight mesh or closely spaced slats; a sturdy automatic swing in which infants can observe their surroundings but be safe from toddlers; an infant seat with a safety strap; a durable plastic toddler playhouse and/or slide; a small table and chairs; a climbing cube; small riding toys; a cupboard for storing fitted sheets, receiving blankets, spare clothes, and teaching materials; a laundry basket for soiled linen; and a CD/cassette tape player with CDs/cassette tapes of children's Bible stories, nursery activities, and familiar songs.

Frequently, people will want to give used items to the nursery. Developing a policy for such items will prevent hurt feelings or acceptance of inappropriate furnishings. Accept items with the understanding that they will be used only if they are safe, appropriate, and needed. Items not needed can be given to a local charity or other recycling agency. Unsafe items should be disposed of properly.

Other Essentials

Additional features are
- a small window in the door so that parents can check on their child after separation;
- a phone or intercom connecting the nursery with emergency assistance;
- a smoke alarm, a fire extinguisher, and directions for a fire escape route (include multiple exit strategies);
- emergency instructions for choking and for CPR;
- capped electrical outlets;
- a thermostat;
- a refrigerator for bottles and snacks;
- a speaker from the sanctuary with a volume control;
- a ventilation fan;
- excellent lighting from artificial and natural sources;
- appropriate heating and air conditioning for small children who will be on the floor;
- emergency numbers posted by the phone (abuse hot line, church office, fire department, hospital, police, poison control, and so forth);
- First-aid kit and current first-aid manual.

Every piece of equipment should pass safety regulations. Smooth, rounded corners are important on all equipment, and only durable, chip-proof, nontoxic paint should be used on the surfaces of furnishings. Check equipment frequently for loose or broken parts and areas that might cause a safety hazard, and repair them before problems or injuries occur.

A Final Word

When you have collected everything you think you will need to furnish your nursery, get down on the floor, look around, and ask yourself, *If I were an infant, toddler, or two-year-old, would I feel happy, comfortable, secure, and loved in this facility?*

Decorating the Nursery

Janellen Evans
Livonia, Michigan

In decorating a facility for infants, toddlers, and twos, remember two important words: *light* and *bright*. Children are affected by their surroundings and stimulated by their environment; therefore, the appearance of the nursery is important. In addition, parents need to see a pleasant, well-organized room to feel secure about leaving their children.

Windows

Keep window treatments to a minimum to provide maximum light distribution. The direction of the sun, winter drafts, and the amount of ventilation needed should be considered when choosing the window covering. If blinds are used, keep the cords out of reach of small hands, and cut the loop end for safety reasons. Depending on the window placement, window guard rails and/or locks may be a necessary security addition. A dropped ceiling with fluorescent lighting is ideal for insulation and light. Track lighting to spotlight specific areas and dimmer switches in the crib area are optional.

Walls

Although there are many wall coverings available, nontoxic, lead-free, washable paint is the least expensive decorating tool. It looks clean, can be wiped with a damp cloth, is easily touched up, and provides a background for anything you wish to hang. If walls are painted white or a light color, the room will appear larger, and a variety of colors can be used as accents. Bright rainbow colors create a warm, cheerful atmosphere.

In choosing wall decorations, remember that young children distinguish shapes and contrast before detail, so keep designs simple. To enhance learning, choose themes that are familiar to children, such as animals, nursery rhymes, Bible stories, and things that go. Cute as they may be, try to stay away from commercial characters as a theme. Use fabric wall hangings, banners, self-sticking vinyl animals, or painted pictures to decorate the walls and to use as discussion pieces or distractions to soothe an unhappy child. Photographs of the children and their parents can be used to decorate an area. Label them with names and birth dates of children to help caregivers and families become familiar with one another. Seasonal decorations relating to the weather or church holidays may be hung from the ceiling or fastened on bulletin boards. (A church youth group might be interested in creating decorations for your area.) Unbreakable mirrors and plastic-coated pictures mounted at the child's eye level will provide visual stimulation.

Toy Storage

Paint low, open bookshelves with nontoxic, bright-colored paint, and stock them with unbreakable, easy-to-clean toys to attract the children's interest. Be sure to bolt the shelves to the wall, or secure them in some other fashion, to prevent injury to the children. Use sturdy plastic baskets or crates to organize toys on the shelves. Avoid toy boxes or large receptacles for the following reasons: Lids on toy boxes can injure children; toys can become damaged if tossed or crowded in a container; and toys are not as visible or accessible if piled together. Shelving gives a sense of order to the room and allows children to make choices. Also, if toys are visible and in similar locations as children return each week, they will develop a sense of belonging and feel comfortable in God's house.

Diaper Bag Storage

To hold diaper bags and children's outerwear, consider mounting hooks or pegs ten to twelve inches apart on a long, narrow board that can be fastened on the wall out of the children's reach. Painted numbers or commercial adhesive numbers located above the hooks will provide a reference to the sign-in sheet to identify children with their belongings. If space is available, individual cubicles for children's belongings can be made.

Fabric

Brightly colored fabric that is washable and durable is great for decorating. Make smocks or aprons for your caregivers to wear to protect their clothes and to identify them as people in charge. Cover large sheets of foam to keep on the floor for crawling infants to climb on. Add color and comfort to rocking chairs by using back cushions. Spread a piece of fabric or a vinyl tablecloth on the floor to provide a picnic area for small children to use at snack time.

Bulletin Board

To communicate important information to the child's family, place a bulletin board near the entrance. Create one from corkboard or by covering a ceiling tile with fabric. Thick yarn tied around the board provides a place where nametags can be attached using diaper pins. Cut simple shapes out of vinyl purchased by the yard at a fabric store, and use a permanent marker to print each child's name. Pin the nametags on the children's backs, as this will not disturb their play. On or near the bulletin board, place a current list of the nursery-age children. You may wish to include the children's birth dates and parents' names to better acquaint caregivers and parents with one another. Consider using a dry-erase marker board outside the door to list the names of the caregivers on duty.

Play Area

A carpeted low step to a raised platform area, or a sloped floor in one area, is great for crawlers to test their abilities. Low-mounted handrails may be installed for the children to strengthen their muscles by pulling themselves up.

Furnish the room with a sturdy plastic slide, cube, rocking boat, playhouse, table and chairs, rocking horse, and ride-on toys. Little Tykes, Playskool, and Fisher-Price make sturdy, safe play equipment suitable for twos and under. Durability is important, since many children of various sizes will be using this equipment. Invest in items that will not require frequent repair or refurbishing. All items need to be washable, as germs are easily transmitted among this age group. Consider purchasing several of the same toy, rather than several unique ones, as young children are not developmentally ready to share. Each child may want a red ball.

Finally

Remember that you are decorating this facility for infants, toddlers, and/or twos. Strive for simplicity and avoid clutter so that the children will not be over stimulated. Introduce new decorations, toys, and equipment to satisfy the children's curiosity for discovery and exploration in learning. Rotate items for variety. To prevent possible injuries, use only materials and equipment that are safe and age-appropriate. Keep the facility light and bright to create a happy, welcoming mood. Use your imagination and enjoy decorating and designing a place to entertain and serve the youngest members of God's family.

Nursery Floor Plan

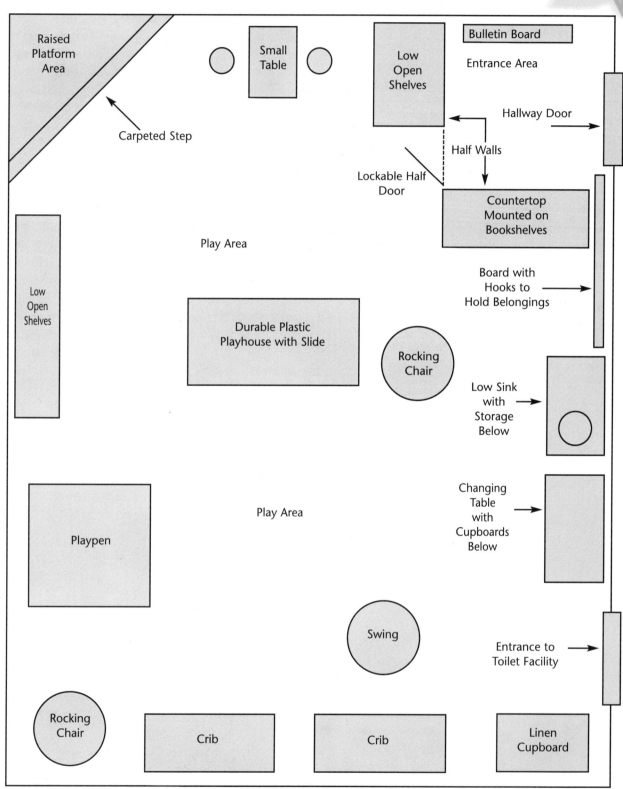

Raised Platform Area

Carpeted Step

Small Table

Low Open Shelves

Bulletin Board

Entrance Area

Hallway Door

Half Walls

Lockable Half Door

Countertop Mounted on Bookshelves

Play Area

Low Open Shelves

Board with Hooks to Hold Belongings

Durable Plastic Playhouse with Slide

Rocking Chair

Low Sink with Storage Below

Changing Table with Cupboards Below

Play Area

Playpen

Swing

Entrance to Toilet Facility

Rocking Chair

Crib

Crib

Linen Cupboard

Using the Articles in This Section

The articles in this section will help nursery coordinators, trustees, finance committees, and other groups within the church that have responsibility for legal and financial stewardship.

Section Seven: Legal and Financial Issues

Contents

Other Related Articles

Liability Issues

Steve Zekoff
Evanston, Illinois

One of the first risk-management steps for every church with a nursery program is to review the current insurance policy to confirm that there is adequate protection in place. The liability coverage provided under insurance policies for local churches usually includes bodily injury and medical payments. Separate policies or endorsements may exist for vicarious liability for physical or sexual abuse and for daycare centers. Check with your church's insurance agent to determine what is covered by the policy, and at what limits. You do not want to discover that you do not have enough insurance in the event of a loss. Also confirm that liability protection is afforded nonmedical personnel who administer first aid to children and others in the nursery or elsewhere in the church facility.

An assessment of liability exposures is recommended. Evaluate your supervision, security, safety, and sanitation procedures to assure that you have taken the preventive steps to avoid an accident or incident.

Adequate supervision of children in the nursery is crucial. If supervision is not properly maintained, it may result in tragic consequences. Have the nursery caregivers been church members for at least six months? Have they completed an application process? Has a background check been done? At least two nursery attendants should be on duty at all times, with a ratio of at least one nursery worker to every four children (one to three for infants). Are your nursery attendants an appropriate age for this responsible assignment? (At least one of the workers should be age eighteen or older. It is inappropriate to have older children and youth responsible for the church nursery. Adult supervision is required.) Have you thoroughly screened your nursery workers to determine qualifications? Have you checked references for any history that would disqualify any of the workers to serve in the nursery?

Security is an important issue. Is your nursery located so that access from outside the building is regulated? Are the restrooms used by the nursery attendants and children adjacent to or near the nursery? Do others, such as ushers or church school superintendents, check on the nursery periodically to see that things are all right? Is a phone readily available so that in an emergency police, fire, medical, and church personnel can be summoned quickly if necessary? Remember to post emergency phone numbers, including direct-dial numbers as an alternative to the 911 service.

Are there procedures in place to allow only authorized individuals to pick up children after worship or other church events? Your church does not want to contribute to unauthorized pickup, whether it be by a stranger or by a noncustodial parent or other relative. Many churches have a sign-in/sign-out policy that uses matching identification tags for the child and parent, in order to prevent children from leaving with an unauthorized adult. Some churches use pagers so that nursery caregivers have immediate connection to parents, and pagers can be exchanged for a child to assure appropriate access to children.

Consider safety issues. Are all the toys and furnishings in proper repair? Are the toys and equipment age-appropriate? Are objects stacked so that they will not become unstable and fall on children? Are children prevented from wandering off unobserved? Are electrical outlets guarded and fans and other electrical appliances out of the reach of children? Do cribs meet safety-code standards? Are nursery caregivers certified in CPR and first aid? Is a first-aid kit stocked and replenished regularly?

Sanitation care of the nursery includes cleaning toys, furnishings, and washroom facilities with a disinfectant on a regular basis; having proper disposal facilities and safe handling procedures for soiled diapers; having first-aid supplies readily available for emergency use; and having safe procedures in place to avoid disease transmittal as a result of treating wounds.

For further information, contact the loss control specialists of your insurance company. Many county and state departments of health and child protective services agencies have helpful resources available.

Set a regular time to review liability aspects of nursery care. Decide who will be responsible for initiating the review.

Screening Nursery Workers

Steve Zekoff
Evanston, Illinois

Caregivers are the key factor in a positive nursery experience. Local churches typically conduct minimum application, screening, and supervision of their paid and/or volunteer nursery staff, which is a crucial step to successful nursery operation. Typically, people looking for inappropriate involvement with children can find that access in churches without fear of being checked out. This has left churches vulnerable to violation of the trust given to nursery workers by church leaders, parents, and children. It is crucial to develop a policy requiring a complete and formal application process for nursery positions. That policy must be implemented and applied consistently.

Experts suggest using an application form to check the background, training, and experience of individuals volunteering their services and of people applying for paid nursery positions. The significance of any position is affirmed when people wishing to serve must apply for the opportunity.

It is essential to request information about current employment, previous church membership, volunteer work, qualifications, and a possible criminal record. It is appropriate to ask why individuals wish to work in the nursery. References should be carefully checked, and a written record of that process should be kept in the person's file. Previous incidents or allegations that could disqualify them may be discovered. Nursery worker applicants with criminal records, child abuse history, or alcohol and other drug abuse problems should not be entrusted with the care of children.

Similar queries should be made of applicants for paid positions, although the types of questions that may be asked of people applying for paid positions vary from state to state. Generally, applicants for paid positions may be asked only questions that are relevant to the position being sought.

Application and reference forms used in your local church should be reviewed prior to implementation by legal counsel familiar with state employment laws.

Be sure applicants understand that all nursery workers serve a probationary period and that they can be let go after that time. It is better for all parties involved to have a clear probationary and termination procedure than to face the difficulty of releasing an ineffective or unqualified nursery worker after weeks or years of service.

Some church members may resist the idea of screening nursery workers. Two common remarks are, "No one would ever harm any of our children" and "It's hard to get anyone to volunteer to work in the nursery as it is." Without a consistently enforced policy in place, a church may find itself letting an applicant with a potentially inappropriate background work in the nursery, and, at the same time, having no assurance that others already working in the nursery are appropriately placed.

Document all of your personnel processes: hirings, probations, incidents, and dismissals. Maintain your documentation with the full knowledge that others may read the records. Take care to include factual details, not speculative commentary. All employment and volunteer application forms should be retained permanently, locked up and available only to properly authorized church staff and members. Typically, personnel records for former employees should be maintained for three years after termination. However, information on church workers with children should be maintained for a longer period, given the statute of limitations on abuse or misconduct incidents.

Appropriate screening of nursery workers will go a long way toward developing an excellent church nursery that you can be proud of and parents will be pleased to have available.

For additional help in developing policies and procedures to reduce the risk of abuse, order the book *Safe Sanctuaries: Reducing the Risk of Child Abuse in the Church*, by Joy Thornburg Melton. This book provides a guide for developing and implementing policies as well as sample forms. It can be ordered from Discipleship Resources (800-685-4370, www.discipleshipresources.org).

Trustees and the Nursery

Marti Biegler
Burnsville, Minnesota

As trustees, it is important that you know and understand the needs and operations of the nursery. Since most accidents on church grounds involve children, the nursery requires special attention to prevent injuries to infants and toddlers. Consider these suggestions:

1. Get down on your knees and survey the room, looking for potential dangers to infants and toddlers.
2. Cover all outlets. Purchase plastic plugs or install rotating covers. Replace any broken outlet covers and switch plates.
3. Check all wall, ceiling, and floor surfaces. Are they clean and fresh? Repaint any surfaces painted with lead-based paint.
4. Install cabinet latches on all lower cupboards.
5. Check cords that operate curtains or blinds. If a cord is long or forms a loop, install a hook four to five feet above the floor to loop it up and away from the children.
6. Look for sharp edges (baseboard heaters, countertops, windowsills, cabinet corners, shelving) that could injure an unsteady or falling child. Provide corner guards to pad such areas.
7. Does the carpet meet fire safety regulations? Repair loose threads. Steam clean the carpet at least quarterly. Vacuum before each use.
8. Check the room temperature. Is it comfortable year-round? Is the temperature on the floor comfortable? Can heating and cooling be regulated for the children's comfort?
9. Talk to the nursery committee. Do they clean the toys on a regular basis and check them for any dangers (for example, small, loose parts that could choke a child)? If you do not have a nursery committee, determine who will be responsible for this task.
10. Remove old cribs. Crib slats should be no more than two and three-eighths inches apart, and cribs should have no decorative knobs on the corners.
11. Check playpens. Is the mesh small enough that small items such as buttons cannot be caught in it? Are the sides secure? Be sure the supports cannot pinch little fingers.
12. Have a specific place in the room for diaper changing. Keep the changing table in public view to reduce the risk of abuse allegations. Running water should be available in each changing area for hand washing. Each changing table should have a nonporous surface with a safety belt to secure the child on the table. Keep a garbage can with a plastic liner and a secure lid close to the changing table. Post diaper-changing procedures by each changing table.
13. Do microwave doors close and seal properly? Check city codes; an NSF (food service) microwave may be required. Check the temperature of the refrigerator periodically, and clean it regularly.
14. Keep a first-aid kit and current first-aid manual in the nursery. Include the poison control phone number. Post instructions for choking and breathing emergencies. Check to see if caregivers are trained in infant CPR and first-aid procedures.
15. Post evacuation plans for emergencies. Stock a flashlight and battery-operated radio. At least annually, practice emergency procedures with caregivers.
16. Have a phone in the nursery, and post numbers for the nursery coordinator, substitute workers, poison control, church office, and a trustee.
17. Check your church insurance policy. Talk to your insurance representative if you are not covered already. Develop policies and procedures, including the screening of caregivers, to reduce the risk of child abuse. *Safe Sanctuaries: Reducing the*

Risk of Child Abuse in the Church, by Joy Thornburg Melton (Discipleship Resources, 800-685-4370 or www.discipleshipresources.org) is a helpful resource.

18. Make sure the nursery meets local building and safety codes. Equip all doors with panic bars, not dead bolts.

19. Visit the nursery on a regular basis, and keep in communication with the nursery coordinator. Some problems or concerns will be apparent only on-site, when you see the children and staff in action. If repairs are needed, handle them in a timely manner.

Nursery Dollars and Sense

Elizabeth Cox
Bozeman, Montana

Many parents decide where they will attend church based on the quality of the church nursery. So, where does your church find funds to provide an appropriate nursery ministry? With church budgets already stretched thin, how can you even consider creating an elaborate place for babies?

Elements necessary to an appropriate environment for infants and toddlers include safety and health, developmentally appropriate furnishings, and care-givers who are loving and well trained. Depending on the size of your congregation, the kind of facility needed, and the budget available, these may be provided through volunteer workers, paid workers, and donations of funds, toys, equipment, and services.

If yours is a small congregation with only one or two babies, you may want to consider providing a baby swing, a supply of crayons and paper, and a basket of appropriate toys and books in one corner of the sanctuary. You will need spare diapers and baby wipes. These little ones are guests in the house of God. The noises of babies in church are no more disruptive than they would be in your home, and the same etiquette applies.

If you have a separate nursery, consider the following items as you build your budget:

- Staff salaries, training (such as infant CPR), and background checks
- Disposable diapers, wipes, washcloths, and gloves
- Crib sheets/blankets and laundry service
- Covered container and liners for soiled diapers
- Paper towels and facial tissues
- Liquid hand soap
- Spray container for bleach-water mixture
- First-aid items

- Toys (to replace any that are broken, unsafe, or missing pieces)
- Nondurable materials (paper, crayons, and so forth)
- Crackers for snacks
- Paper cups
- Cleaning supplies

It is important to locate the nursery as close to a toilet and sink as possible, preferably in an adjacent room. Another important consideration is rotating toys as children tire of the old ones. Having too many toys is as bad as not having enough. It is good, however, to have several of a favorite toy available to make sharing easier. You may also need a source of refrigeration for infants' bottles and a way to warm them (not a microwave). In addition, you will need a coordinator for the nursery with a written job description to keep everything running smoothly. Some of the disposable items you may want can be found at medical supply stores. Are professional services needed that should be included in the budget (for example, laundry service for linens, carpet cleaning, pager services, window cover cleaning, professional childcare services for nursery worker substitutes)?

A committee of parents, early childhood professionals, and other interested church members will be able to help build the nursery budget. A church member with accounting expertise or the church treasurer can help set up the budget format. The budget should be presented to the administrative board or other responsible committee, along with your rationale for the budget.

Your nursery ministry requires priority status. These little ones are not tomorrow's Christians; they are today's Christians and therefore deserve your highest respect.

Funding the Nursery Ministry

Don Joiner
Nashville, Tennessee

"Some of the most important work of the church is with children." "I'm glad our church does such a wonderful job! I trust that my baby is loved and safe in our nursery." The most-often-heard comment in churches today is in the support of children's ministry, with the nursery being a focal point for parents of young children.

The mistake that many leaders in children's ministries make is assuming that the only way to finance their work is through the church budget. A growing phenomena in the church today is in designated giving, giving money directly to ministries that are important to the giver.

People want to give, and many are not giving all they want to give. Some are looking for a cause to support. They are willing to give extra directly to those ministries for which they can see results. They will give when they see that their money is going to make a difference. Does your children's ministry make a difference? Then why not invite individuals, families, businesses, or foundations to support your work?

Funding

One of the most effective means of raising funds is simply asking for it. Identify those people most likely to respond to your invitation. Everyone is not a likely candidate to support your ministry. Create a list of people who have indicated an interest in children's ministry: parents, grandparents, relatives of the children under your care, teachers and former teachers, and anyone who has come to and through your area of ministry.

Ask yourself why anyone would want to give for your needs. Write a compelling vision describing what you want to do, who will be affected by it, and what difference it will make. Hold an open house to show what you have and what you need. (Make sure to get a list of names and addresses of those who attend.) Hold the open house at a time when young children are not present, as a parade of adults is frightening and increases safety risks.

Three other effective ways to ask for financial help are to visit individually with people to explain your vision and ask for their support; to call them on the phone and invite their response; and to mail letters explaining your vision and inviting their response. Always include a card to fill out and an envelop in which they can send their response.

Begin communication about your vision at least four to six weeks prior to asking anyone for a gift. Generally speaking, the more personal your communication, the larger the response. Also write articles for your church newsletter. People often do not give without some information; however, information alone is not seen as an invitation to respond.

Asking a person directly will often get a better, and bigger, response than just an informal letter. Asking for a specific, large amount will assist you in reaching your goal quicker than a lot of small contributions. Identify people who have already shown their willingness and ability to make an extra gift to your church. Identify groups in your church that can support your project: women's and men's groups, youth groups, adult classes, your church's endowment or memorial program.

Although cash is the most likely gift you may receive, help people see that other kinds of gifts, such as the following, are also welcome.

Appreciated Assets

In the past years, property, stock, investments in mutual funds have all shown a great deal of appreciation. Some people do not want to pay tax on those gains. Giving the appreciated assets directly to the church will allow them to make a larger gift, receive a tax deduction for the gift, and avoid the capital gains tax.

Unused Assets

Assets that people no longer need are lying around in different places. For some, it may be a paid-up life insurance policy they no longer need. They can make the church the owner and beneficiary of such a policy, and the church can cash it in to support your project or ministry. Others may have antiques, a car, or a boat. Do not confine giving to just cash.

Memorial or Honor Giving

An untapped resource for giving is to remember someone who has died, or to honor a person who is still alive. Make a list of what you need, and invite people to make gifts in memory or honor of someone they love.

Grants

Consider asking for grants from companies owned by church members and from foundations in your area. They will want a clear vision of what you would do with their donation.

Estate Gifts

Invite people to make a gift now from their estate and/or to include your work in their estate plans. Some people think that making a gift now will deprive them of some security in the future, but they may be willing to include you in a future gift when they no longer need it.

Events

Though events and fundraising projects often raise a small amount of money, in comparison with the work put into it, they should not be ruled out of your plans. Besides the money raised in such projects, you can use the project as a way to increase the list of names and addresses of people for your prospect list.

Raising money in the church can be one of the most rewarding things you do. Whenever you ask anyone to give, remember that it is not for you and that it really is more than giving to the children. In giving, you are helping people fulfill their need to respond to God's call in their life.

Using the Articles in This Section

If your church does not have a nursery home visitor ministry, the articles in this section will help you evaluate whether such a program is needed in your setting and develop a plan for implementing the program. Current nursery home visitors will find guidance for carrying out their ministry.

Nursery home visitors will want to give copies of many of the articles listed as "Other Related Articles" to parents as they do home visits.

Section Eight: The Nursery Home Visitor

Contents

Other Related Articles

The Role of the Nursery Home Visitor

Mary Alice Gran
Nashville, Tennessee

The nursery home visitor is a vital link in the ministry of the congregation. It is the nursery home visitor who sets the stage for a lifelong bond among a baby, the baby's family, and the church. At a time in a family's life when the new parents look for connections, the door is open for the church to enter.

The role of the nursery home visitor can range from making one visit a year to one home with a new baby to spending several days a week on the road and at the desk caring for many families of young children. The following list of tasks and concerns will guide you in making decisions about the role of the nursery home visitor in your congregation.

Family Connections

For some families, the first primary connection to the church may be through the nursery home visitor. Through personal visits to the family home, phone calls, mailings, caregiving activities (arranging meals, caring for siblings, and so forth), and helping the family understand what the church has to offer, the nursery home visitor can provide a strong link between the family and the congregation.

Record Keeping

Accurate record keeping facilitates the communication that allows the entire church to be in ministry to and with families of young children. Information that may be important includes names, birth dates, baptismal dates, parents' and siblings' names, addresses, phone numbers, e-mail addresses, and fax numbers. It may also be helpful to record if the family is new to the congregation and if the family includes others who are also members of the congregation.

Make decisions about what records will be kept in the church office, the nursery, or other appropriate places. Create a system for updating information.

Church Communication

Set up systems for communicating information to appropriate people and groups in the congregation. Who creates birth announcements for the church newsletter and worship bulletin? How will the nursery home visitor communicate information to the pastor or other church staff? Who will notify the nursery home visitor of a birth or miscarriage?

Parent Education

A primary role of the nursery home visitor is to provide support and information for parents. Build expertise in four areas for helping parents at appropriate times: (1) nursery policies and congregational life, (2) faith development of young children, (3) parenting helps, and (4) community supports. You may want to consider regular parenting meetings or classes for exchanging information and networking.

Advocate

The nursery home visitor is an advocate for the young child and the family within the life of the congregation. If, for example, new families have expressed the need for a refrigerator in the nursery area for milk and food, the nursery home visitor can become an advocate with the trustees to provide a small refrigerator for this purpose. Or perhaps the nursery home visitor notices that a parent attends church with three small children and struggles to get them into the church building. The nursery home visitor could arrange for church members to be prepared to help the parent.

Congregational Relationships

The nursery home visitor should develop close relationships with nursery caregivers and leaders, as well as a solid understanding of nursery policies and procedures. When visiting with families, there will be many opportunities to answer questions and to reassure parents. If there are questions that the nursery home visitor cannot answer, he or she should be willing and able to find answers and report them to the families in a timely manner. Otherwise, families may lose trust in the skills and abilities of this person. The nursery home visitor should also be alert for other ways in which the church could minister with families, such as weekday ministries for young children, a United Methodist Women's group for mothers with young children, a parenting class, a baby-sitting class for teenagers, a co-op childcare group.

The nursery home visitor should look for opportunities to help the members of the congregation, individually and in groups, to develop an understanding of today's families. Educating members will encourage continued support of families of young children by increasing numbers of church members. Provide programs for groups, write about specific families (only with their permission) in your church newsletter, cite examples of ministry needs in regular reports to groups, and encourage study of generational theories and other contemporary understandings.

Using Technology

Today's technology can serve as useful tools for the nursery home visitor. Forms and records can be kept up to date on a computer, and form letters can be developed, which will save time and can be personalized for each family.

Additionally, e-mail is an excellent means for making connections within the church family and in the community. The nursery home visitor can easily send messages of encouragement and announcements of church events to families to be received at times convenient for the family.

Consider setting up a church website for families of nursery-aged children, with access to a chat room for them to link together for mutual support.

Report and Support

In all this, the nursery home visitor needs others for mutual support. This may be the nursery committee, the children's council, the education/nurture committee, the staff-parish relations committee, or perhaps a nursery home visitor committee. Whatever the case, regular times should be set aside to listen to and to support this valued person in the work of caring for families of young children.

Starting a Nursery Home Visitor Program

Mary Alice Gran
Nashville, Tennessee

A nursery home visitor provides ongoing care for a family during a child's early years, which creates a special connection between the congregation and the home. The nursery home visitor embodies the church to a family at an important stage of life. A wise congregation selects its best nurturers for this task and provides a clear structure for this ministry.

How to Begin

A nursery home visitor ministry is most effective when supported by the congregation—not just one person, no matter how caring that person may be. What group in your congregation (nursery committee, education committee, nurture committee, children's council) will offer guiding support? Whatever the group in your congregation, involve them from the beginning. Set aside a meeting time for discussion and planning. Perhaps after some preliminary decisions, a small task force will work out a proposal from which the committee can work. Answering the following questions will form a basic support structure for the nursery home visitor ministry. Hint: Try not to limit the thinking to any traditional past program or ideas. Be creative and think broadly.

1. Why?

Why does your congregation want or need a nursery home visitor ministry? It may seem obvious, but put words to the response. Your response to "Why?" will form the foundation for this important ministry. This must be done before any other questions can be answered adequately.

2. How?

What will the ministry look like? Who will be served? Who will be responsible? What are the desired results? What organizational structure within the church will support this ministry?

3. Who?

How many families will be supported within the first year? second year? third year? With a ratio of five to ten families per nursery home visitor as a guideline, how many people will be needed as visitors? What will

be included in the job description? Who will support the nursery home visitors? What other tasks will need to be handled, and who will be responsible?

4. When?

When and how will connections with families be made? When and how will connections with the church staff/pastor be included? When and how will the congregation be involved?

5. What?

What will be provided for families? What support services will the church office provide? What will be the costs, and how will the budget be formed? What will be the forms of communication with the families? (Will there be packets prepared for families, and what will be included in them?) What methods of communication will be used with the congregation? What kinds of forms are needed? What evaluation procedures will be used, and when?

Next Steps

After these questions have been answered and a ministry has begun to take shape on paper, what are the next steps within your congregation?

- Is there a board or committee that needs to hear about the plans?
- Are there key people who need to know what is about to happen?
- Does the pastor/staff have full knowledge and the ability to report information to others in a positive, informed manner?
- How will the funding be handled?
- How will the congregation hear about this ministry and be able to support it?
- Who will recruit the nursery home visitors? Who will provide training?
- How will this new ministry be celebrated?

At each meeting during the first year, plan to hear a report and to work the bugs out of the system. At the end of the first year, plan a formal evaluation and report ending with a special celebration.

Making a Home Visit

Mary Alice Gran

Nashville, Tennessee

Making a visit to a family in their home is one of the most important tasks of the nursery home visitor. As a representative of the church, you bring the congregation with you. Your presence affirms how important that family is to the total church family.

A visit to a family's home involves a greeting, words of affirmation, and taking leave. But it is also much, much more.

Preparation

Pray. As you are thinking about the family and preparing for a visit, pray for them and for yourself. Prayer will make a connection between you and the family that can be made in no other way.

Gather materials. Will you be taking a packet or other materials with you? Is it ready?

Phone. Do not make an unannounced visit. Call ahead and arrange a convenient time.

Check your notes. Who are the members of the family? Is there information you need to discover, such as older siblings in the family? Have they been attending activities at the church? (They may be ready to get started back to church; they may not be ready at all; or they may attend regularly.) Consider taking a gift for older siblings, such as Sunday school student activity sheets, *Pockets* magazine, or children's bulletins from past worship services. (*Pockets* is a devotional magazine for children that is published by The Upper Room, 800-925-6847 or www.upperroom.org/bookstore.)

Consider needs. What are the needs of the family, considering the ages of the children? Is there pertinent information about other church happenings that you might wish to tell about? Are there church connections you could assist them in making? Are they ready to make a first visit to the nursery? Can you meet them and help with the transition?

Review nursery schedules. Have there been any recent changes in the nursery: facilities, staff, hours, weekday programs, and so forth? As families with young children are frequently irregular in attendance, it is helpful to have current information to give them.

The Visit

Know the name of each person in the family, and greet each by name. Wearing a nametag or other identification will make it easier for them to remember your name.

Your primary responsibility while visiting with the family is to listen. Be attentive to their needs when you are with them. A parent may need a friendly adult ear, and an older child may need extra attention. Do not dominate the conversation with your agenda.

Listen. Hear what is bringing them joy and where they are having difficulties. Care about them as God's special creations.

Stay only a brief time. Things can be hectic in a family with young children. Do not let your staying become a burden. Be prepared to offer a prayer before leaving, but ask first. They may not be ready for you to pray with them.

Make sure they have your name and phone number before you leave. It will be reassuring for them to know they can call you whenever they have a need. Tell them when to expect to hear from you again.

Follow-Up

Record the date of the visit and any comments that will help you prepare for the next visit with the family.

Communicate new information or needs with the pastor/church staff. Also notify the nursery caregivers of any helpful information.

If you find your thoughts turning to the family before the next scheduled visit, pray for them, send them a note, call them to say you were thinking of them. Your caring will tell them the church cares for them.

You will find your visits with the family, whether a family of two or of twelve, to be a blessing in your life. God is with you.

Staying in Touch

Mary Alice Gran
Nashville, Tennessee

Everyone enjoys getting personal mail. New parents are always pleased to have someone notice their child and to acknowledge the joy and stress that a baby brings. A note saying you are thinking of them is especially welcome a few months after the baby is born, when the demands of the baby may leave new parents exhausted. A congregation can keep in touch with families of young children by

- sending the church newsletter to parents. This is an easy task and an excellent way to communicate with families in a nonthreatening but helpful way.
- periodically (quarterly, semiannually, annually) sending form letters personalized to each family from the pastor, nursery coordinator, or other church staff. Such letters provide a friendly connection with the family, with no required response.
- sending a personal note to the family from the nursery home visitor, nursery caregiver, pastor, or other person who knows the family. Keep it brief, friendly, supportive, and caring. A simple note stating "I just wanted you to know I was thinking of you" or "I said a prayer of thanksgiving for you today" can give a real boost. If the church has postcards/notecards featuring a picture of the church, use them. They make great keepsakes. Let this be not a chore but a joy. Recruit someone who is limited in his or her ability to leave home to maintain written contact. (Retired school teachers make great communicators.)

Parent Support Leaflets

The parent support leaflets (pages 191–205) are designed to provide ongoing support to parents as they raise their young children in a Christian home. Each contains brief articles of support, a Scripture reading, statements of encouragement, and two prayers: one for the parents and one for the parents to use for/with their child. Each leaflet is designed to fit on one side of a sheet of paper. Side two should be reserved for congregational information and, if mailing as a newsletter, for the mailing address of the family to whom the leaflet is being sent.

If you choose to send parent support leaflets, consider the following:
- What will go on the back of the leaflets?
- When will they be prepared (first of each month, once a quarter)?
- Will they be mailed or delivered personally?
- Will they be included in a packet delivered by the nursery home visitor or pastor?

Be sure the finished leaflet makes a statement of quality, as it will strongly influence the parents' feelings about the nursery and about the church.

The Nursery Home Visitor Packet

When a nursery home visitor makes a visit to a family, it is an appropriate time to deliver information. Consider these items when developing your packet:
- Will packets be produced and collated for periodic delivery to families of young children?
- How frequently will packets be delivered?
- Will they be mailed or delivered personally?
- Will the packets contain parent support leaflets, or will the leaflets be mailed separately?
- Who will prepare the contents of the packets?
- Who will collate the packets?
- How many packets will be prepared at a time?

Preparing Packets

Consider using large envelopes to hold the items to be delivered, and collate enough packets for a year's supply for each child. Mark the envelopes according to the child's age at the time of delivery.

The "Sample Family Visit Record" (page 106) will help you organize your information and ideas. The content you choose to include in your packets will, of course, be based on your local situation.

Sample Family
Visit Record

Family: _____

Name of Child: _____ Date of Birth: _____

Age of Child	Delivery Month/Year	Resources to Be Delivered	Actual Date of Delivery	Comments

Using the Articles in This Section

The articles in this section can be mailed to parents of young children or can be distributed through the church's nursery home visitor program. These articles can also be used with parenting classes or parent support groups.

Section Nine: The Parent

Contents

Other Related Articles

Preparing for the Baptism of Your Child

Ron Anderson
Indianapolis, Indiana

As you begin thinking about the baptism of your child, first reflect briefly on your understanding of baptism. Were you baptized as a child, or did you come to the Christian faith as an adult? What do you remember about your own baptism? If you were baptized as a child, what do your parents remember about your baptism and their decision to have you baptized?

Baptism is multi-layered in meaning. When we turn to the services of the Baptismal Covenant in *The United Methodist Hymnal* (pages 39–43), we find that baptism is first of all God's gift to us, offered without price. It is also new birth offered through water and the Holy Spirit, incorporation into God's mighty acts of salvation, and initiation into Christ's holy church. We are reminded that, before it is our act, baptism is God's act in Christ through the Holy Spirit. It is God's gift to us, to the church, and to our children. But even as it is God's word to us, proclaiming our own and our children's adoption by grace, it is also our word to God, promising our response of faith and love.

Remembering that baptism is God's gift helps us understand how and why we baptize both infants and adults in The United Methodist Church. While they appear to be different, infant baptism and adult baptism both involve invitation and reception into a community of faith that includes one's immediate family, the local church family, and the family of the church through the ages. We baptize people of all ages because the church is a great family that includes people of all ages.

As you prepare for the baptism of your child, you will be called upon to do three things: to welcome, to hold or nurture, and to believe. These tasks can be described as the welcoming, holding, and believing environments in which you and your child live and grow.

Welcoming

The task of welcoming builds on all that you did prior to the birth or arrival of your child: learning about the developmental needs of the child, preparing the child's room, making the necessary arrangements with the hospital and doctors for the day when the child is to be born, and, especially for mothers, learning how to take good physical care of yourself so that your child will be healthy. The task of welcoming calls attention to the ways we show children that they are wanted and loved, that there is a safe place for them to live, and that we receive them, even as they come to us as a gift from God.

One way to formalize this welcome is through a celebration of thanksgiving for the birth or adoption of your child (see *The United Methodist Book of Worship*, pages 585–87). Such a celebration may occur at the hospital shortly after birth, at home when the child arrives there, or at church on a Sunday morning shortly after birth or arrival. Such a celebration should not be confused with a dedication of your child. The celebration of thanksgiving is an act of prayer and thanksgiving, perhaps a preliminary stage before your child is baptized. Of course, this assumes that you have a church home for yourself and your child. If that is not the case, finding such a home is an important step in providing a welcome for your child.

Holding

The second environment is that of the holding place. Even as children need a place to call home, they also need a place in which they can learn before being required to act, test things about themselves, ask questions and safely doubt, and engage in that sacred play we call worship. When your child is baptized, you will make a commitment to providing such a holding place. The service of baptism asks that you promise to nurture your child in "Christ's holy church, that by your teaching and example they may be guided to accept God's grace for themselves, to profess their faith openly, and to lead a Christian life." (From Baptismal Covenant II, in *The United Methodist Hymnal*, page 40. © 1976, 1980, 1985, 1989 The United Methodist Publishing House. Used by permission.) To provide a holding place for your child is to provide a place in which he or she can learn the stories of the Christian family, learn how to pray, and learn how to be in relationship to God.

One of the questions you will want to ask your pastor concerns sponsors or godparents. Traditionally, the godparent or sponsor is another person of faith who, like the parents, guides the child by teaching and example toward the Christian life. Given this role, godparents or sponsors are often chosen by the congregation rather than by the parents. As they function on behalf of the church, they should be members of the church as well.

Believing

These first two tasks or environments point us toward a third, that of the believing environment. If you are to nurture your children by your own teaching and example, then you must be people of faith. Preparation for the baptism of your child invites reflection on your own faith. It requires that you ask yourselves if you are willing to live out these commitments to your child and to the church.

When you bring your child to be baptized, the rite of baptism is an act of faith by you and the church. The faith you will confess is the faith that will become, by your welcome and nurture, your child's faith as well. While at some time in the future your child will want to formally claim that faith as his or her own by a public affirmation of faith, it is your belief that now offers a place in which he or she will be nurtured and welcomed. Providing this believing environment suggests that you must attend to your own nurture and growth in faith by your active participation in a community of faith through prayer, worship, small-group participation, Bible reading, and study.

Finally, as you move toward the baptism of your child, you will want to talk with your pastor about when baptisms are scheduled in your church, what preparation processes and structures are in place, and when you can begin the process. If your church is too small to hold such pre-baptismal classes on a regular basis, talk with your pastor about a less formal preparation time. Perhaps there is another family in the congregation that would wish to join in this time of preparation. You might begin by carefully reading through the service of baptism in *The United Methodist Hymnal* (pages 33–39 or 39–43) and talking about the meaning of the vows you will take during the baptismal service.

Taking Your Child to Worship

Sue Isbell

Knoxville, Tennessee

David, nearly two, took his place in the front pew with his family. Under the watchful eye of his father, young David explored the offering envelopes in the pew rack. He searched around until he found the nearest pencil; then he tested it to see if it worked. He knelt in the pew to survey the crowd behind him. Then he got down on the floor to check the view from underneath.

As the chimes rang to signal the beginning of worship, David sat bolt upright in his seat. With a gasp he turned to his dad, raised a finger in the air, and said in a loud whisper, "Bell!" For a brief second his eyes scanned the sanctuary as if he were searching for the origin of the wonderful sound. With the enchantment of the bell still fresh in his awe-filled mind, David spotted the acolyte processing with the light. Another gasp. "Light!" David said, pointing toward the flame. On the edge of his seat, he watched motionless as the acolyte lit the candles. Later in the service, as the congregation sang a hymn, David left the service to share his exuberance with the caregivers in the nursery for the remainder of the hour.

David's parents have discovered three key elements that can make worship a meaningful experience for you, your child, and the congregation around you: (1) understanding your child's capabilities and needs, (2) having realistic expectations of your child's behavior, and (3) maintaining a patient and positive attitude about worshiping with your child.

Young children have short attention spans. Unlike infants, who may sleep or be content to be cuddled, toddlers need to move. Walking, climbing, and crawling are newly found skills that employ the large-motor skills that are so rapidly developing in your child. Your toddler or two-year-old also operates in a world of discovery. Your child is stimulated by a multitude of sensory experiences. At this age, your child has a natural desire to touch and explore, as well as a need to see what is taking place in the world around him or her.

Recognize these needs in your child, and expect behavior that realistically reflects your child's age and development. If your infant sleeps most of the time, where you sit in worship may not be an issue. If, however, you think you will need to feed, rock, or walk your baby during the service, plan to sit near an outer aisle so you can take your child to an area that will not distract the rest of the congregation. Many churches have speakers in hallways where a parent can be with a child and still hear the service. The rear of the sanctuary may also provide you with more space to move with your baby. All babies fuss or cry at some point, and for many people an occasional crying child is a reminder that the church is alive and growing. Excessive crying, however, can be disruptive both to the pastor in the pulpit and to the worshipers in the pews. If your child cannot easily be calmed, feel comfortable taking your baby to the nursery.

With toddlers and two-year-olds, plan to sit near the front where your child can see what is happening in the service. Do not expect your toddler to sit still for an hour or for even half the service. Choose seats near an outer aisle so you can easily leave when you think it is time to let your child enjoy more freedom in the nursery. Provide limits for your child within the pew. Allow the natural exploration of the items around you with minimal disruption to other worshipers. Recognize the signs of boredom, hunger, and fatigue early, before leaving becomes a power struggle. If your child begins to resist, carry your child lovingly but firmly from the sanctuary. Do not use going to the nursery as a punishment or threat, but make it part of your plan. Tell your child that, after a certain prayer or during a particular hymn, it will be nursery time, and make it part of your child's day.

While in the service, help your child discover the wonders of this special place and time. Point out the colors of the windows, paraments, and flowers. Listen for the sounds of the chimes or the playing of the organ. Watch for the lighting of the candles or the procession of the choir. Children like to do what their parents are doing. Let your child hold the hymnal, draw on the bulletin, and touch the offering plate as it passes by. As your child gets older, plan to bring a special worship bag with you containing a favorite book, a small toy, and simple drawing supplies (paper and two jumbo crayons or a washable marker). Have a special bag of things just for worship.

Remain patient and positive as your child is growing and learning about worship. You are the most important influence in your child's faith development. Corporate worship is the most important thing we do in the church. It is the time and place where the traditions of the community of faith are passed on. By allowing your child short, happy worship experiences with you at an early age, you are teaching your child the importance of worship to your own family as well as helping your child become a participating member in the family of God. Worshiping alongside young children can have a lasting impact, not only on the children themselves, but also on the adults who worship around them. The freshness of a child's first discovery of things that adults take for granted can be a powerful reminder that Jesus said: "Whoever does not receive the kingdom of God as a little child will never enter it" (Luke 18:17). Understanding your child's needs, knowing the limits of your infant or toddler, and being patient as you share your child with others worshiping around you can be a happy time for you, a rewarding experience for your child, and a blessing to your entire congregation.

Leaving Your Child in the Nursery

MaryJane Pierce Norton
Nashville, Tennessee

Separation Anxiety

Most young infants make a smooth transition into the nursery, smiling happily at parents as they leave and at caregivers who take them. But most babies experience separation anxiety around six to eight months, when they are beginning to understand that they are separate from their parents. They realize that parents are actually leaving and are not simply where they cannot see them.

This is a healthy, natural part of growth and is simply a sign that your child loves you and wants to be with you. However, it can be hard for parents. Teachers and caregivers know that the infant will most likely stop crying soon after being left. But as a parent leaving a crying child, you will probably be thinking, *Maybe I shouldn't have left him this time. I wonder if he's still crying. Am I a bad parent to have walked out with my child wanting me?*

For some children, separation anxiety does not completely end until age three.

What to Do

Arrive early enough to allow time for a routine: signing in, placing the child's belongings in a cubicle, hugging, and waving goodbye.

Greet caregivers and other children warmly and cheerfully, and refrain from making negative comments.

Observe the group, but do not get down to play with your child, as this raises the child's expectations that you are going to stay.

Prolonging the goodbye time can sometimes make things more difficult. With each successive hug, kiss, pat on the back, and goodbye, children build up hope that the parent will stay. Thus, when the parent leaves, the protest becomes even more vocal. Each child and each parent is unique, so stay as long as you wish if your child seems to be experiencing particularly intense separation anxiety.

Let the caregivers help with goodbyes, and encourage them to involve your child in an activity or to hold him or her to help the transition. Remind the caregiver of your child's favorite toys and activities. One of my son's teachers always greeted him with, "Bradford, I've been waiting for you! Let's go get your favorite book." He had something to look forward to, I felt relieved, and we both began the day happier.

Tell your child when you will return: "I'll be coming back for you at the end of Sunday school." If you can, peg your routine to an activity your child will recognize, such as "right after snack" or "after nap time."

A familiar routine for leaving the nursery is as important as a familiar routine for entering. Children handle the return of parents in many different ways. Some rush to a parent with open arms. Some ignore the parent or refuse to leave, clinging to the teacher. Follow a familiar pickup routine: signing out, checking the child's cubicle for belongings, and saying goodbye to friends, favorite toys, and caregivers.

What Does Not Help

Sporadic attendance makes it difficult for children to adjust. Attend regularly, thus helping your child recognize the caregiver as teacher, friend, and trusted adult.

Slipping out unnoticed, without goodbyes, tears down the feeling of trust. Your child will miss you and then usually cry when he or she realizes you have left. Trust is the basis for faith at this age; and when trust is shaken, it is hard to build this foundation for faith.

What to Bring

Bring the following items to the nursery in a bag marked with your child's name:
- Diapers (more than you expect to be used)
- A change of clothes
- A bottle or cup of milk, juice, or water that is labeled with your child's name
- Any favorite item, such as a blanket or pacifier, also labeled with your child's name
- Written notes about your child's sleeping habits, routines, and so forth

Illness Procedures for Parents

All children are important, for they are God's gift to us, given for our care and love. We strive to provide a healthy, safe, clean, loving place in which children can thrive. We depend on you, the parent, to help us. Please do not bring a sick child to the nursery.

If your child exhibits any of the following symptoms, please keep him or her at home:

- Diarrhea (more than three times in the last twenty-four hours).
- Vomiting (two or more episodes in the previous twenty-four hours).
- Temperature above 101 degrees.
- Skin infections or infestations (impetigo, head lice, ringworm, or shingles) until at least twenty-four hours after treatment begins.
- Pink or red eye with eye discharge.
- Nasal discharge that is greenish in color.

The following are some of the diseases common to infants and toddlers and the contagious times for each. Please keep your child at home during these times.

Chickenpox

This is highly contagious as long as the pox are open and weeping. When the pox are scabbed and dry, the child can return to the classroom.

Ear Infections

While ear infections are not contagious, the upper respiratory infections that cause the ear infections are. In addition, at the early stage of an ear infection, children are often uncomfortable and cannot be cared for adequately with other children around.

Impetigo

Children need to be on antibiotics for twenty-four hours before returning to the classroom.

Pinkeye

This is another highly contagious disease. Most children need twenty-four hours after treatment has been initiated before returning to the classroom.

Strep Throat

Once a child has had twenty-four hours of antibiotics, he or she is not contagious and may be brought to the class if he or she is feeling better.

Will You Please Sign In?

An unsteady toddler tripped and fell with such force that she split her lip, and blood and tears began to pour. A caregiver picked her up and started searching for her parents, but neither parent was in the place he or she could normally be found on Sunday. Finding the parents required some anxious searching through halls and classrooms. If there had been a sign-in sheet, they could have been found more quickly, and the child could have been comforted by her parents sooner. A sign-in sheet provides security for both parents and caregivers. Please fill one out as completely and accurately as possible.

Praying With Your Child

Judith Mayo
Livonia, Michigan

One of the most precious gifts we, as parents, can give our children is to teach them to pray. An active, rich prayer life, begun as a child, will grow and mature through the years, providing a constant source of strength and comfort.

Unfortunately, many of us find it difficult to teach our children to pray. We might teach them a memorized prayer for bedtime, complete with "God blesses…," and that is good. We encourage our children to say a memorized grace at dinner, and that is good. But many of us leave our teaching of prayer there and do not model an active prayer life for our children.

Getting Started

The most effective teaching parents do is modeling. If prayer is an important and natural part of your life, your child will sense that and will make it an important part of daily living. When you stand over the bed of your newborn and marvel at the miracle of birth and life, speak your prayer of thanks. Get into the habit of praying aloud in the presence of your newborn before your child can even understand your words. Thank God for your child; pray that God will help you to be a loving parent; pray for your child. Your child will gradually understand that prayer is important to you and will begin to make prayer an integral part of his or her own life.

Beginning a prayer life with your child at this early stage will make it easier to continue praying together as your child gets older and begins to talk. Prayers of thanksgiving are meaningful for even the youngest children. When you and your toddler are enjoying an activity together, pause to thank God for dandelions, for the smell of baking cookies, for snow, for rain that helps the flowers grow, for ice cream, for sunny days, for people who love us, for time together. Prayer is appropriate any time. Do not just save it all for bedtime. Help your child feel comfortable telling God in prayer about fears and concerns. The magical years of early childhood bring with them difficulty distinguishing what is real from what is imagined. Monsters live in closets and under beds, and darkness is a cover for all sorts of evil beings. Television shows and the evening news can be frightening to a child of two or three. Often, no amount of rational explanation is sufficient to lay these fears to rest.

Pray together, asking for God's presence to be known to your child. Ask God to calm your child's fears and to help your child know that God is always present, no matter what. A time of fear is a good time to practice breath prayer, a simple prayer said while exhaling or inhaling a breath.

Many families have a wonderful bedtime ritual with their young children: They rock and tell or read stories, talk about the day, and then, perhaps, say a prayer together. Encourage your children to not only talk with you about the important, fun, sad, angry events of their day, but also to bring them to God. If prayer has been a regular part of your life until now, then your children will recognize that God is always present with them. Your children will, with a little encouragement from you, begin to have conversations with God, bringing all the important events to God.

You can help your children learn to frame their prayers by suggesting how they might approach God with these thoughts. For example, "Ryan, it sounds as if you're still angry with Kevin. Maybe you could tell God how you felt when Kevin kicked over your block tower this afternoon. Then you might ask God to help you forgive Kevin." Often, parents help their children memorize a prayer. These prayers regularly conclude with, "God bless Mom, Dad, Grandma, Fido…" Consider, instead, helping your children develop a habit of spontaneous, conversational prayer.

While memorized prayer helps establish a habit of a prayer time, it often results in a rote exercise with little meaning. Instead, encourage your children to communicate naturally and spontaneously out of their own experiences and thoughts. Many families find mealtime to be a time when their family can pray together. The family ritual often involves joining hands around the table as an important part of the mealtime prayer. You might use this time to take turns praying. Or you could ask each family member to contribute to the prayer. Use this time as an opportunity to thank God for the good things that happened during the day, for the food, for particular people, and so forth.

Sometimes, you could read a psalm or sing a hymn of thanksgiving or the Doxology. Vary your prayer offerings, so that they do not become routine. Children can learn that prayer is appropriate anytime, anywhere. When you are in the car and an ambulance screams by, offer a prayer that God will help the paramedics and will be with the person who is hurt. Very young children do not automatically identify with another person, so intercessory prayer does not come naturally for them. You can help your child develop compassion and the habit of intercession by speculating on the feelings of others: "I wonder how Ashley felt after she broke her ankle. Let's pray that her ankle will heal well."

As children grow, they will be comfortable with prayer if you have started from the very beginning. As they are able to express themselves, begin to introduce the concept that prayer is also listening. Prayer is not an attempt to ask God to change God's mind, but rather to help us know God's mind and to take that knowledge and use it to inform our own lives. With a natural and spontaneous prayer life, children will begin to experience and know God in a personal way. As they grow and mature in their prayer life, they will grow and mature in their experience of God.

Sharing Your Faith With Your Child

Judith Mayo

Livonia, Michigan

"How can I share my faith with my three-month-old daughter?" Cindy asked. "Some days I'm not even sure what I believe. Besides, what can a three-month-old understand?" Indeed, how can we share our faith with a three-month-old, or even a three-year-old? Why is it necessary? Isn't that the job of the Sunday school?

Parents are powerful people. Children will adopt your faith as their own first faith. You have the power to communicate your faith in life-giving ways, or you can communicate its unimportance by avoiding it. We live in a society that puts a high value on privacy and individuality. Have you heard people say, "My faith is private"? We are not comfortable speaking of God's activity in our lives and feel awkward and insecure when we try to explain our own relationship with Jesus Christ. We think we need poetic language to pray. Talking about these deep feelings is difficult for us, so we often rely on liturgy to speak the words that begin to describe our faith. We lack role models of our own, and we lack experience to give us the confidence to speak our most deeply held beliefs. But you can break this cycle, giving your own child permission to live naturally with his or her own faith. You can provide the words to help your child think and talk about a relationship with Jesus Christ.

You might say, "What if I'm wrong? I don't want to teach my child something that will create a separation from the church. Besides, I have more questions than answers." Children need to know that you, too, are on the journey. No one has all the answers about God. Your honest searching is part of your growing faith. And your acknowledgment of your search is a gift you give to your child, because it validates your child's inevitable search. In the meantime, take your questions seriously. Visit with your pastor. Join a Bible study. Join an adult Sunday school class that is also searching for answers. Become a Sunday school teacher and use your preparation as a way to learn.

The Power of Actions

You share your faith with your young children, whether or not you do so deliberately. If you talk about God often and naturally, your child will begin to understand that God is important to you. If you convey discomfort in discussing your faith, your child will feel discomfort in discussing his or her faith with you. If you leave your infant in the nursery with confidence and a positive attitude, your child will learn that you believe the world to be a good and dependable place. If you read your Bible often, your child will learn that this is a book you value.

As you and your toddler sort your recyclables, talk about caring for God's creation. Include young children in family financial stewardship discussions and decisions. Support your church's canned food appeals, and allow your young child to choose the cans to bring. Talk about how important it is to share among all God's children. All your actions speak loudly about what you value. How you speak to and treat others tells your child whether you really believe you are God's child. How you spend your money and your time tells your child what you value, what you worship. How you handle difficulties tells your child whether you really believe God is dependable. The way you treat your child will form your child's understanding of God. If you are trustworthy, your child will trust God. If you are loving and affirming, your child will understand God as a loving God. If you are negative and punishing, your child will understand God in the same way.

The Power of Story

We are formed by stories. Stories tell us who we are, where we have come from, and what is expected from us. Stories inspire us with heroic deeds and wonderful insights. Parents communicate their faith through stories. You can tell stories of your own childhood or family legends to teach your child about the people he or she comes from: what they valued and what they believed was important. You can tell stories of ways you have experienced God, even in simple terms a two-year-old can understand. What child ever tires of this story: "Mommy and I waited and waited, and finally you were born. You were so sweet, and we were so happy that God had chosen you to be our child." Or: "It was such a beautiful fall day when Grandma, Grandpa, Aunt Sue, Daddy and I, and all the people in our church family gathered for your baptism. We all promised to teach you about Jesus. Then we remembered that God loves you and that you are part of God's church." Look at pictures of your child's baptism, and use dolls to pretend baptism.

The Power of Prayer

If God is personally important to you, then your child will not be surprised that you communicate with God through prayer. Through prayers of praise and thanksgiving, your child learns that you recognize that all good things are from God. Through prayers of supplication and intercession, your child recognizes that you believe that God has compassion for all children and is a personal God who cares about each of us. When you pray with your child, you invite him or her into your own intimate and personal relationship with God, and your child not only learns about, but also experiences, your faith.

Parents are powerful people. We have the power to shape our children's early faith by the faith we communicate to them. In their 1990 study, Search Institute found that the most important factor in faith growth and maturity in adults and adolescents is the extent to which they talked about their faith with their parents, beginning as young children. We do not need to have all the answers. What we do need to do is to create an environment that is open and inviting. We need to create an environment where no question is shocking—where, in fact, we celebrate and explore all questions and affirm children in their faith journeys.

Using the Articles in This Section

The articles in this section will help the pastor understand how he or she can support and strengthen the church's ministry with young children and their families. Nursery coordinators may want to give copies of these articles to their pastors and then set up a time to discuss the articles and their implications for the congregation.

Section Ten: The Pastor

Contents

Other Related Articles

Ministry to Young Children and Their Parents

Nancy Jane Cheshire

Fairmont, Virginia

"I am the good shepherd. I know my own and my own know me, just as the Father knows me and I know the Father" (John 10:14-15a). As followers of Jesus Christ, we are called to love one another and to spread the good news of God's love. As we follow the Good Shepherd, we are helpers and are called to care for the Shepherd's lambs. God has given us a special opportunity to minister with young children and their families. How fortunate we are to be able to welcome the youngest children of God into the world, into our congregation, and into the family of Christ.

Nothing is more moving and inspiring than holding a newborn child. In the infant we see the wonder and miracle of God's love and the special gift of life. When an infant is brought into the church, we seem to flock around the tiny child with smiles on our faces. Each infant brings the gifts of joy, wonder, and hope. As we hold a baby in our arms, we are reminded that we are a part of God's plan. God gives us the opportunity to nurture and guide this small lamb so that it can grow to know and love the Good Shepherd.

The Scriptures tell us that each lamb is important to the Good Shepherd; thus, we accept each child as a person of value, a person deserving respect. Each child is a gift of God, so we happily recognize and welcome the birth of a child into our church family. Whether the birth is announced by word of mouth, in the Sunday bulletin, in a newsletter, on a bulletin board, or by a flower on the altar, let it be a joyful announcement

of a new child in our care. Then let us accept our responsibilities to help guide and direct the child's growth in the Christian faith.

As we serve Jesus Christ, we have an opportunity to meet the needs of young children and their families. We live in a mobile society where parents and children miss the support and fellowship of the extended family. We in the church family can provide that nurture and help. Following Jesus' example, we will grow and be stronger in our Christian faith by nurturing and loving children.

A church that is alive and growing will be a family of all ages serving the Lord together. Each generation has special gifts and wisdom to offer. A church without the laughter, noise, and activities of children is missing an opportunity for the Spirit of God to be in that place. Children and their families come to churches where they feel welcome, accepted, at home. We can open our hearts and the doors of our buildings to young children and their families.

The Good Shepherd leads sheep to green grass and clear water so they can be nourished. We can answer the call of ministry to feed the lambs by providing safe, healthy, quality programs for the care and education of our young children. We begin our ministry to the child as we celebrate the infant's birth. We have our church prepared and ready to welcome the child and to meet his or her needs. We minister to infants, toddlers, two-year-olds, and their parents as we welcome them into a safe, warm, nurturing sheepfold.

Baptismal Ministry With Young Children

Ron Anderson
Indianapolis, Indiana

The Book of Discipline (¶ 225) charges the pastor of each charge to "earnestly exhort all Christian parents or guardians to present their children to the Lord in baptism at an early age." (From *The Book of Discipline of The United Methodist Church—2000.* Copyright © 2000 by The United Methodist Publishing House. Used by permission.) As each pastor knows, however, this is only the beginning of our baptismal ministry with young children and their parents. It is the beginning of an important relationship between pastor and family, as well as between family and congregation. Infant baptism provides an important point of entry or reentry into active participation in the life of the local church.

As pastors, our baptismal ministry has three primary characteristics: evangelism, education, and sacrament.

Evangelism

In regard to evangelism, we focus on our work with the parents of the young child. First, in speaking to parents about the baptism of their child, we offer a welcome both to the child and to the parents on behalf of the church. Our welcome is a way of speaking and offering the good news of God's grace in Jesus Christ, recognizing that Jesus both welcomed and invited people of all ages and abilities to a new relationship with God. Part of this welcome includes the visit with the family at the hospital following the birth of the child, or at the family home sometime after the birth of the child. Another part of this welcome may include a time of prayer and thanksgiving. *The United Methodist Book of Worship* (pages 585–87) provides an order of thanksgiving for the birth or adoption of a child, which can be used in hospital, home, or church.

Second, the evangelical characteristic of our ministry also suggests that these initial visits with a family are a time when we might begin to speak with the family about their own faith. As we begin to talk with the family about the baptism of their child, we have an opportunity to help them understand that Christian baptism holds together personal faith and the faith of the church. Baptism is an act that speaks about our relationship both to Jesus Christ and to the community of faith, the church.

Such conversation suggests a third, often neglected task we have with families: helping parents discern whether baptism is appropriate at this time or should be delayed until later. A decision to delay baptism should not be based on an argument against the baptism of children. Rather, two reasons suggest a delay of baptism: (1) if the parents are not themselves baptized people of faith, and (2) if the parents do not intend to fulfill the commitment to be made to the child in the sacrament of baptism. In the first case, you have an opportunity to work with the entire family as you invite them into a process of preparation for the baptism of parents and child. In the second case, you will want to invite the family to continue discussing their faith and their understanding of baptism.

Education

Our second characteristic as pastors is educational. We are called to be caregivers with parents, children, and whole congregations. As resident caregivers and theologians in the congregation, we are responsible for helping parents and the congregation understand the practice and theology of baptism in The United Methodist Church. We give particular attention to the service of the Baptismal Covenant (*The United Methodist Hymnal*, pages 32–54, and *The United Methodist Book of Worship*, pages 81–114) and the statement on baptism, *By Water and the Spirit: A United Methodist Understanding of Baptism*, adopted by the General Conference (*The Book of Resolutions of The United Methodist Church*, pages 798–817). We are helping families and congregations understand not only what baptism is and means for us but also what baptism is not.

As caregivers in our congregations, we can help develop and implement educational structures and processes that lead people of all ages into a fuller understanding of our baptized life in Jesus Christ. Our educational role takes our baptismal ministry from an initial focus on parents preparing for the baptism of their child to ongoing learning and reflection on baptism with people of all ages and levels of Christian maturity. If such processes do not exist in your congregation, you may want to suggest them to the work areas responsible for nurture and Christian education.

Sacrament

The third characteristic of our baptismal ministry to children and their parents is the more specific sacramental ministry we have as pastors. Here we focus on the celebration of the sacrament of baptism itself. Such attention suggests ways we can help make baptism an important event in the life of the child, the child's parents, and the congregation.

First, baptism should happen in the context of the congregation's regular worship when children are present. Its importance for the entire congregation as a response of faith is emphasized when it has an intentional and dominant place in the service, as indicated in both the *Hymnal* and *Book of Worship*. Schedule baptisms on those Sundays of the church year that lend themselves to baptismal themes, such as the baptism of the Lord, Easter (or the Easter vigil), Pentecost, and All Saints' Day. When there are no baptisms on these Sundays, you may use the "Congregational Reaffirmation of the Baptismal Covenant" (Baptismal Covenant IV, in *The United Methodist Hymnal*, pages 50–53; or *The Book of Worship*, pages 111–14).

Second, it is helpful to remember that water is the primary symbol of baptism. Water should be used amply and should not be obscured by other acts or symbols.

Third, we are reminded of baptism and its central place in our Christian identity when the font remains visible in the church. It should not be stored away until needed.

Finally, we can involve members of the congregation, including children, in pre-baptismal visitations with families, in developing and teaching pre-baptismal classes with other parents, and as sponsors or godparents.

Through evangelism, education, and sacrament, we engage in a vital ministry with young children, their parents, and the congregation.

Baptism Resources for Pastors

A Place for Baptism, by Regina Kuehn (Chicago: Liturgy Training Publications, 1992).

Baptism: Christ's Act in the Church, by Laurence Hull Stookey (Nashville: Abingdon Press, 1982).

By Water and the Spirit: Making Connections for Identity and Ministry, by Gayle Carlton Felton (Nashville: Discipleship Resources, 1997).

Celebrating New Life: The Pastor's Practical Guide to Baptism (Nashville: Abingdon Press, 1998).

Come to the Waters: Baptism and Our Ministry of Welcoming Seekers and Making Disciples, by Daniel T. Benedict (Nashville: Discipleship Resources, 1996).

Remember Who You Are: Baptism, a Model for Christian Life, by William H. Willimon (Nashville: The Upper Room, 1988).

The Godparent Book, by Elaine Ramshaw (Chicago: Liturgy Training Publications, 1994).

Worship Matters: A United Methodist Guide to Ways to Worship (Volume I), edited by E. Bryon Anderson (Nashville: Discipleship Resources, 1999).

Worship Matters: A United Methodist Guide to Worship Work (Volume II), edited by E. Bryon Anderson (Nashville: Discipleship Resources, 1999).

Sample Letter to a Child at Baptism

As a pastor, you can help a child remember his or her baptism by writing a letter after the baptismal day. Encourage the parents to keep the letter and reread it to the child on the anniversary of the child's baptism. The following sample can be adapted to fit your particular situation.

Dear Child of God,

It was my privilege and joy to baptize you on (date) at (name of church). Baptism is a sacrament of the church; that is, a symbolic act with special meaning. The symbol used is water, which refreshes, cleanses, and renews life. You were baptized by (sprinkling of, pouring of, immersion in) water. I also, with your family, laid hands on you in blessing.

Baptism initiated you into God's family, the church. Baptism celebrated the gift of your life, affirming that you are loved by God and others.

Your parents took vows to help you grow as a Christian, to teach you that you are a child of God, and to help you understand the meaning of your baptism. The whole congregation promised to assist in your Christian nurture and care.

I pray that you will grow in your understanding of the meaning of your baptism and the use of your gifts and graces to God's glory.

Your pastor,

(*signature*)

The Challenge of Families With Young Children

Kim Giana and Judith Mayo
Jacksonville, Florida, and Livonia, Michigan

The Current Situation

Young families face tensions and challenges the church never considered a generation ago. Rising education costs leave many young parents in debt from their own college education. High costs of housing and transportation add to their tensions.

Young parents face new, complex parenting dilemmas. Through cable TV, they can introduce their children to many wonderful and enriching educational topics. They can also expose their children to graphic violence, sex, and adult topics. The information superhighway runs through their living rooms, and virtual reality looms on the horizon.

Multiculturalism at school, at work, at church, and in the neighborhood affords opportunities for enrichment as well as challenges to communication and coexistence. Ethnic diversity brings opportunities for new experiences and new ways to understand the world. It also puts new pressures on limited resources, sometimes resulting in competition and misunderstanding.

The nature of the family itself continues to change. Blended families, single-parent families, teen-parent families, and grandparents raising grandchildren are common. The nuclear family is isolated from the extended family and even from supportive neighborhoods. Many families are living in poverty. These situations challenge the church to care for young children and their families.

Our Scriptural Heritage

"Hear, O Israel: The LORD is our God, the LORD alone. You shall love the LORD your God with all your heart, and with all your soul, and with all your might. Keep these words that I am commanding you today in your heart. Recite them to your children and talk about them when you are at home and when you are away, when you lie down and when you rise" (Deuteronomy 6:4-7).

These words tell us that the primary caregivers and the primary setting for the education of children in the faith are the parents and the home. The church can provide settings to help children acquire words, become familiar with stories, and reinforce the teaching of the home, but the church cannot do it alone. It is in the home that Christian values are lived and stories are appropriated, where young children begin to make meaning out of their experience and respond in faith. But considering all the stresses on young families, they cannot do it alone. The church must empower and support them.

Strong families with strong Christian values are our hope for nurturing young Christians. We must find many ways to support, nurture, and empower families of all descriptions in their growth and to provide safety nets at their points of crisis.

Making Your Church Family Friendly

If you want your church to be family friendly, you must send the message that you care about families. What message does your congregation send? Is childcare provided for all worship services, meetings, and programs? Are there enough childcare providers for the number of children needing supervision? Are childcare providers properly screened and trained? Is your nursery clean, bright, safe, and well equipped? Are there procedures for contacting parents if they are needed in the nursery? Are there highchairs and booster chairs for congregational meals? Are people of all ages welcome in worship and at the Lord's table?

Reaching Out to Families

Many people return to the church when they become the parents of young children. Often, they are people who grew up in church-going families but, for various reasons, stopped going to church on a regular basis. Awareness of their responsibility for instilling in their children values and morals often draws them back to the church.

Look for a moment at your church's nursery area through the eyes of a first-time visitor. For a visiting family with young children, their first impression of your church's nursery area will have a dramatic effect on whether they choose to return for a second visit. What impression does your church and nursery leave? Ask a parent who does not attend your church to visit and tell his or her initial impressions of your nursery.

No matter how brilliant a pastor's preaching or how beautiful or new the building, if parents are not satisfied with the quality of care given to their infant or young child, they will not return. The strength of a nursery ministry can bring new families to a church.

Creating a Positive Impression on Arrival

- A knowledgeable person is available to direct the parent to the appropriate room. This person accompanies the parent, or at least gives clear directions on how to get there.
- A warm, smiling face is there to welcome the child and parent. This person gets on the child's eye level to greet the child.
- A nametag is prepared quickly and placed on the child's back.
- The parent is asked to fill out a form providing basic information about the child before leaving.
- The physical environment of the nursery area is clean and well lit.
- Any noticeable odors are those that are clean and fresh smelling.
- Equipment, toys, and furnishings appear to be in good condition and are clean and sanitary.
- Enough cribs are available to accommodate visiting babies. A clean sheet is already on the bed.

Creating a Positive Impression at Departure

- The caregiver briefly tells the parent about the child's nursery experience that day.
- The caregivers say, "Thank you for bringing your child. We hope you'll visit again."
- Procedures are followed that allow only authorized individuals to take the child from the nursery.

Providing Ways to Support Families

While the church nursery is critically important, it is not the only way the church can support families with young children. Consider the following:

1. Baptismal seminars prior to baptism. Families with children to be baptized meet and work together to understand the promises they will make and to explore ways family members can participate in the ritual of baptism. You may also want to recruit sponsors from the congregation for all baptized children to help support the family in its task of Christian nurture of their child.
2. Classes and preaching that help the congregation understand its role in Christian nurture.
3. Experiences that empower parents to find words to articulate their faith to their children and to make meaning in their own life. Bible studies that provide images, stories, and Bible competency for adults who may have had minimal Bible exposure will help empower parents to give faith to their children.
4. Support groups and classes that deal with a variety of life issues, such as entering or reentering the job market, dealing with addictions, caring for parents and children, single parenting, parenting skills, money management, conflict resolution, and so forth. When parents feel supported by the church, they have increased strength to support their children.
5. Networks for families to form supportive friendships, such as parents' day out programs; story hours; family outings and events; newsletters written for, about, and by young families; play groups; family camps; recreational teams; and so forth.
6. Mentoring relationships between experienced parents and newer parents.

Setting Priorities

If you want to care for young families, your congregation may have to make choices. Redecorating the parlor may need to be delayed, in order to furnish the crib room. Childcare, paid or volunteer, may need to be provided for all church events. Program decisions need to be made with an awareness of the needs of all generations. You will need to cultivate an openness to welcoming people where they are, rather than welcoming only those who fit the present agenda.

You have a challenge before you. If your congregation truly wants to care for young families, you will make them a priority.

The Young Child in Worship

Susan A. Patterson-Sumwalt
Denver, Colorado

The new minister of education was appointed to a church where there were no children. The congregation wanted children and had searched for the person to help them attract young families. The pastor arrived and began programs to do that. Soon, families with young children who did not have a church home came to worship. The parents wanted their children to be included in the worship service. Adults accustomed to worshiping in an adult atmosphere now had the opportunity to sit with children who had never been in worship, but they expected the children to sit quietly or to go to the nursery. The families began to feel unwelcome, and, if something had not been done, they would have left the church.

How did this church resolve this dilemma? Let's take a look.

One of the most striking generalities about today's parents is that they had choices growing up and therefore want their children to have choices. When they enter that door to attend worship for the first time, they expect to have the choice of keeping their child with them or of sending the child to a high-quality nursery program.

The greeter or usher at this entry point to the worship service becomes the pivotal person on whom the friendliness of the church is based. This person needs to greet the parents and child and then offer options: "Would you like to be seated for worship, or would you like to know about our nursery?" Or: "Would your child like to stay with you, or would he (or she) like to stay in the nursery during the service?" The ushers and greeters should have information about the location of classes, ages the classes serve, where a changing table is available, and so forth. Ushers and greeters also need to feel comfortable addressing both mothers and fathers in these matters.

Today's families often include two working parents or a single working parent. Because they are separated during the week, they look for opportunities to participate in activities as a family and to spend time together. The eagerness to leave a child in the nursery is not as prevalent as it once was. Where the church welcomes families to worship together, the families feel welcome and supported.

Worship is a place where young children, their parents, and those without children can experience the love of our Lord Jesus Christ through one another. The worship experience can be one of a happy family in Christ. Achieving that experience requires education that can happen in several ways:

1. Communication. Newspaper articles, bulletin notations, bulletin inserts, visitor information sheets, Sunday school handouts, and so forth can be used to discuss the importance of children in worship. Topics for these communiqués might include helping children understand worship, helping parents care for their children in the pews, what happens in the nursery, why include children in worship, a child development guide for people who do not have children, recognition of births, and facts about children in the congregation.

2. Preaching about the importance of families worshiping together. Welcome young children during announcements. Invite feedback from the congregation on integrating children into the worship service. Include child-appropriate examples in the sermon. Use a variety of storytelling methods in teaching Scripture.

3. Offer age-appropriate books, drawing materials, or toys for use by children during the sermon.

4. Learn the children's names, and greet them individually before or after worship. Include them in the life of the congregation holistically, but particularly during worship or other experiences in the sanctuary.

Children need to be a part of the worshiping community, as the worshiping community is greatly enriched by the inclusion of children.

Making worship child friendly means making the environment inviting to both the child and the parents. Considering the needs and expectations of today's parents will help enhance the worship service and the life of the congregation.

When a Young Child Dies

Charlotte T. Brent
Welsh, Louisiana

It is Monday morning and you are in the middle of writing your reflections for the church newsletter when the phone rings. When you answer, you are startled to hear, "Pastor, can you come right away? We have just found our baby dead in the crib! We are all in a terrible state over here." You hang up and try to organize your thoughts. This family was just in church yesterday; the baby was in the nursery and seemed so lively and healthy. You are about to go on one of the most difficult pastoral calls you will ever have to make. What do we do when a child dies?

Before rushing out, take a few minutes to stop, pray, and think about the needs of the parents, siblings, and family. Remember, they called you primarily because you are their tangible connection with the love and concern of God, a visible reminder of God's presence. There will be time later for theological discussion of "Why?" and "What does this mean for our family?"

If these are people for whom the reading of Scripture and prayer will be a comfort, select a few passages before leaving your office, and consider what prayer would be supportive and helpful. (You will probably need to make a second visit to plan a funeral or memorial service.) Before leaving the church, call your Christian educator, nursery coordinator, or nursery worker to begin your congregation's follow-up plan for when a young child dies. Are there other children in the family? Know their names. The brief time you and other staff initially spend in prayer, thought, and contacts with other ministry staff will be helpful as the congregation begins to reach out in ministry to this family.

What About Miscarriage/Stillbirth?

Miscarriages and stillbirths are experienced by many families in your congregation. Each of these deaths is the loss of a child who will be mourned, and each calls for pastoral and congregational care. In recent years, medical and mental-health professionals have come to see the importance of support at such times. No other children—or the promise of future children—can take the place of the one lost. Perhaps it is in the community of faith that we recognize most clearly the importance of each individual person.

As pastor, you will want to make a hospital or home visit as soon as possible. Encourage the parents to name any child carried to a possible viable age (as early as the sixth month) and to have a memorial or funeral service. For earlier-term miscarriages, a home service to honor the brief life of this child in the family would be helpful. These rituals can be extremely important as the parents and others enter the bereavement process.

What About Long-Term/ Chronic Illness?

You may have a child in your congregation who suffers from a life-threatening illness. During the course of the disease, the parents will need consistent pastoral care. They may experience anticipatory grief, shock, anger, or guilt. As their pastor, you will share this experience with them, perhaps even receiving some of their frustration and anger. Remember that it is their trust in you that allows them to vent pain and anxiety in your presence.

The parents will be sad over the loss of untasted joy and fulfillment that they had anticipated. You can offer hope in their darkness and support in their pain. Because of your consistent and caring ministry throughout the illness, your presence and help during the time of death and bereavement will be a strength to the grieving and to your own sense of loss.

The Grief Process

The grief process can take two to four years or more, depending on the closeness of the relationship. It takes at least a year to walk through the special days—Easter, Christmas, birthdays, and other significant family occasions—without the presence of the child. Follow-up is extremely important. Visits, phone calls, or cards throughout that first year reassure those who are grieving that their loved one has not been forgotten. You may want to call on your staff to assist in these gestures of care and concern. This could be a part of the plan carried out by you and the nursery staff that allows you to maintain contact with parents during the first year after the death. Let others help you and share in this meaningful ministry with the family.

Planning

You can prepare yourself, the other pastors with whom you work, and nursery workers by planning death and grief workshops and seminars. The content might include the normal grief process and what to expect when a child dies. Practical suggestions are always helpful, especially about what to say and what to avoid saying. Consider offering a churchwide experience resourced by a person in your community who is trained in grief work. These experiences can go a long way in helping you and your congregation make the most effective, loving response to families when a child dies.

Things to Remember

- Presence (yours and that of other church helpers) is paramount.
- Support groups and seminars can help.
- Design a care plan and include yourself, staff, and nursery workers.

- Fathers, as well as mothers, grieve.
- Grandparents grieve, and they are often forgotten.
- The loss of a sibling is sensed by infants and toddlers.
- You and your staff will experience the loss. Do not forget to discuss your own feelings.
- God knows the pain at the death of a child. Discuss this understanding with parents and friends at the appropriate time.

Resources for Further Help

Talking About Death: A Dialogue Between Parent and Child (Third Edition), by Earl A. Grollman (Boston: Beacon Press, 1991).

American Association of Pastoral Counselors, 9504-A Lee Highway, Fairfax, Virginia 22031-2303. Phone: 703-385-6967. Website: www.aapc.org.

National Sudden Infant Death Syndrome Resource Center, 2070 Chain Bridge Road, Suite 450, Vienna, VA 22182. Phone: 703-821-8955. Website: www.circsol.com/sids.

The Compassionate Friends, P.O. Box 3696, Oak Brook, IL 60522-3696. Website: www.compassionatefriends.org.

Using the Articles in This Section

The articles in this section are important for nursery coordinators, teachers, and caregivers. The articles can be used in caregiver training manuals and to support caregiver training.

Section Eleven: Safety and Health

Contents

Other Related Articles

Keeping the Nursery Safe

Steve Zekoff
Evanston, Illinois

Is your church nursery safe? Churches providing nursery care have taken on increased responsibility for protecting the safety of children while their parents worship and participate in other activities. Physical injuries to children left in a nursery could range from minor cuts and bruises to more serious injuries, such as broken bones and concussions. Falls, electric shock, food poisoning, or the spread of communicable diseases could be seen as the consequence of a poorly supervised nursery or an unsatisfactory physical environment.

Building and room inspections should be undertaken at regular intervals, with a focus on the physical condition of ceilings, walls, floors and floor coverings, lighting, and general housekeeping. A "kid's eye view" inspection of the church nursery, adjacent areas, and washrooms used by nursery students is recommended. When you inspect your nursery, get down on your hands and knees and observe the room from the height and perspective of the children who use it. (If it is not clean enough for you to get on the floor in your Sunday clothes, then it is not clean enough for your young children!) Check for potential hazards.

If snacks or beverages are provided by either the church or parents, it is essential to have provisions for keeping the food at the proper temperature until it is consumed. Clean up thoroughly after the children eat refreshments to avoid food poisoning from the consumption of spoiled leftovers or spillage, and to avoid attracting insects or vermin. If nonperishable food is kept at the church, store it in a sealed container. Never give very young children popcorn, nuts, hard candy, peanuts, sliced hotdogs, or other foods that can become lodged in a child's throat.

Churches with nurseries in a location at some distance from the church sanctuary, fellowship hall, church office, or another location where adults are present when the nursery is in use will want to consider the installation of a remote audio monitor. Adults away from the nursery listening in on the activities can speed the response should an emergency require additional assistance. A buzzer system accessible only to adults and incorporated into the monitoring system allows for a "help" signal to be sent when necessary. Vibrating pagers can be given to parents and other adults meeting within the building in case of a crisis.

The fire and emergency evacuation plan should be posted and known by every nursery worker. At a minimum, two remote fire exits with illuminated exit signs, and preferably with panic hardware on the doors, should be provided. Never lock exit doors with padlocks or dead bolts. Emergency lighting should be installed to provide necessary illumination in the event of a power failure. An approved automatic sprinkler system is the best defense against the peril of fire and may be required due to your building construction or local ordinances. Check your local building code to verify that you are meeting all ordinance requirements.

Approved fire extinguishers should be properly placed, available within seventy-five feet of the nursery and accessible to adults but not to young children. Extinguishers should be inspected or recharged and tagged at least annually. All possible sources of fire should be eliminated or properly controlled. Boilers and furnaces should be enclosed within a room that is fire-resistant for a minimum of one hour and that is located well away from the nursery.

Conducting a safety check of your church nursery facilities should be a high priority and should be done at least twice a year. Make it a routine activity for those responsible for the operation of the nursery.

A Child-Safe Place— Safety Checklists

Stephen D. Krau and Steve Zekoff

Nashville, Tennessee, and Evanston, Illinois

It seems that most accidents that occur with young infants are the result of their natural curiosity, vitality, and lack of comprehension about potential danger. Although it is impossible to totally safeguard every child in every situation, there are things you can do to make the physical environment as safe as possible, and behaviors you can exhibit to promote safety.

Safety Checklist for Toys

____ 1. Toys are appropriate for child's age level.

____ 2. Toys are not small enough, nor do they have detachable parts small enough, to be swallowed.

____ 3. Toys do not have sharp edges or points.

____ 4. Toys are not made of glass or brittle plastic.

____ 5. Toys do not make loud noise that could injure a child's hearing.

____ 6. All toys are in good repair and clean.

____ 7. Stuffed toys have no holes or detachable parts.

____ 8. Climbing toys are appropriate for nursery-age children. Those that are not age-appropriate are removed.

____ 9. Toys and furniture are not left stacked so that a child would find them inviting to climb, possibly resulting in physical injury.

Safety Checklist for Indoor Environment

____ 1. Lighting is adequate. There are no burned-out light bulbs.

____ 2. All windows, screens, mirrors, doors, and gates are in good repair. Cords to draperies and blinds are cut off and/or anchored where children can't reach them.

____ 3. Cabinets have childproof safety latches.

____ 4. Carpets are clean, with no loose or frayed areas.

____ 5. Walkways and stairs are not obstructed by furniture, toys, or other "trip and fall" hazards.

____ 6. Any stairs used by nursery children have antislip treads and child-height handrails.

____ 7. All furniture is in good repair. Sharp corners are padded. Heavy furniture and equipment that could tip over are anchored to the wall.

____ 8. There are no hidden traps, such as toy chests, forts, playhouses, and appliances such as refrigerators that could enclose a child out of your view.

____ 9. Electrical wiring, switches, and outlets meet local electrical codes.

____ 10. Electrical outlets are covered when not in use with an immovable piece of furniture or safety caps.

____ 11. Extension cords are never used as permanent wiring and are never accessible by children, even when used temporarily for electrical devices such as video or tape players.

____ 12. All electrical cords are out of the reach of children.

____ 13. There are no signs of rodents or insects.

____ 14. All cleaning and medical supplies are secured out of children's reach.

____ 15. There are no plumbing leaks or spills on the floor.

____ 16. Safety hazards are reported to the appropriate person promptly. All caregivers are aware of any problems that cannot be remedied immediately.

____ 17. All cribs and playpens used in the nursery meet current safety standards. Cribs have been checked with a ruler to ensure that the distance between slats is no more than two and three-eighths inches (six centimeters). Any equipment that does not comply has been discarded. Corner posts do not extend above the rest of the crib slats so that children cannot get hung on them. Mattresses fit snugly inside of cribs and are set at their lowest height if the children using them can pull up to a standing position. Mattress sheets fit snugly, with plenty of overhang under the mattress so that they do not pull off easily.

___ 18. Gates are installed on stairwells and windows that are accessible to young children.

___ 19. Doors are closed to prevent children from wandering off, but access into the nursery for parents and other adults is maintained. (A safety glass viewing port in the door, or the use of a split door, can provide a solution.)

___ 20. Cleaning supplies, insecticides, matches, power tools, and any other hazardous materials are properly and safely stored in child-resistant, locked enclosures away from the nursery area.

___ 21. Any supplies utilized in nursery activities, such as paints and crayons, are nontoxic.

___ 22. Nursery furnishings, equipment, and toys are sanitized on a regular basis. Crib and playpen mattress coverings are made of washable vinyl. Proper disposal facilities for soiled diapers are available. All trash cans in the nursery are securely covered.

Safety Checklist for Outdoor Environment

___ 1. Entrance from outdoors to classroom/nursery area is uncluttered and safe.

___ 2. Outside area is safely fenced.

___ 3. Outdoor equipment is in good repair and age-appropriate for children using it. Any swings are not heavy or made out of wood, metal, or other rigid materials. There are no potential traps, such as chests or closed-in playhouses.

___ 4. The area is inspected for signs of unwanted animals, such as rodents, reptiles, biting insects, and stray dogs and cats. The area is also inspected for poisonous plants. Such animals or plants have been removed.

___ 5. Play surfaces have no sharp edges, splinters, or other hazards. Surfaces underneath play equipment that children can climb are covered with impact-absorbing material according to safety guidelines (see *Handbook for Public Playground Safety*, Pub. No. 325, U.S. Consumer Product Safety Commission, Washington, DC). The following have not been used in these areas: asphalt, concrete, soil, hard-packed dirt, grass, turf, linoleum, carpet.

___ 6. Litter and trash are picked up.

___ 7. All outdoor equipment (lawn mowers, rakes, shovels, and so forth) is safely stored in an enclosed area away from the children's play area.

Caregiver Behaviors for Safety of Children

It is sometimes difficult to allow the child to explore his or her environment without being too prohibitive or restrictive. There are some caregiver behaviors that promote safety and help make this an easier task for you.

___ 1. Never leave a child alone, even if you think the child is asleep.

___ 2. Do not allow children to stand on tables or chairs or to climb shelves. If a child does climb onto an unsafe location, simply remove the child and explain why it is not a safe place. Interest the child in another activity.

___ 3. Dispose of small objects that children might swallow.

___ 4. Be on constant lookout for potential hazards, such as a parent's hot coffee or a hot water tap at the sink left running.

___ 5. Safely dispose of all packaging materials that come with new toys, including plastic wrapping and plastic foam padding.

___ 6. Always support the head of a newborn or infant when holding the child, even if the child seems able to hold his or her head up.

___ 7. Never lift a child off the floor by his or her arms.

___ 8. Be sure that places children like to hide are well ventilated, cannot be locked, and are easily accessible to you.

___ 9. Be well rested and alert.

___ 10. Put personal belongings in lockers or in a closed closet, keeping children away from potential dangers such as medications, metal nail files, and drawstrings.

___ 11. Know what to do in case of fire.

___ 12. Know what to do when an emergency does occur.

Keeping the Nursery Clean

Stephen D. Krau

Nashville, Tennessee

The best way to prevent the spread of communicable diseases among children and workers in the nursery is to follow good sanitation practices. The number and severity of illnesses among children in nurseries and daycare are related to the sanitary practices of the facility and the personal hygiene of the staff. Certain factors increase the risk of transmitting diseases in such settings. Generally speaking, the more children in a space the greater the risk. The presence of diapered children in the area also increases the risk of transmitting diseases associated with diarrhea. You are responsible for minimizing these risks.

Hand Washing

Frequent hand washing (of staff and children) is the most effective action you can take to prevent the spread of diseases in the nursery. Wash your hands upon arrival, before feeding or serving food, after diaper changes, after outside activities, and after wiping runny noses.

For hand washing, a foot-operated soap pump and automatic sink are ideal! If that is not possible, an effective alternative is a liquid soap dispenser. Use paper towels for drying hands and also to turn the faucet off so that you do not touch the dirty faucet handles with clean hands. Clean the sink area regularly with disinfectant.

Food Preparation

Feedings or snacks should not be prepared or served by the person who changes diapers that day, if possible. If potty chairs are used, rinse them out in the toilet area. (Be sure to wear disposable gloves.) Never rinse potties in the same area where food is prepared.

If refrigeration is required for feedings and snacks, the refrigerator should be checked weekly for neglected foodstuffs and should be wiped out at least monthly. If your church provides formula or snacks, be sure to date the containers. Discard open formula after forty-eight hours. Inspect refrigerated snacks prior to serving. Remember, if in doubt, throw it out!

Toys

To avoid transmission of bacteria from toys, wash the toys after each session if they have been kissed, drooled on, and chewed on. Use only washable toys in infant and toddler rooms. Keep two plastic containers for "mouth toys" and rattles; label one "clean" and the other "dirty." Use toys only from the clean container and, once used, place them in the dirty container. Wash dirty toys in soapy water; then put them in a solution of one-fourth cup of bleach to one gallon of water (prepared daily) for at least two minutes. Allow to air dry. Machine wash and machine dry fabric toys.

Cleanups

Spills, runny noses, and spit-ups are frequent occurrences in any nursery. Keep abundant supplies of paper towels, facial tissues, and disposable wipes on hand.

Noncarpeted floors should be mopped and cleaned after each session. Clean carpets in high traffic areas frequently. Give furniture, toys, and supplies designated locations out of the main traffic area. At the end of each session, clean used items and return them to the appropriate locations. Remember to remove sheets from the cribs and place them in a laundry bag.

Final Words

Not only does cleanliness cut down on transmission of disease, it minimizes accidents that result from excessive clutter. A clean, orderly nursery also reassures parents that their children are cared for by people who want to provide the best environment possible.

When Accidents Happen

Stephen D. Krau
Nashville, Tennessee

It seems that no matter what precautions are taken, and no matter how cautious and mindful the caregiver, accidents will occur. These occurrences are often beyond the control of the caregiver and are in no way a reflection on the adult's competence. What is within the control of the caregiver is the capacity to respond rapidly and effectively in these situations to minimize the degree of injury to the child.

It is important to remain calm. Keep in mind that the actual event is already traumatic for the child. Your composure affects not only the child involved in the accident but also any children who are bystanders. If you become frantic or distraught, impressionable bystanders will perceive the event as more traumatic than it may actually be, and the children will become anxious. As a result, you may have to deal with the accident event and with the anxious behaviors of the other children. This can cause you to become distracted, diverting your attention from the child who needs help. Maintaining a tranquil demeanor during the event will also help you think more clearly and respond appropriately.

Remember that *first* aid is the care that is delivered immediately. As appropriate, another adult should immediately contact the child's parents and a physician or other emergency service. Caregivers should always know the location of the parents and the nearest telephone, as well as emergency numbers, including 911, fire and police departments, poison control, the nearest hospital, and the church office. Post the church's address with the telephone numbers.

Following is a review of common events that occur with toddlers and infants and require first aid. It is not an exhaustive list, nor should it be considered a substitute for a first-aid manual or a replacement for teacher education in first-aid procedures.

Falls

If any bones are out of alignment and a fracture is suspected, do not attempt to move the child. One adult should stay with the child while another gets the parents and calls for medical assistance.

If a child's head hits a hard surface, observe the child for vomiting, paleness, dizziness, sudden drowsiness, or unequally dilated pupils. These are all indications for immediate medical attention.

Bleeding

Clean the wound with soap and water. Let the water from the sink run over the wound to flush it thoroughly. Blot the area dry with a sterile gauze or pad, and cover it with a bandage to prevent infection.

If bleeding is severe, put a sterile gauze over the area and, with a gloved hand, apply direct pressure. Elevate the wound while holding pressure. If bleeding fails to stop, send someone to get the parents, and obtain medical assistance. Avoid direct contact with the blood.

Once the child is taken care of, clean surfaces in the areas that are bloodied, and disinfect them with a bleach solution (one-fourth cup bleach to one gallon water, prepared daily). Remove cloth articles (sheets, toys, and so forth) that have been contaminated with blood and put them in plastic bags until they can be washed.

Nosebleeds

Put the child in a sitting position leaning forward or reclining with the head and shoulders raised. Apply direct pressure by pinching the child's nostrils together between your thumb and forefinger. If bleeding continues, notify the parents and recommend medical attention.

Bites

First, comfort the child.

For an insect bite, remove the stinger or insect with tweezers. Wash the area thoroughly with soap and water. Cover it with a dressing and apply a cold pack. Watch for allergic reactions: sudden difficulty breathing, nausea, dizziness, swelling. A reaction requires immediate medical attention. Because the children are so young, parents may not be aware that their child has such allergies.

For an animal bite, clean the area with soap and water. Restrain the animal for medical inspection.

For a bite from another child, clean the area with soap and water. Fill out an incident report and notify the parents. If the bite causes bleeding, contact the health department for advice. Biting is a common behavior in young children who are teething or who are not able to put their frustrations and feelings into words. Firmly tell the biter that biting hurts others and that you will not allow him or her to bite. *Do not* bite the child to show him or her how it feels. Instead, watch the child closely to try to figure out and eliminate the reason for the biting: offer a teething ring to a teething child, help a tired child get more rest, purchase a duplicate of a favorite toy that children fight over, try to give positive time and attention to a child needing more attention, and try to stick to a calm and predictable routine that can help children feel more in control of their world.

Choking

For toddlers and older children, if the child does not cough up the object after a few seconds, hold the child's head down and, with the bottom of the palm of your hand, deliver five to seven sharp taps between the child's shoulder blades.

Hold infants in one arm with the child's head down. Use your other hand to deliver five to seven sharp taps between the child's shoulder blades.

Send someone for medical help if the object does not come out or if the child has difficulty breathing.

Mouth-to-Mouth Resuscitation

If a child stops breathing, artificial respiration is required. Once any obstructions are removed from the mouth, the child's air passage must be opened. Tilt the child's head back, cover the child's mouth and nose with your mouth to make a seal, and blow gently into the child every three seconds. Continue until the child breathes on his or her own. Seek medical assistance immediately. Do not leave the child alone. In cases where emergency medical treatment is warranted, one adult should notify the parents while another adult contacts emergency medical assistance.

Reporting an Emergency

When reporting an emergency, the caller should do the following:

1. Tell the contact person what has happened and the nature of the emergency, including the child's age and what is presently being done for the child. Be calm and clear.
2. Give the name and phone number of the church; the address of the church, including the entrance most accessible to the child; and the caller's name.
3. Do not hang up until the contact person has hung up. The person on the other end may have more questions and may have paused to write information down. Do not assume that the conversation is over. Listen for any advice or further questions; let the contact person hang up first.

Stay Calm

In any emergency event, be reassuring. To convey that the situation is under control, a calm, reassuring manner is imperative. Toddlers who witness an emergency may not be able to express their concerns and fears. Talk in simple terms to children who witnessed the event. Explain what happened and what is being done to help their friend. It is vital to convey to all witnesses and to the victim that you are there to protect and care for them. Provide the same reassurance to the parents of the child who had the accident, as well as to the parents of children who witnessed the event, who may need to discuss it or answer questions later.

As soon as everything is under control, all caregivers present should record what happened. Even minor falls and cuts should be recorded and parents told. Clearly record all details, including time of occurrence. Date and sign the report and write on it the time at which it was filled out.

Clearly communicate to the parents of the child what has happened. Tell the facts of the event as you know them. Listen to any concerns they may have. Be caring and reassuring.

Using the Articles in This Section

Teachers, caregivers, and nursery coordinators will find these articles helpful as they seek to provide a stimulating and safe environment for younger children.

Section Twelve: Supplies, Toys, Equipment

Contents

Other Related Articles

Stocking the Nursery

Nancy Jane Cheshire

Fairmont, Virginia

As the saying goes, A picture is worth a thousand words. Picture the room or areas your church provides for infants, toddlers, and two-year-olds. The rooms we provide for these youngest members of our church family show, without words, if we are following the example of Jesus as he welcomed the children with open arms, saying, "Let the little children come to me" (Matthew 19:14).

Get down to the children's eye level and move around in the play areas of the nursery. The room should say, "Come in, children! Here is a room planned just for you, a place where you can have fun as you learn that God loves you. You are an important part of our church family." Providing for the needs of infants and young children through loving, consistent care helps them develop trust in the caregivers and instills a feeling that the church is a safe, friendly place.

Pictures and Toys

When stocking the nursery room, put pictures and unbreakable mirrors at the children's eye level. Be sure pictures include children of diverse racial and ethnic groups, ages, and so forth. (Check Sunday school files for possible pictures.) Include pictures depicting Jesus interacting with children. Mount photos of children engaged in a variety of activities. Provide many textures for them to feel. Use carpet and fabric pieces to make wall murals at their eye level. Soft pillows and a quilt in a little nook make a cozy place for a child wanting some quiet space.

Children learn through play. Play is their work. Place their toys on low, open shelves so children can see them, choose the ones they wish, and, later, put them away. Provide toys that will not break or crack and that do not have small parts that can be swallowed. All toys do not have to be put out at once. Rotate some of the toys for variety. Too many toys can cause confusion for the children. However, the thinking skills of young children have not yet developed to allow for sharing toys easily, so have more than one of the favorite play toys available.

Because infants grow and develop rapidly during the first two years of life, stock the nursery to meet a variety of individual needs. The supplies and equipment provided help the children grow mentally, physically, socially, and emotionally.

Safety and Comfort

Infants need a place to sleep in safety and comfort. Provide a sanitary diapering area so that all infants and caregivers can be kept safe and healthy. Include a comfortable chair so that infants can be held while being fed. A rocking chair serves nicely and also allows the adult to rock, soothe, sing to, talk to, and respond to the infants. Crib mobiles are attractive and fascinating to infants but can be dangerous. Hang them high enough that the infants can't reach them, and remove them before the infants are able to grasp them or to stand up. You can then hang mobiles from the ceiling, out of reach, instead.

As infants become mobile, they need a safe space for crawling, "toddling," and exploring. In this space, they need furnishings that allow them to safely pull to standing and then to move about, climb, and jump, as they learn to use their bodies. They learn about their world not just by seeing objects but by tasting, smelling, hearing, and touching them. Stock the nursery with a variety of toys children can hug, shake, throw, bang, push, pull, stack, open, and close. Remember that inexpensive toys (boxes, plastic bowls, spoons, and so forth) can be just as entertaining and instructive as expensive ones.

Perhaps God planned for mobile infants to be quick and active because there are so many wonderful things to see and experience in God's world. We fill an important role for these children by providing an appropriate setting in the church nursery where they can learn, grow, and develop feelings and attitudes that will stay with them throughout their lives.

It is natural for infants to discover how toys and supplies "taste," so supply play items that can be sanitized after being mouthed. Protect these active explorers with gates or half doors at the entrance to the nursery. To assure that no one can easily step on or rock on little fingers while caring for other children, position furnishings in such a way that they divide the room to allow an open, safe area for mobile infants to discover and experience the world around them.

Activity Centers

Encourage toddlers and two-year-olds as they develop independence and autonomy by arranging their space into activity centers. A housekeeping center allows role play, language development, and social skills. Multicultural dolls help teach the belief that all people are valued children of God. A block area encourages dramatic, creative play. A plain wooden truck can serve as a variety of vehicles. Home living and block centers allow children to experience Christian living in work and play.

Encourage creativity in an art center, where children can draw, tear paper, and paste. Plain colored paper (rather than printed activity pages or coloring books) can blossom into a creation of the child's imagination.

Children's books should be available. Sturdy hardboard books with rounded corners are durable and colorful. And don't forget the joy and fun that music brings to children! Manipulatives (puzzles, small building sets, playing dough) help small motor development. Toys children can ride, climb, and actively manipulate help with large motor development.

Together, the equipment and supplies provide activities for developing the whole child in a Christian environment.

Sources for Supplies and Equipment

Following is a brief listing of companies that sell equipment and supplies for young children:

- Community Playthings
  P.O. Box 901, Route 213
  Rifton, NY 12471
  800-777-4244; Fax 800-336-5948
  www.communityplaythings.com

- Constructive Playthings
  13201 Arrington Road
  Grandview, MO 64030
  800-448-7830
  www.constplay.com

- abc school supply, inc.
  3312 N. Berkeley Lake Rd.
  Duluth, GA 30096-9419
  800-669-4ABC; Fax 800-933-2987
  www.abcschoolsupply.com

- Lakeshore Learning Materials
  2695 E. Dominguez St., P.O. Box 6261
  Carson, CA 90749
  800-421-5354; Fax 310-537-5403
  www.lakeshorelearning.com

- Kaplan
  P.O. Box 609
  Lewisville, NC 27023-0609
  800-334-2014; Fax 800-452-7526
  www.kaplanco.com

Checklist for the Infants' Room

Nancy Jane Cheshire

Fairmont, Virginia

Use checkmarks to record discoveries as you tour the facilities for infants.

___ 1. As you enter the room, does it appear attractive, clean, and welcoming?

___ 2. Is a convenient place provided for recording information about each child upon arrival?

___ 3. Are there clear guidelines for parents regarding where to put diaper bags, coats, and so forth?

___ 4. Are all diaper bags, bottles, and pacifiers clearly labeled for each child?

___ 5. Is the entry area protected so that crawlers are not endangered when people enter and exit the room?

___ 6. Are there attractive pictures on the wall at adult height that can be shown to infants being held?

___ 7. Are there pictures at low heights for crawlers to enjoy?

___ 8. Are there unbreakable mirrors at the children's eye level?

___ 9. Are there clean, safe cribs available for resting or sleeping infants?

___ 10. Is there a safe, clean diapering area?

___ 11. Is the diapering surface sanitized after each use, or are disposable paper table coverings provided?

___ 12. Are disposable gloves provided for diapering?

___ 13. Is a covered receptacle for dirty diapers provided?

___ 14. Can caregivers easily wash their hands after diapering an infant?

___ 15. Is there at least one adult rocking chair?

___ 16. Is there refrigeration for bottles?

___ 17. If children stay for an extended period of time, is there a safe, clean feeding area?

___ 18. For extended care, are there facilities for heating food?

___ 19. Are there safe chairs for infants being fed?

___ 20. Is there a privacy area for nursing mothers?

___ 21. Is there a safe area for infants to crawl and explore?

___ 22. Are toys neatly and conveniently placed on low, open shelves?

___ 23. Are mobiles at a safe height to prevent injury?

___ 24. Are there vinyl or heavy cardboard books with rounded corners and high contrast illustrations?

___ 25. Is music available?

___ 26. Are toys available that
  ___ are soft and cuddly   ___ can be pushed and pulled
  ___ make sounds or music   ___ offer a variety of textures
  ___ can be filled, emptied, or stacked

___ 27. Are equipment and supplies available for sanitizing toys that are mouthed after each use?

Checklist for the Toddlers' and Two-Year-Olds' Room

Nancy Jane Cheshire
Fairmont, Virginia

Use checkmarks to record discoveries as you tour the facilities for toddlers and twos.

____ 1. As you enter the room, is it attractive and welcoming?

____ 2. Is the entry area safely protected so that a child is not lost through an open doorway?

____ 3. Is there a convenient check-in area?

____ 4. Is the room appealing at the children's eye level?

____ 5. Are there pictures at the children's eye level?

____ 6. Is there at least one unbreakable mirror at the children's eye level?

____ 7. Are tables and chairs appropriate to the children's size?

____ 8. Are there many different textures in the room?

____ 9. Is there sufficient lighting?

____ 10. Is there a safe, clean diapering area?

____ 11. Is the diapering surface sanitized after each use, or are disposable paper table coverings provided?

____ 12. Are disposable gloves provided for diapering?

____ 13. Is a covered receptacle for dirty diapers provided?

____ 14. Can caregivers easily wash their hands after diapering a child?

____ 15. Are cots or resting areas available?

____ 16. Is music available?

____ 17. Is there an adult-size rocking chair?

____ 18. Are there child-size tables and chairs for snacks or feeding times?

____ 19. Is refrigeration available?

____ 20. If children stay for an extended time, is there a food preparation area?

____ 21. Is the room planned so that there are different play areas or learning centers where one child or a small group of children can play?

____ 22. Are toys neatly arranged on low, open shelves so that children can easily choose them and put them away?

____ 23. Is there a low table or shelf where nature items can be experienced?

____ 24. Is there a home living area? Does it include

     ___ kitchen appliance   ___ multicultural dolls   ___ table and chairs

     ___ doll bed   ___ two phones   ___ cooking/eating utensils

     ___ child-size rocker   ___ dress-up clothes   ___ unbreakable mirror

____ 25. Is there a block center? Does it include

     ___ building blocks   ___ variety of vehicles

     ___ small animals and people (but large enough not to be a danger)

____ 26. Is there a creative art area? Does it include

     ___ an easel   ___ a table for art activities   ___ paper, large crayons, paste

____ 27. Is a variety of children's books available?

____ 28. Are books in a cozy, easy to enjoy setting?

____ 29. Are there several manipulative toys such as puzzles; snap-together blocks; toys for stacking, pushing, pulling, filling, and emptying; and playing dough?

Purchasing and Paying for Supplies and Equipment

Nancy Jane Cheshire

Fairmont, Virginia

"We really want to improve our nursery, but we can't afford to purchase new supplies and equipment." If this sounds familiar, don't give up! You can find a way. If you have evaluated the nursery and found need for improvements, then get ready to take the first big step. That doesn't mean get ready to shop; it means begin with prayer. God can show us solutions to our problems and guide us toward our goals.

Don't hide your wish list under a basket. Let the needs of the nursery be known. A note in the Sunday bulletin or church newsletter may bring in donations of one or two needed items, but when many people and groups in the church help with a project, the potential for success is great. Your enthusiasm and positive approach will be contagious!

If your wish list is overwhelming, set priorities and start at the top of the list. Break a large project into small units. Large needs, such as carpeting, can be broken into square feet or square yards that can be purchased from donations. Or set up an angel tree, listing needed items on paper angels hung on a tree. Individuals or groups select an angel item and either donate the item or the funding for it. Acknowledge all gifts or donations with thank-you notes, and list them in a special book at the church. (Donations can be made in honor or memory of a loved one.)

A catchy theme will help your project.

- Create a wall hanging from donors' handprints to allow everyone to have "a hand" in the project. Trace donors' hands onto a cloth sheet with brightly colored fabric markers. Write their names on their handprints. Quilt and bind the wall hanging. The church will have a beautiful keepsake and the nursery will have needed funds.
- Constructing a new building? Sell handprints that will remain in concrete for generations.
- Have a baby shower where all the babies that use the nursery are recipients, and all gifts are given to the nursery.

- Have a nursery open house. Post pictures of needed items at the locations where those items would be found in the nursery. Post beside each picture the cost of the item and a sign-up sheet. Let donors sign up to donate funds needed for specific items.

Before purchases are made, comparison shop. Ask for recommendations from childcare centers, other churches, the early childhood department of a local college, or a local elementary school. Look for small items at yard sales or flea markets, but be sure they meet safety standards. Be sure to choose items appropriate for use by more than one child.

When others are doing the actual purchasing or are donating used equipment, be clear about expectations of quality, size, and other pertinent information. Have a policy in place that allows for acceptance of only those items that are safe and actually needed in the nursery.

For low shelves and other simple installations, consider purchasing wood and asking people in your church or community to donate their labor. Patterns for many items are available at the local public library or a bookstore, even patterns for the kitchen appliances for the home living center. Set safety guidelines, such as rounded corners and nontoxic finishes, for locally made items.

Use your financial resources wisely. Toys and equipment serving many children must be both safe and durable. A more expensive item may actually prove to be more cost-effective.

Be sure toys, books, and pictures show diversity and inclusiveness. Show sensitivity to the uniqueness of each individual child and family unit.

Improving the church nursery is time well spent. When we welcome children with rooms that are safe, healthy, and equipped to meet individual developmental needs, we are living our Christian faith. Each child of God deserves the best. Pray, dream, and work toward your goal of following Jesus' example in welcoming little children into your church family.

Policy for Donations and Gifts to the Nursery

Nancy Jane Cheshire
Fairmont, Virginia

My neighbor gave me a round coffee table in excellent condition. It was no longer needed at her house, and she asked if I had any use for it. I was delighted. It was just what we needed for an activity table in the older nursery room. Her trash was my treasure.

Not all gifts are so useful. How should you respond when someone gives you a donation that cannot be used with young children? When this happens, you will be thankful if your church has a policy or written statement concerning donations. It will help avoid hurt feelings that can result when a gift is not accepted.

When asking for donations, remember that you are responsible for the health and safety of the nursery children, so be specific. If you put a notice in the newsletter saying, "The nursery needs another baby crib," you may get what Mrs. Jones considers a real treasure. The only problem is, the crib Mrs. Jones brings to the church is thirty-five years old and doesn't meet the safety standards we recognize as being important today. When requesting donations, specify criteria for acceptance.

When requesting small items, you might try a project with a theme. For example, "A Budding Nursery" bulletin board could feature flower petals lying in grass. Write on each petal the name of a specific item needed. People wishing to help with the project could choose a petal and donate that item.

Always acknowledge donations with a written thank-you. The church should record gifts and donations in a book as a lasting way of honoring and thanking donors.

Each church family is made up of unique individuals. What is appropriate for one church may not be best for another church. Your church can decide on a policy by considering a few questions:
- How can donations be made to the church nursery?
- Who accepts donations?
- How is the gift acknowledged?
- Who determines if the gift is safe and can be placed in the nursery room?
- Are all gifts to be accepted?
- What procedure will be followed if the gift is not safe or is not needed?

When you have an answer to each of these questions, and have hurt no one in the process, then you have a good procedure or policy. A printed statement might read as follows:

> *We put our faith into action by sharing with others and by being good stewards. We are thankful for donations and gifts to the nursery. Due to limited space, health regulations, and safety standards, we cannot always use donations as intended by the giver. We will do our best to see that each donation is used to benefit or help the children of God.*

Using the Articles in This Section

Nursery coordinators or administrators will find the articles in this section helpful as they design and implement training for volunteer or paid staff.

Nearly all of the articles in this book are potentially valuable for training. The articles listed here as "Other Related Articles" provide particularly useful content to support your training plan. These articles can become the basis for workshops or can be used in one-on-one training.

Section Thirteen: Training Plan

Contents

Other Related Articles

Developing a Training Plan

MaryJane Pierce Norton and Mary Jane Van Hook

Nashville, Tennessee, and Bloomington, Indiana

Training helps new teachers begin to feel comfortable with the task ahead and to have a better idea of what is expected of a teacher of infants, toddlers, and twos. It gives them an opportunity to explore the space where they will be teaching, locating available furnishings and supplies. It also gives them the support of other caregivers like themselves as they begin their planning.

Training helps experienced teachers know more about others who are teaching. They are able to share past experiences and gather new ideas, to find support for what they have done in the past and for ways they are growing in their task. They are able to offer guidance to others who are just beginning to teach.

For all who work with infants, toddlers, and twos in the church, training can set up connections among Sunday school workers, evening childcare workers, daycare workers, and parents. It enables them to better support one another in their common task of caring for infants and toddlers. They can exchange ideas about working with young children and about setting up the best environment for the children, including developing guidelines and standards for the equipment and supplies that will be available to teachers and children.

A training workshop energizes attendees for the new year, creates excitement about the work ahead, and establishes a sense of community. It can open the door for the workers to give prayer support for one another.

If you wish for support or help in planning training for caregivers, contact a professional Christian educator at a church of your denomination in your area, or the director of a weekday ministry that receives strong, positive community support.

Remember: You know your setting better than anyone. You know the needs. Follow your own instincts and develop a plan that best fits your needs.

Planning a Training Workshop

1. Choose the format that is best for your church.
2. Select a date and place. Be sure to consider the church and community calendars.
3. Secure leadership. Reserve audiovisual equipment and acquire other materials. (Check with conference media resource services for potential training videos.)
4. Invite teachers, caregivers, and parents.
5. Plan for refreshments as needed.
6. Design an evaluation tool.
7. Relax and enjoy the experience with your partners in infants-toddlers-twos ministry.

Suggested Workshop Schedule

(The following schedule is designed for a three-hour teacher training session. It can be expanded or reduced according to the needs of the teachers.)

9:00 A.M.—Greeting, nametags, refreshments
9:15 A.M.—Opening worship
9:30 A.M.—Preview resources
10:00 A.M.—Break
10:10 A.M.—Age-level overview
10:40 A.M.—Planning a session
11:10 A.M.—Break
11:20 A.M.—Room setup and supplies
11:45 A.M.—Evaluation
11:50 A.M.—Closing worship
12:00 noon—Dismissal

Topics for Training

Following are some areas to consider in your plans for training workers:

Age-Level Characteristics

What do we know about six-month-olds? What is important to a two-and-a-half-year-old? How do children at each age level interact with toys and with other people? How do they understand God?

Parents as Partners

We know that faith development begins in the home. How can nursery caregivers best support parents in that nurture? What can help with the transition from home to church? What can be done to help parents feel confident in the care their child is receiving?

Separation Anxiety

During the first three years, there are times when children separate easily from their parents and other times when the process can be traumatic. What can be done to support everyone through this process?

Preparing the Room

Young children use all of the space available to them. How can the physical setting meet each child's needs?

The Value of Play

Play is the way young children begin to make sense of their world. What is the adult role in a child's play?

Faith Development

Faith is developing in the first three years. What is the importance of trust, grace, creative activity, and wonder in the formation of that faith?

Using the Printed Curriculum

There are wonderful resources available to teachers. How can printed curriculum fit your setting and a particular group of children? You can order approved United Methodist curriculum through Cokesbury, 800-672-1789.

Communication Skills

The first three years are extremely important for language development, as well as for learning to care about others. How can adults talk in ways that encourage children to listen, and listen in ways that encourage children to express their thoughts and feelings?

Health and Safety Issues

Above all, ensure the safety of the children. How do adult workers prevent accidents, control the spread of germs, and create a safe environment for every child? Address issues of child abuse, and provide caregivers with abuse-prevention training.

Bias Issues

Everyone has biases. It is essential, however, that we are aware of those biases so that the children with whom we have contact will not suffer because of them. Children's self-esteem is crucial to their successful development.

Activity Experiences

Caregivers enjoy learning new activities to use with children, and understanding the reason those activities are helpful to children's development. Do a workshop on reading, or music, or rhythm activities, or some other developmental activity.

Additional Resources for Training

Many of the articles in *The First Three Years* provide valuable information that can be incorporated into a training plan. Articles that are particularly helpful for training include

How to Organize and Plan a Training Session

Susan Groseclose
Nashville, Tennessee

Juanita, a single mom with a two-year-old, is searching for a United Methodist church that cares about her child. She is looking for a nursery that is clean and safe; a place where the caregivers understand the needs of young children and model Jesus' love; a site where children experience love, trust, prayer, and forgiveness; an environment where the caregivers play with the children, provide a variety of toys and creative activities, treat children equally, and allow children to expand their imaginations.

Juanita is looking for a church that supports her as a single mom; a church that offers a Sunday school class for parents of young children, parenting classes, and resources about parenting available for her to study on her own time. She is looking for personal support through staff and church members who can understand the joys and stresses of being a parent, particularly a single parent. Juanita wants to participate in the total life of the church, but she must depend on quality childcare being available for all times of worship, committee meetings, fellowship gatherings, and study opportunities.

Through an ongoing training plan for caregivers, parents, and part-time volunteers, you can create in your nursery ministry the atmosphere Juanita is seeking. This article describes the basic steps for creating a training plan. You will find many possibilities that are adaptable to your congregation. At the end of the article is a step-by-step guide to use in your planning.

Developing a training plan includes identifying needs, prioritizing and setting goals, and planning, implementing, and evaluating training events. Evaluation leads back to identifying needs. Each step supports the preceding step, and steps will overlap during the process. For example, as goals are written, you will clarify needs, gaining a sharper focus on planning.

Step 1: Identify Needs

Determine the needs of your caregivers, parents, and part-time volunteers. In casual conversations and through observations, begin to identify areas that will benefit from training. You may hear, "I wish I could manage my child better," or, "It's been a long time since I've had CPR classes." You may observe caregivers or volunteers bringing out the same toys or playing the same games repeatedly. You may observe parents talking with one another about their child's development. These are clues to identifying needs for training in discipline, CPR, creative curriculum planning, and child development.

You can also identify training needs through a more formalized approach. Make a list of possible training topics in the form of an interest survey for caregivers. One-on-one interviews with caregivers will provide helpful insights. Ask parents and leaders of the Children's Council, Nurture Committee, or Work Area on Education to share their own personal needs. These committee members can create a mail or phone survey that polls caregivers and parents about their needs.

Prayer is a powerful tool in identifying needs. In times of meditation we are often able to see the needs of people in the congregation and community more clearly and to hear more clearly the voices of staff members, church and community leaders, and/or parents. In the midst of conflict or frustrating situations, prayer leads to a more focused understanding of the root issues and needs. Become aware of your own thoughts and longings as you pray.

Enthusiasm is generated as you plan training that truly meets the needs of the caregivers, parents, or volunteers. If individuals are enthusiastic, they will attend and will encourage their friends to attend. It makes for successful training!

Step 2: Determine Priorities

List the needs identified by caregivers and the needs identified by parents. Prioritize the two lists. Identify similarities and differences. Often the needs will overlap, either because the caregivers are parents or because they have the same concerns as the parents. On the other hand, issues such as policies and procedures or curriculum concerns relate more directly to paid or volunteer staff. This process helps determine if the priority is training for either the parents or the caregivers or training for both groups. As you and the committee review the lists, you may find that a number of individuals expressed the same needs, making those needs priorities for training among both groups.

Step 3: Develop Goals

Review the prioritized lists and write goal statements. Select the top three or four needs for focused training for this year. Ask yourself, "By identifying this need, what skill or knowledge is the learner seeking?" Decide if the training for each need will be for caregivers, for parents, or for both. Now your group is ready to write training goals.

Goals are general statements that provide direction for training and that become the basis for evaluation. Goals describe what the caregivers and parents want to learn through the training experiences. Make the goal statements specific, measurable, and attainable. Include in each goal statement when the training is going to occur, what is going to happen, and who is attending. Reread the statements to ensure that they establish goals that can be evaluated; for example, "Next spring, the Children's Council will offer behavior management training for parents and caregivers." Write a goal statement for each identified, prioritized need.

Step 4: Plan Training

Use the goal statements to plan training events. You may choose to address only one topic at first, then plan, implement, and evaluate that training experience before planning the next event. Or you may create a training plan and schedule for a full year. Advantages to planning for the year include (1) securing support for the entire plan rather than seeking it for each individual event; (2) publicizing the dates a year in advance, which can improve attendance; (3) more freedom to pursue creative approaches, such as planning with another congregation; (4) higher likelihood of successfully scheduling with preferred resource people.

In planning training events, the following questions need to be explored. They are not listed in any particular order of importance, but your answers to each will have an impact on the other questions.

What is the primary focus? Gaining information? Developing a skill? Creating support? Seeking spiritual enrichment? Informational training focuses on learning about a new procedure, a new ministry, child development, parenting styles, or behavior management. Skill development focuses on learning techniques, such as first aid, CPR, or praying with children. Support groups offer an opportunity to share joys and frustrations and to offer hints for dealing with situations.

Spiritual enrichment training focuses on ways for individuals or their families to develop a closer relationship with God. A training event could incorporate several of these foci, but it usually focuses on one primary area.

What training format will you use? Three popular formats—workshops, one-on-one training, and experiential training—offer a variety of options for caregivers. At the beginning of each year, consider providing to all paid and volunteer staff a list of local church and community workshops to be offered throughout the year, as well as suggested training videos. In addition, describe the experiential, lab training option (described below). Encourage each paid staff person to choose four to six hours of training from the options, and each volunteer to choose two to three hours. In this way, training meets the specific needs of individuals and allows for flexibility in scheduling.

Workshops can be scheduled in many possible formats: a one-day event with intense training in one topic, with the focus on information and skill building; a one-day event where attendees choose from several workshops; a weekly series of one- to two-hour sessions; quarterly workshops addressing a different topic each quarter. The workshop topic, amount of content, and leader's style and availability will help determine the best workshop format.

One-on-one training is customized to meet the specific needs of an individual, with a leader serving as a consultant. This format can be offered through personal contact or media contact. The staff member or parent can view training or parenting videos—either commercially produced or produced from your workshops—at home, then discuss the videos at a later date with a leader/consultant. Because media one-on-one training is individualized, convenient, and concise as a training format, it is growing in popularity.

Experiential training is active learning through observation and through practicing new approaches in an environment conducive to experimenting and trying new methods and activities. For example, in a model similar to a lab format, a staff person schedules a one- to two-hour session with the nursery coordinator to explore the children's needs and to plan next week's play activities and room setup. The next Sunday, the coordinator or an observation team observes the children's interaction and reaction to the planned activities. Afterward, the observers meet with the staff person to offer feedback from the observations and to discuss ways of enhancing the next session. Or, in a model similar to an apprenticeship, a trained, experienced staff person is paired with a new staff person to work together for a period of time. The trainer is responsible for teaching proper procedures, curriculum planning, and caregiving techniques, and for offering support throughout the year.

When will the workshop take place? What is the best time for most people to attend? This will usually be during a regularly scheduled program in the church, such as a monthly staff meeting or a midweek dinner with adult programming. If this is not possible, check church and community calendars as you plan. Consider the activities of your caregivers and parents to determine if a weekend or weeknight is best. If a weeknight is chosen, consider starting with a snack dinner and ending early to accommodate parents of school-age children.

How will spiritual undergirding occur? Prayer is essential. Pray for ongoing planning, for the resource person, and for participants. When the group gathers, offer a personal prayer to greet God's presence and transforming power working in and through the speaker and the participants. Incorporate a time for spiritual enrichment. Through Scripture reading, Bible study, hymn singing, moments of reflection, and prayer, participants grow closer to God and depend on God to direct and change their lives.

What resources are available for training? The term *resources* includes printed materials, media, and people with training and experience in a particular subject. The United Methodist Church provides print and media resources through Discipleship Resources, Cokesbury, The Upper Room, the Service Center, the General Board of Global Ministries, the General Board of Church and Society, and the General Board of Discipleship. Each agency/publisher provides catalogs and other instruments that list resources and people available to assist you.

Does your conference Council on Ministries office have a media loan library or a list of skilled people who lead training? Contact your conference Christian Educators Fellowship or The Fellowship of United Methodists in Music and Worship Arts for training recommendations. Is your conference or district planning training events that match your goals?

Within your community, contact directors of weekday programs, others who minister with children, the Red Cross, hospitals, and local chapters of the National Association for the Education of Young Children to learn what resources have been useful for them. Networking is key in locating available resources.

Cost must be considered in identifying available resources. The church budget is a starting point for specifying funds available for supplies, food, and a speaker's expenses and honorarium. If the budget is small, consider charging a nominal fee and inviting other churches to send their caregivers. Contact community agencies that offer training free or with a nominal contribution. Consider sharing costs with another church by planning a joint event. Another creative approach is to develop a job share with another church. Identify the areas of training you or another leader can lead and offer yourself to another congregation at no charge. Then a childcare leader in that church reciprocates by leading a training event for your parents or caregivers.

Inevitably, part of the funding discussion will focus on the issue of whether or not to pay staff for their time to attend training. This decision will have to be made based on already established expectations of staff, desire for staff to attend, and fairness. If the cost is too high, consider offering the training during regularly scheduled staff meetings, or offer training during the staff's work hours and secure parent volunteers to fill in for staff while they attend training.

Money is not the only cost factor. Consider the time and energy of the planning committee. This committee will lose interest and enthusiasm if the training plan becomes too cumbersome. Delegating tasks of planning, publicity, room arrangement, food, and cleanup will generate a feeling of congregational involvement and enthusiasm.

What methods and materials will be used in the workshops? Basically, this question will be answered by the workshop leader. In addition, however, ask the scheduled speaker to model the techniques being taught and to provide a handout of key points and, if possible, a display and bibliography of resources available for further study.

Step 5: Publicize

Publicize the training at least two months in advance. Plan on publicizing in at least three different ways. Some options are church newsletters, church bulletins, Sunday school flyers, bulletin boards, personal invitations, banners, outdoor signs, newspaper ads, and so forth. Use creative language, graphics, design, and color. The more appealing and eye-catching the publicity, the more likely it is that people will read it and get excited about it.

One clever approach used anticipation and biblical characters to publicize a workshop on storytelling in the family. Two months prior to the workshop, signs reading "It Is Coming—March 28" appeared around the church. A month prior to the workshop, the signs were replaced with silhouettes of biblical characters saying, "Tell My Story—March 28." Two weeks prior to the workshop, people dressed as the various biblical characters visited each Sunday school class to give complete details about the workshop and to encourage parents, grandparents, and caregivers to experience ways to share their faith through stories with children, young and old. This approach created enthusiasm and a sense that something exciting was going to happen.

Developing training based on identified needs, thorough planning, and excellent publicity creates contagious enthusiasm that excites people about the training.

Step 6: Implement

Create a warm, welcoming atmosphere that invites parents or caregivers to learn together. Set up the room to facilitate the movement of the workshop, promote interaction, and provide a comfortable environment. Demonstrate to staff that room setup is important in teaching. When people arrive, let posted signs direct them to the correct room and a greeter welcome them. Ask everyone to wear a nametag so that people are able to talk with one another freely.

If the training is for parents, be sure to provide childcare. Plan for easy accessibility into the building and room, an interpreter, close-captioned media resources, and large-print handouts so that people with special needs can participate fully and feel welcome. Refreshments or a simple meal promotes fellowship and informal sharing among participants.

Step 7: Evaluate

After planning and completing the training, it is easy to breathe a sigh of relief without evaluating what has happened. Evaluations are a learning experience, not a judging session. The purpose is not to evaluate the effectiveness or ineffectiveness of the planners or leaders but to determine how the group progressed toward its goal and to give feedback about the process. Through evaluations, you identify which activities promoted learning and which ventures could be reworked to create successful new ideas for the future.

Through friendly conversations and observations, you will gain insight into individuals' reactions to the training. Talk with people as they arrive to learn what piqued their interest in attending the training. Listen as they express their thoughts and insights during the training. Observe individuals' expressions, movements, and interactions. As people leave, ask about their reactions or provide evaluation forms for them to complete. These forms could include verbal or written sentence completions, a feelings checklist, thumbs up/thumbs down ratings, space for comments and suggestions, and so forth. As you and your committee review the evaluations, discuss the committee members' own thoughts and possible new approaches and future needs.

Step 8: Begin Again

The final step is to begin the cycle over again. An ongoing, well-organized training plan provides staff and parents continuous opportunities to broaden their knowledge and to feel confident in their responsibilities. And it demonstrates that the church cares enough about children to provide the skills, support, and information needed by the parents and caregivers.

Worksheet for Developing a Training Plan

Identify Needs: List the needs of parents and caregivers in your congregation.

Needs of parents	Needs of caregivers

Prioritize: Number each of the above needs in order of priority. Choose three to four needs for which you will offer training this year and write them below. Identify who will attend the training.

Develop Goals: Write a specific, measurable, attainable goal statement for each need below.

Needs that training will be provided for . . .	Who will attend	Goal
1.		
2.		
3.		
4.		

Plan: Develop and schedule the training events for the entire year. For each event, ask the following questions:

	Event 1:	Event 2:	Event 3:	Event 4:
1. What is the primary focus? (gaining information, developing a skill, creating support, or enriching spiritual life)				
2. What is the training format? (workshop, one-on-one, experiential, or a combination)				
3. When is the event scheduled?				
4. How will spiritual undergirding happen?				
5. What resources will be used—print? video? People?				
6. What methods will be used? What materials will be needed?				

Publicize: Create and implement a two-month publicity plan.

Implement: Identify how you will create a warm, welcoming environment.

Evaluate: Through informal and formal methods, identify activities that promoted learning. What should be different for the next training event?

Worksheet for Developing a Training Session

Goal: _____

Date of Event: _____

Total Budget: _____

Description: _____
_____
_____
_____
_____
_____

Event Coordinator: _____

Committee Members: _____
_____

Plans (publicity, media/equipment needs, room setup, childcare needs, event leadership needs, cleanup crews): _____
_____
_____
_____
_____
_____
_____
_____
_____
_____
_____
_____

Task	Person Responsible	Deadline	Estimated Cost	Supplies/ Resources

Training Event Evaluation Form

Training Event: _____

Date: _____

Event Coordinator: _____

Committee Members: _____

1. Did you meet the goal? Why or why not?

2. How was this training beneficial to the caregivers and/or parents?

3. How was this training not beneficial to the caregivers and/or parents?

4. What needs to be considered when planning the next training?

5. What additional information, skills, and/or support of spiritual enrichment do the caregivers and/or parents need?

Using the Articles in This Section

Most of the articles throughout this book apply to both weekday programs and Sunday programs. However, weekday programs have some unique issues. The articles in this section address some of those issues and help congregations consider whether a weekday program is something that could be added to the church's ministries with younger children.

Section Fourteen: Weekday Ministry

Contents

Other Related Articles

Noisy Weekday Church

Fran Moran

High Point, North Carolina

My church is a busy place every day of the week. There are always lots of children and lots of children sounds. As I walk down the hall, I hear the babies. Through the door I hear Tyler cooing as he's being rocked. Sarah's sitting on a colorful quilt on the floor laughing out loud as Miss Laura plays peek-a-boo with a bright orange ball. Samuel reaches toward the mobile hanging above his crib, listening to the song it plays as his eyes track the movement. Juan is exploring a rattle, using his sense of taste.

The sudden sound of a Sousa march has captured my attention as I glance toward the toddler room. Colorful scarves are being waved about as the caregivers lead the procession of enthusiastic marchers. Demetrius peeks at me from the room next door, where the two-year-olds are involved in a kaleidoscope of activity. I hear the beginning attempts of sentences and emerging words decorating the air as blue fingerpaint is smeared across shiny paper by little hands. Hats of all kinds are the "costume of the day" as firefighters, construction workers, and nurses play make-believe, mirroring the world they see. Part of the class is busy building block towers and knocking them down. Robert and Shamika are sitting in the rocking boat, singing a song together.

I hear giggles coming from the three-year-olds' room. Following the sound of laughter, I discover Beth and Madhu feeding the pet guinea pig. At the art table, Rebecca and Claire are creating their very own masterpiece with bits of ribbon and foil. Sandy encourages them to tell a story about their picture. The walls are full of colorful recollections of their day.

The four-year-olds are busy about their room, painting at the easel, building elaborate structures with blocks, creating stories using handmade puppets, and making amazing discoveries in the science center.

As I continue my walk through the halls of this busy weekday church, I also see adults arriving for a Bible study. I know they'll walk down this hall by choice because they love to see the action of God's children at play. They love the smiles and sounds of discovery, laughter, new words, and even tiny tears.

As lunchtime approaches, the sounds of cleanup time emerge. Blocks are placed with care back on the shelf. The children and teachers are singing little songs to make cleanup time fun. Friends are helping one another. I hear the sounds of stories being shared, a time to reflect on the day so far. I see eager faces anticipating the next event as they gather to wash their hands. I hear little footsteps, challenged to "make a line," but resembling more of a cloud shape. I hear chattering and murmuring as the four-year-olds socialize, taking turns at the water fountain. In the midst of all this, far from my field of vision, I hear the two-year-olds singing to the tune of "Jesus Loves Me," "God is great and God is good. Let us thank God for our food. By God's hands we all are fed. Give us, God, our daily bread. Amen." I never get tired of hearing that blessing. My weekday church is a place where children can grow and learn about themselves, about others, and about God.

It may also be a noisy place, but imagine the alternative. Take away the banging blocks and the marching band record. No brand-new words or spontaneous laughter. Imagine the smell of that quiet church—a building closed up tight all week smells faintly musty. Children bring life. A church that has been opening its arms all week to children and their families is ready on Sunday to embrace God through worship. The church facility benefits in many ways. Stewardship provided by the use of the building keeps it alive, not stagnant. The congregation benefits by participating in hands-on ministry. The midweek Bible study group, though not actively involved in the care of children, delight in their presence. They have even made some friends among the staff and children.

The church needs the children as much as the children need the church. The members of the congregation that delight in the sounds of children are blessed. Children who feel welcomed and wanted by "their" church feel kissed by God. Your church can be the grand and glorious noisy weekday church!

Making the Decision: A Weekday Ministry?

Sharon Nimtz Hill

Billings, Montana

As congregations become concerned for the children in their congregation and their community, a frequent desire is to explore a weekday ministry. With excellent nursery facilities being used only occasionally and with the increasing need of parents for weekday care for their young children, the church is a natural choice for weekday infant/toddler care.

Who Helps Make the Decision?

When an initial interest in weekday ministry arises, an appropriate group should be directed to explore and coordinate the course of action. Depending on the size of your church, any combination of the following may be involved: pastor, nursery coordinator, Christian education director, deacon, diaconal minister, children's council chair, education committee representative, administrative council representative, representatives of other weekday programs, trustee, parents. It is helpful for the congregation if regular progress reports are made public. Listening/discussion meetings for the entire congregation may be welcomed and helpful.

Communicate clearly and frequently. Although the final decision must be made by the administrative council, total congregational support is needed for a successful weekday ministry.

What Questions Need to Be Asked?
Basic Questions and Licensing

Is there a need for a weekday childcare program? How should this need be determined? Why does the church want to do this? How would a weekday program relate to the church? What kind of program is proposed? What will be the facility's statement of purpose?

Who would oversee the operation of the program? Would a separate board of directors make the policies for the program? How would this be organized?

What are the requirements for the program to be state licensed? What are the specific space requirements? What is the staff/child ratio? Are fire and health inspections necessary? What are the local build-ing codes? Can the program be located anywhere in the church building? Will building renovation be needed? When is relicensing needed?

Facilities

How many rooms are available for the program to use? What ages would be in the same space? Is there sufficient room for mobile and nonmobile children? Is there space for diapering, napping, active play, eating, and storage?

Is there adequate heating, cooling, ventilation, and lighting? Are heating pipes covered? Are heater units child-safe? Are all rooms safe? Is the facility free of asbestos? Has nontoxic paint been used? Has the water been tested for lead content? Is the water heater set at a temperature that ensures that young children cannot be burned? Are smoke detectors tested regularly? Is a sprinkler system necessary? What pest control system is safe for use around young children?

Is there a water source for caregivers to wash their hands, mix formula, and wash/ rinse/sanitize dishes? Is there a refrigerator located conveniently to the room? Is there a way for food and formula to be heated?

Is there a bathroom for toilet training? What will be the program's philosophy about toilet training, and how will that affect the facilities? Is the bathroom able to accommodate more than one child at a time? Are there proper disposal areas for diapers and garbage?

Is there space for each child to have a cubby hole labeled with his or her name for storing diapers, wipes, and a change of clothes, and space there or elsewhere to store each child's diaper bag, coat, hat, mittens, boots, and papers to go home?

Where will children sleep? Is there room for the children to have individual cribs? Will mats or cots be used for sleeping? Is there storage space for them?

Is there an area of some privacy designated for mothers who come in to breastfeed their children?

Is there a place for isolating children who become ill during the day until their parents can pick them up?

How will communication be handled? Will there be a parent bulletin board? a message center for caregivers? a bulletin board for information for the congregation? Is equipment available for these communication methods?

Is there a telephone in the room or in close proximity for emergencies and for calling parents? Will the program have its own number, or will calls be forwarded from the church office?

Is there an indoor gym? Is there a safe outside play space?

Is there an office area for keeping records and files? Can access to confidential information be controlled? Is there a break room for staff?

How will people enter and exit the weekday facility? Where will staff and parents park their vehicles? How will this affect regular weekday church activities?

Funding and Financial Operations

Will the program be self-sufficient, wholly church-funded, or a combination? Will the church provide rent-free space and utilities? Will the program provide partial support for utilities and room usage?

Will the program use the church's tax identification number?

How could a scholarship fund be established? For what will it be used? How will grants be discovered and written? Is the program able to apply for church foundation money? What kinds of fundraising will be done? How will fundraising be coordinated so that it is not in conflict with a similar church activity? How will the start-up funding be provided?

Will the church or the program manage the finances and bookkeeping? Who will handle the payroll and pay the bills? How will FICA and Worker's Compensation be handled? Who will control the money? Will an audit be required? If so, by whom and how often?

Will a computer be available for parent communication? for financial records? for student records?

What are the insurance and liability needs? Is the program covered on the church policy? Does the policy have a sexual misconduct rider? What recommendations does your insurance company make for risk management?

Is the program accountable to the church, the church board, or the program's board? What is the procedure for the groups reporting to each other?

Who will determine the budget? Will there be a registration fee? Is it refundable if the child does not attend? Will there be other fees? How frequently will parents pay the fees? Will there be an hourly rate, a weekly rate, or a monthly rate? Will there be a sibling discount? Will credit be given when a child is sick and

unable to attend? How will parents be reminded that the next payment is due? Who will contact parents who do not pay on time?

Program

Will the program be in session year-round or just during the school year? What days and hours will it be open? What procedures will be used when the program is open different hours from the church?

Will children be able to attend both full-time and part-time? How will children be scheduled to attend? Will the program be open to children in the community or only to those associated with the church? Will the program accept children from families receiving federal subsidies?

How will the program be advertised? Who will handle public relations? Is an open house planned?

What curriculum will be used? How does it differ from that used in Sunday school? Are religious teachings consistent with the church's theological position? Who will guide curriculum development?

How will the program's calendar be coordinated with the church calendar?

Staff

Who will be responsible for the day-to-day operation of the program? Who will prepare an employee policies handbook? Who will write job descriptions for the various positions?

How many staff will be needed? Who will interview and hire the initial staff? What will their qualifications need to be? What criteria/requirements will be considered: college degree? CDA (Child Development Associate) Credential? high school diploma? parenting? college enrollment? practical experience? other? What paperwork will staff be required to complete for employment? Will this include a statement of health, written letters of reference, authorization for release of information from police files, and a tuberculosis test?

Will there be a probationary period of employment? What method of staff evaluation will be used? How often will this be done? What will the termination policy be?

How much will staff get paid, and what benefits will be provided? Will staff hours depend on the enrollment of children? Who will substitute for sick staff?

How will the staff be trained? Will the program pay for staff to attend workshops that provide additional training? Will CPR and first-aid training be required?

What is the dress code? Will the program provide smocks for the staff?

Policies

Will communication with parents be handled via written notes, monthly newsletters, written progress reports, conferences, telephone calls, or personal visits? What will be included in the parent handbook?

What methods of behavior guidance and discipline will be used?

What emergency numbers will be posted by the phone? What emergency procedures will be needed? What will the plans be in case of fire, tornado, hurricane, or a major snow or ice storm? What will be done about any intruders? How will the security needs of the staff, children, and building be met?

Will children bring their own lunches? Will the program provide nutritious meals and snacks? What kind of refrigeration, storage, or cooking facilities will be needed to support these policies?

What provisions will be made for children with food allergies or milk intolerance? What arrangements will be made for skin sensitivities to soap, wipes, scented detergent and fabric softeners, or paper products? Will cloth diapers be permitted?

Will children go for walks? Will strollers be available for younger children? Will a walking rope be used for older children?

What is the policy that determines if a child is too ill to attend? How will parents be notified if their child gets sick while at childcare? What is the health policy? What immunizations do children need? How will these be recorded? What will be the policy for accepting, storing, and administering over-the-counter and prescription medicines? Will covered containers for refrigerated and nonrefrigerated medicines be kept within the room? What provisions will be made to keep them safely away from children? Are written accident reports necessary?

What will be the policies for dropping off and picking up children at the facility? Will parents sign their children in and out, or will staff mark attendance? Will children's records clearly indicate who is allowed to pick the children up from the facility? Will the records clearly state custody arrangements with parents in situations of divorce or separation?

Equipment and Supplies

Will the church provide necessary equipment for diapering, napping, active play, eating, and storage? Will equipment and consumable supplies be shared by Sunday and weekday staff? Who will pay for what? Who will be responsible for repairs or replacements?

Can cribs be provided that meet safety requirements for width of space between slats and other safety requirements?

What other equipment will be necessary?

Will toys and puzzles be carefully inspected for small parts that could be easily swallowed? Will broken and rough-edged items be removed from use?

What supplies will the program provide? Will parents provide any supplies?

Maintenance

Who will be responsible for maintenance and cleaning? Where will cleaning supplies be kept? Who will do the laundry? Is the floor carpeted? Can it be vacuumed daily and cleaned on a regular basis? Will furniture need to be moved within the room to satisfy either the Sunday or weekday program? Who will do this?

What provisions will be made for cleaning toys and equipment? Will all toys (including stuffed animals) be completely washable? Will rest mats have removable, washable covers? Will mats be made of materials that can be disinfected?

Where Are the Answers to Be Found?

The Book of Resolutions of The United Methodist Church—2000 contains the policy statement "Childcare and the Church" (pages 172–178), which outlines the responsibility of all United Methodist churches involved in weekday ministries. A copy of this policy can also be found at www.gbod.org/children/articles/childcarepolicy.html.

The Department of Family Services, the Human Resources Development Council, the Department of Health and Human Services, the fire marshal, the Resource and Referral Agency, or a similar organization in your community can provide a copy of licensing requirements. The health department provides information about health practices, immunizations, and inspections. The fire department provides information about safety, codes, and inspections. The state agency that relates to the United States Department of Agriculture Food and Nutrition Service (Child and Adult Care Food Program, CACFP) informs programs of nutritional requirements.

Consider collaboration with a nearby program for three-, four-, and five-year-olds that has an unmet need of caring for younger children. Perhaps the need can be met by your church.

Groups within the church (such as United Methodist Women or United Methodist Men) may be able to subsidize the program to keep the fee scale lower or may be able to make some of the items that are too costly to purchase for a beginning program. They may be able to provide a wide variety of support for the weekday program. "Rockin' and Readin' Grandmas and Grandpas" would be a real plus for a weekday nursery program.

A written shared-space agreement between the church and the program would help alleviate potential misunderstandings. Ongoing, open communication among Sunday and weekday people who use the same space is vital.

Materials that focus on specific types of programs are available from Cokesbury, 800-672-1789. Numerous publications describing developmentally appropriate programs, curriculum, and room environments are valuable and readily found in early childhood catalogs. Professional organizations such as the Ecumenical Child Care Network and the National Association for the Education of Young Children (NAEYC) provide additional resources and information. Local childcare associations can provide expertise on many issues. Check with your annual conference or regional office for possible statewide denominational weekday ministry groups.

Setting Up a Weekday Ministry

Susan A. Patterson-Sumwalt
Denver, Colorado

Your church has decided to begin a weekday ministry for young children. Good for you! This can be one of the most exciting ministries for your church. It also fills a great need for parents of young children, as quality care for infants and toddlers is hard to find. When you begin this ministry, you want to start with everything in place. Refinements can be made as time goes on, but you should begin with the highest level of quality possible.

First, contact the licensing agency. In most states it is the Department of Social Services, childcare licensing division. In some states, municipal (city or county) social service departments are responsible for licensing. Write or call for guidelines and regulations for licensing the age group you plan to serve.

Regulations differ from state to state and for different age groups. Unless your ministry includes having parents present on the premises during operating hours, it must be approved by the Department of Social Services. These regulations are tedious and take an extensive amount of time to complete. They are, however, in the best interest of the children's health and welfare. Licensing agents are often assigned to help programs get started. Utilize these people to guide you through the process.

Consider the following questions in planning and developing your weekday ministry for infants, toddlers, and twos:

1. Will your weekday ministry be a Parent's Day Out, a daycare, a play school, or a parent cooperative? If it is a daycare, will it provide full-time, part-time, and/or occasional care?

2. Will the weekday ministry be a ministry of the church, or will the church simply lease space to someone else who runs the program?

3. What is the purpose of the ministry? How does it fit into the overall purpose and vision of the church?

4. What congregational committees need to hear of this ministry plan: children's council, education, family life, long-range planning, trustees, council on ministries, administrative council? At what stage does the information go from one committee to the next? Who needs updates? How frequently?

5. What committees are planning, implementing, and evaluating the weekday ministry? Are there subcommittees? Who is writing policies, raising funds, handling publicity, articulating the vision? Who are the early childhood education experts? Who is researching other weekday ministries? Who will make up the board of directors?

6. Will the weekday ministry be incorporated? Will the finances and books be kept separate from the general church accounts? Will the books be open and audited by the church? Will the ministry be subsidized by the church budget or self-funded? Will the church charge for utilities/building maintenance? Will funds be paid to the trustees for increased liability insurance? How much liability insurance is enough? Will lawyers and accountants be consulted? What are the budget priorities? Who will determine the priorities, and how?

7. What type of staff will be needed: director, associate, assistant, co-teachers, specialty staff, substitute teachers? What education/experience levels will be required? What about administrative support and custodial support? How will staff training be provided? Will staff be church employees (with the advantage of participation in conference benefits such as pension and insurance)? What benefits will you provide: pension, medical and life insurance, vacation, holidays, sick days, continuing education, childcare, Social Security, Worker's Compensation? Will employment policies encourage long-term employment, promote staff morale, provide fair compensation?

8. Will church members receive special considerations, such as lower tuition and priority registration?

9. How will this ministry relate to other ministries that share the same space? How can they work cooperatively? Will equipment and supplies be shared? If so, what responsibilities will each group have toward maintaining order and inventory? Will

there be a common supply and resource room? Will outdoor equipment and library resources be shared? "Turf" can be an emotional issue. Encourage Christian cooperation and supportive relationships! What policies will be set for sharing space? (What if the United Methodist Women need childcare at the same time and same place as weekday ministry?)

10. What are the perceived and real benefits of weekday ministry to your church? Will this program be a presence and witness to the support of young children in the community? Will it meet needs of parents with young children? Will it be a way to reach out to new members? Will it be a source of Christian education for young children? Will it be a place that offers parents an opportunity for Christian fellowship?

11. How will this weekday ministry be integrated with other weekday programs and ministries of the church? with Sunday worship, Sunday school, church socials? Are church members invited to fundraisers for weekday ministries? Is the weekday ministry staff represented at church staff meetings? Do regular articles about weekday ministries appear in church publications?

As you can see, there are many issues to address. In the long run, however, the success of the weekday ministry relies on the careful, thoughtful planning and preparation completed before the first teacher is hired or the first child comes through the door. Integration with existing church programs and ongoing communication among the weekday ministry staff, church staff and laity, and parents are crucial to ensuring that the weekday program and the church are indeed supporting young children and their parents.

Accessing Community Resources

Chris Evan-Schwartz

Cedar Rapids, Iowa

Communities are often rich in untapped resources that could benefit your weekday ministry. Think broadly and creatively about how resources might be pulled together to benefit your program. Think about new ways of working with existing agencies.

Who do you know? Are members of your congregation working in settings that might support your weekday ministry? Do you have neighbors associated with community groups that might contribute to your project? What about your school system, where all these young children will be headed in the future?

To collaborate means to come together to work toward a common vision. It means to share resources, knowledge, and skills. At its best, it can mean creating networks to share ideas and solve problems, eliminating duplication, and developing strategies to provide for the needs of children and families. Collaboration can provide ongoing relationships that inspire and support growth. The synergy generated through collaborations can work to reduce stress and provide ongoing strength for the work of ministry.

Establishing Collaborative Relationships

First, you must know yourself. That means knowing your plan. What is the scope of your weekday ministry? Are you planning to focus on a particular age group? Will you provide parent education groups? Will children with special needs participate in your program? What is your timeline? Knowing yourself also means being aware of how you work with other people. Do you prefer to talk with people by phone, in person, via e-mail, or through written correspondence? What do you have to offer others? What skills and talents might you share with others in the community?

Second, you must know your potential collaborator. What history does the individual, group, or agency have for working with others? How is the agency connected with other groups in the community? Are there common threads that weave community groups together? Who are the key people in the organization? What ties do you have to anyone

in the group, directly or indirectly? Do you know someone who could introduce you to a key person? Examine the mission statement or the stated goals or purpose of the group. How do these relate to your developing ministry? What connections can you make? Is the organizational style formal or informal? What protocol should be followed in working with the agency? Explore the potential collaborator. Do this through active research. Examine written material from the group. Attend open meetings and introduce yourself when appropriate. Informally explore possibilities that might connect with your mission. Be open, receptive, and interested in the work of the group. Take the time to affirm the group's contribution to the community. Follow up with a letter or note to a key person you met. Plant the seeds for cooperation.

Next, work to build a relationship with a potential collaborator. Articulate how working in partnership will benefit everyone. For instance, in collaboration with a middle or senior high school, you provide an opportunity for young people to give to the community and to increase their awareness of community needs.

One childcare center worked with teachers at a middle school. Students wrote and illustrated original works that they shared with young children in the center. The young children at the childcare center became a real audience for the middle school students.

Another collaboration involved a church providing free space for an in-service session for teachers in a nearby school, giving the teachers a fresh setting away from their building. The school then included the church's weekday ministry childcare staff in their in-service training on conflict resolution. Work to eliminate barriers and to heal issues of turf protection that interfere with productive relationships. The possibilities are endless!

Potential Community Collaborators

Whether you are in the planning stage or implementation stage of a weekday ministry program, now is the time to stop and brainstorm possible resources in your community. Consider funding resources and personnel. Think broadly and without judgment. Let one idea lead to another. Brainstorm not only a list of potential collaborators but also possibilities for support from each. Be creative. Reach high and wide!

Below is a list of community resources that have been integrated in other communities who are working to provide comprehensive programming for young children. Let the list stimulate your thinking about your setting. Think about how your ministry might build upon the strengths of each group's particular mission, and about how you might work together.

- State and county agencies
- Hospitals (Food service departments might contract to cater meals. Students might give health checks.)
- Schools (elementary schools, middle schools, high schools, junior colleges, colleges)
- Head Start, childcare centers, preschool programs
- Other churches and synagogues
- Public libraries
- Education agencies (may be able to observe children for developmental needs or provide needed special services to families)
- Health care providers (may set up an immunization clinic at your site)
- United Way
- Girl Scouts, Boy Scouts, Camp Fire Boys and Girls, 4-H, YMCA, YWCA, and other civic youth-serving organizations
- Foundations (funding resources)
- Planned Parenthood
- Hot lines, crisis lines
- WIC (Women, Infants, and Children nutritional program)
- Symphony orchestras
- Special education services
- Neighborhood organizations
- Local corporations
- National Association for the Education of Young Children
- Ecumenical Childcare Network
- Food pantries
- Homeless shelters
- Community service programs for youth in detention
- Parent/teacher associations (PTA's, PTO's, PTSA's)
- Businesses
- National professional and service organizations
- United Methodist Women
- United Methodist Men
- United Methodist Youth
- Youth Sunday school classes
- Adult Sunday school classes
- Municipal parks and recreation departments
- Family Resource Coalition
- Children's Defense Fund
- Media (radio, television, newspaper)
- Sports clubs
- Local ethnic groups
- Community centers, sports/entertainment complexes

Keys to Successful Collaborations

Find out what resources are available in your community. Do your homework. Research through the phone book, media, interagency groups, the public library, and existing programs. Survey any program or group that might have a connection with young children, always thinking creatively about ways you might partner.

Assess the needs of your weekday program. Critical components of any program for young children include health, nutrition, family support, building self-esteem, cultural identity, and high quality learning experiences. What further support does your staff need in order to provide developmentally appropriate programming?

Initiate relationships with potential collaborators. Be tenacious. Find ways to "get in the door" of agencies or groups that could contribute to your efforts. Approach others with a positive attitude, a vision of working together, and the idea of reciprocity. Build on the strengths of existing groups and be willing to share your resources, skills, and knowledge. Consider all the possibilities of working together!

Take the time to market your weekday ministry. Find ways to let others know about your plans and efforts. Highlight successes through newspaper articles, newsletters, and television and radio interviews. Broadcasters are required to run public service announcements and are always looking for fresh ones. Create a brochure to distribute in a variety of settings. Offer to give presentations at conferences, local interagency meetings, civic group meetings, or church group meetings. Use these opportunities to let others know about your ministry and dreams for the future.

Have faith! Have faith that collaborations will work for the benefit of all the children and families in your community. Have patience and perseverance in establishing positive relationships. Create visions of successfully engaging your community in your ministry.

Using the Items in This Section

This section includes forms and posters to be used or adapted as needed. Remember that you will need to keep information sheets updated in order for them to remain useful to your ministry.

The forms can be used in a variety of ways. Teachers, coordinators, caregivers, and nursery home visitors will need access to the information provided. Display the posters in appropriate places within your nursery facilities.

The Volunteer Application Form and Record of Contact With an Applicant's Reference are designed to aid your recordkeeping with regard to interviewing volunteers for caregiving in the nursery. Similar forms for hiring paid staff will need to be customized to meet the needs of your state. Other childcare professionals in your community and your church's legal counsel will be able to offer help in designing forms.

Copies of the Report Form for Injuries Occurring in the Nursery and the Report Form for Suspected Sexual or Physical Abuse should be kept within the nursery facilities. Each time there is an injury or a reported abuse, these forms should be completed as soon as possible. The reports should then be given to a church official, with a copy kept in the director's secured file. Legal counsel should be sought whenever such a form is completed.

The Nursery Home Visitor Report Form will help organize visits to homes of families.

Section Fifteen: Forms

Contents

Other Related Articles

Child Information Sheet

Today's date: _____ Full name of child: _____

Name child is called: _____ Date of birth: _____

Is child baptized? ___ Yes ___ No

Address: _____

Home phone: _____ Fax: _____ E-mail: _____

Mother's name: _____

Address: _____

Work phone: _____ Cellular phone: _____

Father's name: _____

Address: _____

Work phone: _____ Cellular phone: _____

Who lives in the home with the child? (name, relationship to child, age) _____

_____

Has the child been in group care before? ___ Yes ___ No   If yes, where? _____

_____

Was this group care a positive experience? ___ Yes ___ No   Please explain: _____

_____

_____

Does the child take regular naps? ___ Yes ___ No   If yes, what are his or her regular nap times? _____

_____

If an infant, is the child ___ breastfed ___ bottle-fed?   If breastfed, will the child willingly take bottles? _____

_____

If a toddler, what are some of the child's favorite foods? _____

_____

Does the child have allergies? ___ Yes ___ No   If yes, to what is the child allergic? _____

_____

Is the child on any kind of regular medication? ___ Yes ___ No   If yes, describe: _____

_____

Does the child have any fears? ___ Yes ___ No   If yes, describe: _____

_____

Describe some of the activities your child enjoys: _____

_____

What words would you use to describe your child? _____

_____

Is there anything else your child's teachers need to know to best meet the needs of your child? _____

_____

_____

_____

_____

Add additional comments on back of page.

Sign-In Sheet

Today's date: _____

Child's name: _____

Parent's name: _____

Location of parent:_____

_____

Comments about the child: _____

_____

_____

_____

Time arrived: _____

Time picked up: _____

Signature of parent picking up child: _____

- - - - - - - - - ✂ -

Sign-In Sheet

Today's date: _____

Child's name: _____

Parent's name: _____

Location of parent:_____

_____

Comments about the child: _____

_____

_____

_____

Time arrived: _____

Time picked up: _____

Signature of parent picking up child: _____

Daily Information Sheet for Infant

Child's name: _____
Today's date: _____

(For Parent to Complete)

Bottles
Number brought: _____ Contents: _____
Last bottle taken at: _____
Special instructions: _____
_____

Food
Item(s) brought: _____
Last fed at: _____
Special instructions: _____
_____

(For Caregiver to Complete for Child)

What I Did Today: _____
_____
_____

Bottles/Food
Time given: _____ Contents: _____ Amount taken: _____
Time given: _____ Contents: _____ Amount taken: _____
Time given: _____ Contents: _____ Amount taken: _____
Time given: _____ Contents: _____ Amount taken: _____

Diaper Changes   ## Naps
Time: _____ Dry   Wet   BM   Time: _____ How long? _____
Time: _____ Dry   Wet   BM   Time: _____ How long? _____
Time: _____ Dry   Wet   BM   Time: _____ How long? _____
Time: _____ Dry   Wet   BM   Time: _____ How long? _____
Time: _____ Dry   Wet   BM
Time: _____ Dry   Wet   BM
Time: _____ Dry   Wet   BM

Comments from caregiver: _____
_____
_____
_____

Signature of caregiver: _____

We have enjoyed caring for your infant today. We hope our care records help you in knowing how your child's day has been. If there are any additional questions, please call the caregiver who has signed above.

Daily Information Sheet for Toddler or Two-Year-Old

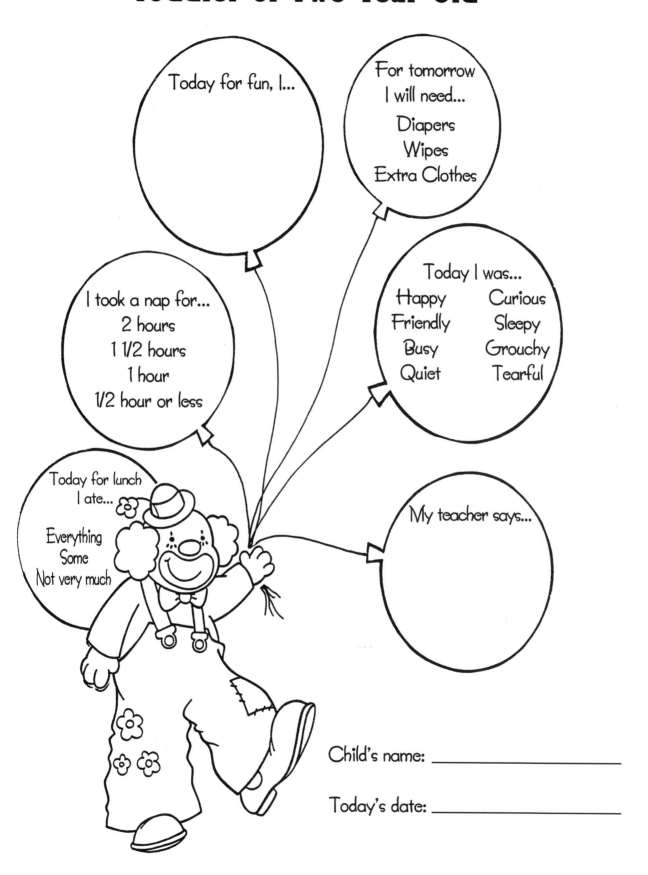

Today for fun, I...

For tomorrow
I will need...
Diapers
Wipes
Extra Clothes

I took a nap for...
2 hours
1 1/2 hours
1 hour
1/2 hour or less

Today I was...
Happy   Curious
Friendly   Sleepy
Busy   Grouchy
Quiet   Tearful

Today for lunch
I ate...

Everything
Some
Not very much

My teacher says...

Child's name: _____

Today's date: _____

Procedure for Changing Diaper

1. **Gather necessary supplies.**

2. **Clean diapering surface.**

3. **Wash hands.**

4. **Cover diapering surface with clean paper.**

5. **Put on disposable gloves.**

6. **Place child on diapering surface.**

7. **Remove soiled diaper.**

8. **Clean child's diaper area thoroughly with disposable wipes.**

9. **Dispose of diaper appropriately. (Place cloth diaper in plastic bag, or secure disposable diaper folded inward. Place in plastic-lined container and close lid.)**

10. **Remove and dispose of gloves.**

11. **Put clean diaper on child.**

12. **Clean child's hands and face, using separate cloths.**

13. **Remove child from diaper area.**

14. **Clean diapering surface.**

15. **Return supplies to proper storage area.**

16. **WASH HANDS!**

Procedure for Washing Hands

1. Use soap and running water.

2. Rub all hand surfaces vigorously.

3. Rinse well.

4. Dry hands with a paper towel.

5. Turn off water using paper towel.

6. Dispose of paper towel properly.

When to Wash Hands:

- Upon arrival each day

- Before eating or handling food

- Before feeding a child

- After handling any body fluids

- After wiping noses, mouths, sores

Sanitizing Solution

	BLEACH	WATER
Large amount:	1/4 cup	1 gallon
Small amount:	1 Tablespoon	1 quart

- **Mix fresh each day.**

- **Use solution in a spray bottle.**

- **Leave on for at least two minutes.**

- **Allow to air dry when possible.**

Volunteer Application Form

The information obtained on this form is for internal use by this local church only. Please provide all information requested. You may continue on the back of this sheet.

Name: _____ Date of Birth: _____

Address: _____

City: _____ State: _____ Zip: _____

Home Phone: _____ Business Phone: _____ Fax: _____

Position applied for: _____ Current driver's license number: _____

Current occupation, employer, and business address: _____

_____

Time at this employment: _____ years _____ months

Names and addresses of other churches you have attended regularly during the past five years:

_____

_____

_____

Name/address/telephone number of references who may be contacted:

Pastor: _____

Employer: _____

Personal: _____

Describe your background working with the program and/or age group requested. (Include information about church-related, volunteer, and paid experience you may have.) _____

_____

_____

Groups in which you are currently active (church, civic, professional, and so forth): _____

_____

Circle yes or no for each of the following questions:

Have you ever been convicted of any criminal offense?	Yes	No
Have you ever been charged with or convicted of child neglect or abuse?	Yes	No
Have any complaints or allegations of misconduct involving children ever been made against you?	Yes	No
Have you been convicted of the possession, use, or sale of drugs?	Yes	No
Within the past thirty days have you abused alcohol and/or legal or illegal drugs?	Yes	No
Have you been convicted of or pleaded guilty to a traffic offense within the last five years?	Yes	No

Please explain fully on the back of this page any YES answers to the above questions.

In addition to the above, is there any fact or circumstance involving you or your background that would call into question your being entrusted with the supervision, guidance, and care of young people? Explain.

The information I have provided may be verified by contacting people or organizations that may have information concerning me. I hereby release and agree to hold harmless from liability any person or organization that provides information, and this release may be sent to any reference. I also agree to hold harmless _____ United Methodist Church and the officers, employees, and volunteers thereof from any use of this application or information. I waive any right that I may have to inspect references provided on my behalf. I certify that the information I have provided is true and correct. If it is found that the answers given are untrue, I understand that it may be cause for dismissal.

Signature _____ Date _____

Record of Contact With an Applicant's Reference

Please complete one form for each reference contacted.

CONFIDENTIAL

1. Name of applicant: _____

2. Reference or church contacted (If a church or organization, identify both the church or organization and the person or pastor contacted.): _____

   _____

   _____

   _____

3. Date and time of contact (List each time if more than once.): _____

   _____

4. Person contacting the reference or church: _____

   _____

5. Method of contact (telephone, personal conversation, letter; Attach any letters.):_____

   _____

6. Summary of conversation (Summarize the reference's or pastor's remarks concerning the applicant's fitness and suitability for youth or children's work.):_____

   _____

   _____

   _____

   _____

   _____

   _____

Signature:_____

Position: _____

Date: _____

Report Form for Injuries Occurring in the Nursery

Today's date: _____ Time report recorded: _____

Injured's name: _____ Age: _____

Address: _____ City: _____ State: _____ Zip: _____

Phone: _____

Parents or guardians of injured: _____

Date and time parent or guardian contacted: _____

Location of accident: _____

Date and time of accident: _____ Staff person in charge at time of accident: _____

Brief description of accident: _____

_____

_____

Other children involved in accident: _____

Other adult or youth witnesses to accident: _____

Action taken: _____

_____

_____

Medical attention required: _____

_____

Treating medical personnel and/or facility: _____

Follow-up required: _____

_____

Insurance-related action: _____

_____

Name of insurance company: _____

Policy term: _____

Agent: _____ Date: _____

Report prepared by: _____

Action taken: _____

_____

Report Form for Suspected Sexual or Physical Abuse

Staff person completing report: _____

Child's name: _____ Age: _____

Parents/guardians of child: _____

Date, time, and location of incident: _____

Brief description of incident: _____

_____

Date, time, and location of initial conversation with child: _____

Notes of conversation: _____

_____

Name of person accused of abuse: _____

Date, time, and location of initial conversation with accused (if staff member): _____

Notes of conversation: _____

_____

Date, time, and location or date and time of phone call of initial contact with parent/guardian: _____

_____

Person spoken to: _____

Notes of conversation: _____

_____

Date and time of call to child protective services agency: _____

Person contacted: _____

Notes of conversation: _____

_____

Date, time, and location of call to law enforcement agency: _____

Person contacted: _____

Notes of conversation: _____

_____

Nursery Home Visitor Report Form

Child's name: _____ Date of birth: _____ Date of baptism: _____

Parents' names: _____

Home phone: _____ E-mail address: _____

Address: _____

City, State, Zip: _____

Mother's work phone: _____ Father's work phone: _____

Directions to home: _____

_____

_____

Siblings (names and ages): _____

_____

Comments: _____

_____

_____

_____

VISIT RECORD

AGE OF CHILD	MONTH AND YEAR FOR CONTACT	ACTUAL DATE OF CONTACT	REMARKS	FOLLOW-UP
BEFORE BIRTH				
AT BIRTH				

Using the Leaflets in This Section

The leaflets in this section are designed to provide ongoing support to parents of young children in raising their children in a Christian home. Each leaflet contains a brief article, a suggested Scripture reading, some things for the parents to think about, a prayer for parents, and a prayer for children. Each leaflet fits on one page, leaving the back free for information from your congregation and, if appropriate, for the names and address of the family to whom the leaflet is being sent.

Some possibilities for the back of the leaflet include
- church name, address, telephone number, staff list;
- information about childcare givers: names, interests, thoughts about children, training, and so forth;
- announcements of church activities that might be of interest to families with young children;
- nursery policies of interest to parents;
- name and telephone number of Nursery Home Visitor.

Plan for who will prepare the leaflets and when they will be prepared (first of each month? once a quarter? as needed?). Decide how the leaflets will be distributed. They may be mailed, delivered personally, or inserted in a packet of other information.

Remember, the quality of the leaflet will make a statement to the family about the quality of the church nursery. Be sure the text and graphics match what you want to convey about your congregation and nursery. Hint: Cover up the page numbers before copying the pages.

Section Sixteen: Parent Support Leaflets

Contents

Other Related Articles

Your Church Welcomes Your New Baby

Dear Parents or Parent:

Congratulations! You have just experienced one of God's best miracles: the birth of a baby, your baby. This precious life was born into this world as a living, breathing person—unique, unlike anyone else in this whole wide world.

Every three months you will be receiving a leaflet similar to this one from your church family. With these leaflets come our love and care as you begin a life adventure with a new child of God entrusted to you. You will find in each of these leaflets a brief article, helpful guidelines for parents, a suggested Scripture reading, and two prayers—one for you to pray for yourself as a parent and one for you to pray for or with your child. The content is designed to help you raise your child in a nurturing, Christian home. May these resources be a blessing in your life.

From Your Church

Scripture

Read Luke 2:25-40. This Scripture passage describes Mary and Joseph taking the baby Jesus to the Temple.

Some Things to Think About

The most effective teaching parents do is modeling. If prayer is an important, natural part of your life, your child will sense that and will make it an important part of daily living. When you stand over the bed of your newborn, marveling at the miracle of birth and life, speak your prayer of thanks. Get into the habit of praying aloud in the presence of your newborn before your child can even understand your words. Thank God for your child. Pray that God will help you to be a loving parent. Pray for your child. Your child will gradually understand that prayer is important to you, and prayer will begin to be a part of your child's own life.

A Prayer for You

Dear God, you have given us a marvelous gift in this child. In this baby's face we see your love. The days are often long and the nights short. Grant me the patience and wisdom to be a loving parent. Amen.

A Prayer for Your Child

May God watch over you when you sleep and when you wake, when you cry and when you laugh, when you play and when you rest. As you grow, may you always know that you are loved, by me and by God. Amen.

Now That Your Child Is Three Months Old

Routines in the life of an infant, such as changing clothes, feeding, and changing diapers, are important parts of the day for your child. Talk to your baby. Explain what you are doing and what will happen next. You are your child's first teacher. Make each interaction with your child a special time. Make happy sounds. Sing (even off-key!). Say happy things about the day. Share your love with a smile, a kiss, and those important words of communication that will help your baby's language development.

Begin now to tell your child: "I love you!" "God loves you." "God made you special!" "I am so glad God made us a family!"

Scripture

Read Psalm 33. This psalm reminds us of the goodness and greatness of God.

Some Things to Think About

We know that adults build strong muscles with exercise and weight-lifting. But have you ever thought about how a baby's muscles develop? The large muscles of the neck, trunk, legs, and arms develop before the small muscles of the wrist, hand, and fingers, so your child will be walking long before he or she is drawing and writing. Muscles also develop from the head down to the toes, so your baby was able to lift his or her head long before he or she will be able to walk. Muscles also develop from the center of the body outward to the extremities. For example, your baby rolls over before sitting up. Isn't it wonderful to watch your baby grow into an independent young child? God's plan for growth and development is miraculous. Thank you, God, for your dependable plan!

A Prayer for You

Ever-attentive God, keep me focused on the partnership I have with you in nurturing my child. As cries of need for food and attention come in the night, let them remind me that you hear and come to my need as a parent as well. Teach me the loving patience you so wonderfully show to your creation; in Jesus' name. Amen.

A Prayer for Your Child

Creator God, what a wonder you created in this child that I hold in my arms. The fingers that curl around mine are such a marvel. Thank you for each breath you give to this tiny miracle. I am awed by this bundle of love. May this child grow in the wisdom of your light, in the comfort of your love. Amen.

Now That Your Child Is Six Months Old

This is an extraordinary time in your family's life. What a heavy responsibility and what a joy-filled responsibility is this young life that is your child, given to you by God and placed in your care. Your child looks to you with eyes of trust, knowing that you will meet physical, psychological, social, and spiritual needs. Take a few moments each day to forget the worries of the world around you and to concentrate on the world of you and your child. Look into your child's eyes. Smile. Laugh. Play. Pray. Be. God has given you these moments. Be thankful!

Scripture

Read Psalm 100. This is a psalm of thanksgiving. As you read it, think about all that you are thankful for.

Some Things to Think About

As your child grows and matures, the world around takes on new meaning and relevance. You are recognized as a "very special person." What a joy the first time your child says "Ma-ma" or "Da-da." With the joy of recognition come added burdens. The child, previously happy to go into anyone's open arms, now may become shy, selecting only those who are very familiar. Appreciate this as a new stage of development for your child. Help your child depend on you and, at the same time, know that being with someone other than you is okay, too.

When your child suddenly becomes anxious around strangers or when you leave, remember that this is a natural part of your child's development. Ask the person meeting your child to try getting your child interested in a toy or activity first, rather than trying to make direct physical contact. Let the child get acquainted slowly. This stage of development will pass. Be patient.

A Prayer for You

Gracious God, giver and sustainer of life, I am so very grateful for your love made visible to me in this child. Guide me as I love and nurture (*name of child*) in the faith. Strengthen me for the task ahead, give me your wisdom as I prepare to answer questions, give direction to one so young and unaware, and give me the peace of your presence in my life daily. I pray in the name of Jesus, your Son and my Savior. Amen.

A Prayer for Your Child

Dear God, thank you for the wonder and delight that come through my child. What a joy it is to watch (*name of child*) discover a new world. In the safety and security of a loving family, learning and exploration come with every waking moment. Help me provide the safety and acceptance (*name of child*) needs to grow in your love. In the name of your Son, Jesus, I pray. Amen.

Now That Your Child Is Nine Months Old

Children will learn more in the first three years of life than ever again in such a brief time span. Their sometimes apparently aimless play has great purpose. The child from birth to three is learning how to move, how to communicate, how to manipulate the environment, how to do most everything! Language, movement, discrimination—all are part of learning for the very young child. Play is the learning setting.

Scripture

Read Matthew 7:7-11. This passage reminds us that just as we want good things for our children, so God wants good things for us.

Some Things to Think About

Have you ever thought about what your child is seeing from the eye level of a crawler? Get down on the floor and take a look. Wouldn't it be fun to put some pictures at the child's eye level? How about a picture of grandma and grandpa, a picture of your church, a picture of familiar objects? There is so much to learn and enjoy in our world. Make your child's "low level areas" bright, colorful, and interesting. Acknowledging where your child can see is one way to say, "I love you and care about you."

Have you ever thought about what your child hears? Are the sounds that surround your child gentle, sweet, and clear? Or do sounds assault your child's ears? Do voices soothe your child and spark your child's interest, encouraging babbling and cooing? Or are voices angry and harsh? God created ears to hear. Be grateful for your child's ability to hear. Providing sounds that are positive and encouraging for your child is one way to say, "I love you and care about you."

A Prayer for You

Holy Spirit, you have made me a steward of this precious young life. Guide me so that this child may see Jesus through me. Amen.

A Prayer for Your Child

O God, thank you for (*name of child*). Thank you that on the day of the birth of this precious child you said, "Good and very good!" May (*name of child*) grow up knowing herself/himself to be loved by you and cherished by us/me. Amen.

Now That Your Child Is One Year Old

Self-esteem means how I value myself. The mature person experiences joyful pride and creative achievement in significant relationships with others. Healthy self-esteem frees a person to love others appropriately. Healthy self-esteem allows a person to behave unselfishly and to have a deepening capacity for joy, peace, patience, kindness, goodness, gentleness, and self-control. We want these characteristics for our children.

Steps for enhancing a child's self-esteem:
1. Keep yourself healthy.
2. Provide a home that is safe, secure, and stable, yet playful.
3. Give empathy and take delight in your child.
4. Let your child idealize you, but be prepared to let it go.
5. Let your child work and play alongside you.
6. Put a toddler's no's in perspective; respect what he or she is trying to accomplish.

Healthy self-esteem enables a child to love self, others, and God appropriately, with an ever-deepening capacity for the fruit of the Holy Spirit: joy, peace, patience, kindness, goodness, gentleness, and self-control.

Scripture

Read Luke 18:15-17. In this passage Jesus reminds us that God's kingdom belongs to children.

Some Things to Think About

If you have not already done so, introduce your child to Jesus. Hang in your child's room a picture depicting Jesus with children. Talk about Jesus as a special person who has much to teach us. Read about Jesus, using a book designed for young children. Sing "Jesus Loves Me." Use simple language that your child understands. Other ways of knowing Jesus will come later as your child grows.

A Prayer for You

Dear God, give me the grace to listen carefully, guide tenderly, encourage generously, and love dearly this precious gift of a child you have entrusted to me. Walk with me as we journey as a family and give me patience, wisdom, and love; in the name of Christ. Amen.

A Prayer for Your Child

Dear God, as my child sleeps, mend the little hurts that this day has brought. Give pleasant dreams that refresh and delight this weary child; in the name of Jesus. Amen.

Now That Your Child Is Fifteen Months Old

During the first three years, your child begins to form understandings about God, Jesus, the Bible, and the church. A child begins to learn that the Bible is an important book full of stories, especially about Jesus. Jesus loved God and people, taught about God, and was born as a baby with parents who cared for him. God loves each person and is the one to whom children can express praise, wonder, joy, and thanksgiving. The church is a special, happy place where the child hears stories of Jesus and prays to God.

Whatever the age, these concepts can be introduced and nurtured through trust, appreciation of nature, and predictability of events. Positive reinforcement of any action that encourages trust, dependability, love, and care should begin from the first moments of a child's life. Trust is the foundation of faith; if a child learns to trust the parent, that child will learn to trust God. In addition, learning to have a genuine appreciation for nature opens up the ability to appreciate the Creator and to experience God's grace in all living things.

Scripture

Read Matthew 5:3-12. This passage is often called the Beatitudes. It reminds us of what it means to live under God's rule.

Some Things to Think About

Teach your children positive self-regard and positive orientation toward others. Acknowledge the important role the church can play in assisting in the Christian nurture of your child. Talk to your young child about God's love just as you speak of your love for your child. Your actions can demonstrate your love and respect for others as well as for your little one. You can express your own faith through prayer times with your child.

A Prayer for You

Loving God, parenting is a responsibility granted by you. May I have the wisdom to make parental decisions that bathe my child in your love. I pray for courage to fulfill my sacred calling to raise this child of yours in a home filled with your ever-present grace. Thank you for entrusting one of your children to my care. Amen.

A Prayer for Your Child

O God, my God, Creator of the treasure that is my child, bless this exploding ball of exploring energy that enlivens each day. Was Jesus so energetic at this age? What a joy—and how weary we all are at the end of the day! How grateful I am for the special delight you bring to me in this child. Amen.

Now That Your Child Is Eighteen Months Old

Your days are so busy! Children don't understand adult schedules. Please allow extra time for the child's slower pace. Children sense our stress and anxiety. Childhood is such a short span of time, and one day all too soon it will be over. Relax and enjoy those "baby steps" and playful moments. What a blessing your child is! While moving slowly for your child, say a prayer of thanksgiving to God for your child!

Scripture

Read Matthew 5:14-16. This passage reminds us that we are to let our "lights" shine.

Some Things to Think About

Reread Matthew 5:16. Think for a moment what this verse has to say to you as a parent of an eighteen-month-old child. How are you sharing the light of your faith with your child? Pray aloud at mealtime, in the car, while dressing your child, while playing in water or petting a dog. Talk about the God who loves us and Jesus who teaches us and loves us. If you have not done so already, take your child to church. Introduce your child to the church family. Talk about church as a place where people will love and care for your child. Invite the pastor or nursery worker to your home so that your child will get to know that person as a friend. Join a group of parents, and learn together about sharing God's love with your children.

What you do and say are important to your child, who is constantly learning from you. May your child receive the light of God's love through you.

A Prayer for You

O God, thank you for the gift of parenthood. Thank you that when my love is less than perfect for this child, your love is not. Teach me to be the parent I so need and want to be. Amen.

A Prayer for Your Child

Holy God, give this child a heart that hungers to know you, and help me to nurture faith in such a way that my child will respond to your grace when you call. May the light of each day reveal your faithfulness, may each loving touch teach that your loving arms embrace and uphold us both, and may each struggle increase strength and bring growth. Amen.

Now That Your Child Is Twenty-One Months Old

Now is the time that the groundwork for faith development can be laid for your child through
1. a positive self-regard
2. a positive orientation toward others
3. a positive attitude toward life
4. a joyful attitude about learning

These attitudes must be reinforced by both parents and caregivers. Thus, religious education for young children becomes attitude education based on faith, hope, and love.

Concepts of God are accepted as single ideas but not formed into a cohesive whole. The toddler's self-worth and self-esteem need to be nurtured within the boundaries of the adult's love and care, which proclaim, "You are a child of God."

Scripture

Read 1 Corinthians 13:1-13. In this passage we are reminded of the power of love.

Some Things to Think About

Very young children do not automatically identify with another person. Intercessory prayer does not come naturally for them. You can help your child develop compassion and the habit of intercession by speculating on the feelings of others: "I wonder how Ashley felt after she broke her ankle. Let's pray that her ankle will heal well."

A Prayer for You

God of love and wisdom, your mercy and grace have been made known again by the privilege of parenthood. The awe-striking responsibility of rearing a child is both astounding and imposing. I am not sure how to do it. Often I feel woefully inadequate for the task, yet I know that your strength will more than overcome my weakness. I cannot do this by myself, but I can do this in you. You will empower me.

I thank you for this precious moment. Fleeting as these early years in my child's life will be, let me give my best for my child, to you, gratefully knowing that you will indeed bless my meager strivings by the power of your spirit. I pray in the name of Jesus the Christ. Amen.

A Prayer to Pray With Your Child

Thank you, God, for (*name all family members*); and thank you, God, for me. Amen.

Now That Your Child Is Two Years Old

We know that little fingers and hands are wonderful for leaving fingerprints on walls and furniture. But aren't you glad that these same little hands can be "helpful" hands? Let your child help dust the table and chair legs. Tell your child that his or her little fingers are "just the right size" for this job. When helping is fun and enjoyable, we teach children to be responsible helpers in our home. And what is more beautiful than these same little fingers and hands folded in prayer as your child talks to God?

Scripture

Read Deuteronomy 6:4-7. In this passage we are reminded of the responsibility we have to teach our children.

Some Things to Think About

Isn't it wonderful the way children learn and develop? It is amazing that by age two many children have a vocabulary of nearly three hundred words, and that in the next year this number will triple! Wow! There is much learning going on each day of your child's life. Remember, talk and sing to your child, read books together, pray together, tell stories together, and have fun!

A Prayer for You

Loving God, sometimes I struggle to deal with this demanding and often unpredictable person who has come to live with us. When tempers flare, help me teach by example how to cope with anger and frustration. By words and acts let me communicate your love to this little person you have given me. In the name of Jesus, I pray. Amen.

A Prayer to Pray With Your Child

Dear God, I'm so glad you made me me! Thank you. Amen.

Now That Your Child Is Twenty-Seven Months Old

While all children are born spiritual, the environment can do much to nurture their spirituality. As a parent, be deliberate about supplying the content for this spirituality. Provide Christian stories, images, and symbols from which your child can begin to fashion her or his own spirituality. The establishment of trusting, caring, dependable relationships also determines whether the child will approach a relationship with Jesus Christ in a positive, trusting way, or whether the child will develop this relationship based on anxiety and mistrust. To nurture the young child's spiritual life, you will carefully select the sources your child uses to construct these images. By the same token, you need to be aware of other images your child is absorbing from the media, from other children, and from the rest of the environment. Telling appropriate Bible stories will supply images that undergird your child's spirituality.

Scripture

Read Psalm 22:9-11a. This psalm reminds us that God is always with us.

Some Things to Think About

Provide your child with Bible story books. Visit your sanctuary. Admire the banners, stained-glass windows, and pictures. Sing hymns. Look at the baptismal font and feel the water. Tell the story of Jesus' baptism and talk about your child's baptism. Provide your child with an unbreakable nativity scene. Tell the story of Jesus' birth using these figures. Wonder together how the shepherds felt when they heard the angel choir. Encourage your child to retell the story using the nativity figures. Provide other manipulatives that can be used to tell and play Bible stories. Get a flannelboard with story figures for storytelling.

Most of all, surround your child with a loving, dependable environment filled with wholesome influences. Respect your child's spiritual nature. Encourage your child to talk with God. Pray together. Admire God's creation. Encourage your child to wonder and to think about and to develop a relationship with Jesus Christ appropriate to your child's maturity and individuality.

A Prayer for You

Dear God, give me strength and patience as I deal with this child. In the midst of the work and struggles, help me not to overlook the joys that are part of parenting this wonder you have placed in my life. Amen.

A Prayer to Pray With Your Child

Dear God, I am so glad you love me. Thank you for stories, playtime, and my mom and my dad. Watch over me as I sleep, and wake me with bright sunshine. Amen.

Now That Your Child Is Thirty Months Old

Remember the joy that filled your heart when you first held your newborn child? You probably said, "Thank you, God, for this beautiful child!" God is as near to you today as on that special birth day. God cares about you and about your child. You don't need an 800 number or a fax machine. God hears your prayers. God cares about you!

Scripture

Read Proverbs 22:6.

Some Things to Think About

Sooner or later, each child goes through a time of asking questions. Each response you give is followed by yet another question. For adults, it is sometimes difficult to be patient with such a cascade of questions. Remember, questions help children learn. They learn specific answers, they practice their verbal skills, they practice reasoning and thinking, and they practice communication skills. Questions must be a special creation of God's, although they sometimes feel like a nuisance.

Handle each question and your response to each question with respect, and later, when your child is a teenager or young adult, you will still get asked questions.

A Prayer for You

Dear God, bless my child as he or she grows and begins to notice your world and all of its creation. May this world provide ways for my child to learn about you. May the forces of nature teach my child about your wisdom, creative activity, awesome power, and comforting presence. May my child discover a sense of wonder and awe as she or he encounters majestic mountains and tiny flowers and all the many other parts of your creation. Guide me as I grow in knowledge and experience of your creation. Help me be able to give answers to my child's questions about your creation and about you. In your name, I pray. Amen.

A Prayer to Pray With Your Child

Dear God, thank you for my family, my (*any pet*), my (*favorite toy*), and my friend, (*name of friend*). I am glad you love me. Amen.

Now That Your Child Is Thirty-Three Months Old

Remember what your child was like just two and a half years ago. That tiny, dependent infant has turned into a child with a mind of his or her own. Not that many months ago your child's primary method of communication was crying. Now your child communicates in a variety of ways. Celebrate all that your child has learned.

Scripture

Read Psalm 133. This psalm reminds us how wonderful it is when we live together in unity.

Some Things to Think About

The kitchen is a good source of learning for children. Gelatin boxes are great for stacking and sorting. Pans are great for stirring and banging. Make a cake, letting your child stir the batter with a spoon. Measuring cups and small bowls are great for measuring water in the sink. Encourage children to help with food preparation and cleanup. Insist on safety. (Do not allow a child to perform dangerous tasks. Explain why you will not allow this.) As your child helps prepare lunch, talk about how God gave us bread to eat and milk to drink.

When in the kitchen with young children, give them time. Don't rush. They sometimes need to move slowly and deliberately. Be patient with messes. Clean them up together. Working together is fun!

A Prayer for You

Dear God who created me, you are a loving parent to me, even when I am less than you created me to be. Teach me patience and wisdom so that my child may see in me glimpses of your steadfast love and forgiveness. Help me teach my child to act justly, to love kindness, and always to walk humbly with you. Give me wisdom to know how to share my faith with this child. May my love for you be clear, and may it draw my child to you; in Jesus' name. Amen.

A Prayer to Pray With Your Child

Dear God, thank you for my mother and father. Thank you for others who care for me. Help me know about your love. Thank you, God, for showing me your love through my family and church. Amen.

Now That Your Child Is Three Years Old

years

A three-year-old is one of God's amazing creations. Your three-year-old is probably beginning to talk in short sentences. Three-year-olds enjoy repeating words and sounds. They like familiar stories told the same way, time after time. The world of three-year-olds is full of wonder, and they spend much time watching, observing, and imitating.

Scripture

Read Matthew 6:9-14.

Some Things to Think About

As your child continues to grow, it is important that you nurture not only your child's spiritual life but also your own relationship with God. Are you part of an adult Sunday school class or some other learning group? Do you read the Bible regularly? Do you begin and end each day with prayer? These spiritual disciplines all provide ways to strengthen your relationship with God.

A Prayer for You

O God, as a parent I pray for wisdom and guidance from you in raising my child. I pray for good character and even temperament. I pray that I can be a part of a childhood that brings about delightful memories, enchanting stories, and winning ways.

O God of light and glory, help me cherish the days of my child's youth by encouraging independence, fostering dreams, and nurturing faith.

And most important, God, please help me lead my child into a relationship with you! Help me teach and model for my child my belief in a deathless God, a never-failing God, an everlasting God who resides in all times and places.

Help me, in my style of living, respond to the challenges of life with a clear, conspicuous, lasting faith in you. Amen.

A Prayer to Pray With Your Child

Dear God, thank you for sunshine and rain, for family and friends, for food to eat and a bed for sleep. And, dear God, help me to be kind and do good things each day. I love you, God. Amen.